AN ANTHOLOGY OF
GREEK DRAMA

First Series

Classical Literature in Rinehart Editions

EDITED AND TRANSLATED BY KEVIN GUINAGH

Vergil, *The Aeneid*

EDITED BY PHILIP WHALEY HARSH

An Anthology of Roman Drama (The Twin Menaechmi, The Rope, Phormio, The Brothers, Medea, Phaedra, Thyestes)

EDITED BY C. A. ROBINSON, JR.

An Anthology of Greek Drama: First Series (Agamemnon, Oedipus the King, Antigone, Medea, Hippolytus, Lysistrata)

An Anthology of Greek Drama: Second Series (Prometheus Bound, Choëphoroe, Eumenides, Philoctetes, Oedipus at Colonus, The Trojan Women, The Bacchae, The Clouds, The Frogs)

Plutarch—Eight Great Lives (Pericles, Alcibiades, Coriolanus. Comparison of Alcibiades and Coriolanus, Demosthenes, Cicero, Comparison of Demosthenes and Cicero, Alexander, Caesar, Antony)

Selections from Greek and Roman Historians (Herodotus, Thucydides, Xenophon, Polybius, Livy, Sallust, Suetonius, Tacitus)

AN ANTHOLOGY OF
GREEK DRAMA

First Series

EDITED WITH AN INTRODUCTION BY

CHARLES ALEXANDER ROBINSON, JR.

Harcourt Brace Jovanovich College Publishers
Fort Worth   Philadelphia   San Diego
New York   Orlando   Austin   San Antonio
Toronto   Montreal   London   Sydney   Tokyo

Library of Congress Catalog Card Number: 49-48280
ISBN 0-03-009415-1
Printed in the United States of America
Typography by Stefan Salter
123   095   45 44 43 42

FOR ALEX, SAM

AND FRANK

INTRODUCTION

IN THE *Persians* of Aeschylus the Persian queen asks a question, to which no one has found the answer: "What is this Athens, of which all men speak?" But the foreigner who has seen the play in modern Athens, and has felt the ripple of proud possession which passes over the audience at the familiar lines, will perhaps recognize that the answer was best suggested by the ancient playwright himself when he set the quality of Athens in the democratic spirit of her people, and let a Persian give his queen the incomprehensible response: "They bow to no man and are no man's slaves."

Aeschylus's play commemorated the Greek triumph over the predatory Persian empire at the opening of the glorious fifth century B.C. Because Athens had led the city-states of Greece during the crisis, it fell to the growing imperial democracy in all the enthusiasm of victory to bring its people to a summit of civilization never before reached by the human race. Now. under Pericles, the Parthenon and other buildings were erected; a galaxy of brilliant men thronged the violet-crowned city; and the drama, which in many ways represents the finest creative achievement of the Greek mind and spirit, reached its height.

Greek tragic drama grew out of the choral dithyramb, and although the details of its origin are obscure, it had a long tradition of epic, lyric, and dramatic poetry behind it, and was probably welded at Athens, the center of Greece, out of diverse primitive elements. It was always associated with religion and religious ritual; yet the plays themselves are concerned fundamentally with human values, with man's dignity and his individual responsibility, with problems raised by the existence of evil, by conflicts of duty and endurance under stress. God had been Israel's discovery, but it remained for Greece to place man in the center of things. The presence of gods or of some superhuman force in these dramas reminds us, however, that man, though free, does not live unto himself alone. The plays are on the level of universal tragedy and bear out the definition, made almost a century after the Periclean Age by Aristotle in his *Poetics,* to the effect that tragedy is an "imitation" of an action that is serious, complete, and of a certain magnitude, while its function is—by rousing pity and fear —to provide a *catharsis,* or purging, of these and like emotions. The ideal tragic hero, continues Aristotle, must be a highly renowned, though not a pre-eminently virtuous, man whose misfortune is brought upon him by some error of judgment or frailty, rather than by vice and depravity. And so in *Oedipus the King,* for example, the feelings of pity and fear are aroused by the tragic situation in which Oedipus finds himself, but with the completion of the play the same emotions are purified in the minds of the audience by the nobility of Oedipus's conduct under stress. Still, had Aristotle lived a century earlier and been influenced by fifth-century standards, he probably would have emphasized that the emotional function of tragedy was secondary to the intellectual one.

The culture of the Periclean Age stemmed from a belief in the all-comprehensive perfection of the state, to whose good the citizens, in war and in peace, were to subordinate their individual interests and devote their lives. It also stemmed from traditional belief refined by an expanding intelligence and humanism—belief in the power, wisdom, and goodness of the gods, in the superiority of the fathers, in the beneficence of the heroes of old. In other words, the central idea of Hellenism embraced the city-state, with all its traditional associations and responsibilities, religious, social, and civic. But during this great fifth century B.C. the hereditary faith of the Greeks was being changed steadily, if slowly, by a growing individualism. Poets and sophists took the lead in questioning the problems of life and the old answers to them, and during the second half of the century the new centrifugal tendencies struggled with the old conservatism in a conflict fiercer and deadlier than the strife between Athenians and Spartans.

Man's love of symbolism and his hope for a future life weakened the hold of the traditional faith. Some people turned from the cold Olympian gods to the new mystery religions and the strange deities—new gods from Thrace, Phrygia, or the East, with their unfamiliar priests and curious rites, emotional and noisy, or secret and mystical—brought in by swarms of foreigners and slaves. All the new religions were individualistic, and though they were scorned by the educated and the conservative, they tended to weaken the position of the recognized civic cults in the community.

A far more active solvent was rationalism. While treating with forbearance the myths that formed the tragic poet's stock in trade and the background of his country's history, Euripides makes it plain that many supernatural powers, traditionally assumed, have no real existence. Homer made the gods responsible for the good and evil acts of men. Euripides rejects the whole theory and lays the responsibility for conduct upon the individual; while the eminent comic poet, Aristophanes, in other ways conservative, ridicules the gods and their weaknesses. The drama thus introduced advanced ideas to a large audience.

The Athenian needed the teaching and inspiration of his great poets, for to meet the various requirements of citizenship in this intense democracy, a man had to be well educated. He began his training on a small scale in the deme (administrative district), where local affairs were freely discussed in the town meeting, and where local offices gave some practice in communal management. Further experience he gained in one or more of the many administrative offices of the state and empire, and in the assembly and law courts. But this practical instruction was narrow. The Athenian received a broader education from the choral songs at festivals and particularly from the drama presented in the theater. During the year more than sixty days were given to festivals, including dramatic exhibitions and the holidays of the demes. Every year, moreover, from one to two thousand boys and men appeared before the public in choruses for the dramatic and other exhibitions that required them. These choral services, as well as others, were generally rotated among the qualified citizens, thus giving all, or nearly all, a training in music and a close contact with literature.

The majority of the dramatists who spoke to their fellow citizens in fifth-century Athens are irretrievably lost; others are known to us by name only. Those who have survived are represented by a mere fraction of their total production. In spite of the loss of so many masterpieces, three of the four greatest tragedians in history are Greeks. The earliest of these, Aeschylus (ca. 525–456 B.C.), was born near Athens at Eleusis, which was the home of the official Mysteries, a fact that doubtless made a lifelong impression upon him. Though the most creative of Athenian dramatists, Aeschylus desired above all else to be considered a loyal citizen who had fought for his country at Marathon. He belonged to the generation of the Persian Wars: in his day the man of deeds was greater than the artist, and it is almost in spite of himself that we describe him as a literary man. Nevertheless, in his hands the drama became a new and fully developed art that had cast off all traces of its primitive beginning.

Aeschylus wrote approximately ninety plays, of which seven are now extant. Of these the *Oresteia,* which deals with the culmination of the succession of curses that fell upon the House of Atreus, is the only trilogy[1] to have survived from antiquity. An ominous gloom pervades the *Agamemnon,* the first and probably the greatest of the trilogy, but it is broken now and then by moments of joy. Above all stands Zeus, who brings all things to pass, but the the characters are strongly drawn and are given some opportunity for the display of personal initiative. Into their mouths Aeschylus, a man of deep religious conviction and a poet of beautiful language and imagery, puts noble sentiments.

According to the ancient story, Thyestes had seduced the wife of his brother Atreus, who in turn had killed Thyestes' children and served them to their father at a banquet. Atreus's sons, Agamemnon and Menelaus, inherited the curse that had fallen upon their father. When Menelaus's wife, Helen, fled to Troy with Paris, it became the duty of Agamemnon, as the strongest king in Greece, to lead an expedition to Asia Minor to bring back the most beautiful woman in the world. But unfavorable winds kept the fleet at Aulis, until finally Agamemnon, on information from Calchas, the seer, sacrificed his daughter Iphigenia, thinking that he would thus appease the goddess Artemis. The expedition then sailed to Troy, but when the city fell after ten years' fighting, Agamemnon dishonored the temples and altars of its gods. At the opening of the *Agamemnon,* Agamemnon's wife has not yet learned of Troy's capture, but she has plotted with her paramour Aegisthus, the surviving son of Thyestes, to kill her husband on his return. Here, then, is to be Agamemnon's reward—death at the hand of Clytemnestra, the strongest human character in the

[1] A group of three plays, often on the same general theme, for consecutive presentation on the same day.

play. In killing her husband she but serves as a link in the resist-less chain of blood-revenge, a tool, as it were, of the inevitable retribution that overtakes evil.

In the next play, the *Choëphoroe* (*Libation-Bearers*), the chil-dren of Agamemnon and Clytemnestra, Electra and Orestes, as the avengers of their father, murder their mother, this monstrous fruit being the by-product of their inherited guilt. In the *Eumenides* (*Furies*), the last play in the trilogy, the dread Furies, who seem to typify both conscience and a Mosaic justice, pursue Orestes, tormenting him with the most intense suffering, but by the agoniz-ing experience he expiates the crime he had to commit as a duty; with suffering come obedience and wisdom. He is, accordingly, purified by Apollo at Delphi and acquitted by the Athenian Coun-cil of the Areopagus sitting under the presidency of Athena. In this way the family is ultimately saved from the recurrence of its guilt. With the gods' aid a family worked out its own redemption in suffering.

This tempering of justice with mercy, symbolized by Zeus him-self, was in keeping with the growing sense of kindliness and the religious spirit of the day, which expressed itself in diverse forms. Progressive though he was, Aeschylus held fast to the hereditary faith of his race, exalted and purified by his splendid intelligence and brilliant imagination. In touch with the best thought of the time, he could only conceive of Zeus as combining in the highest degree power, splendor, and sublimity; he gives us scenes and con-ceptions which, in their grandeur, are altogether too bold for representation.

While it is true that the poets were the teachers of Athens, they had no sense of mission. Certainly Sophocles (ca. 496–406 B.C.) did not consciously regard himself as a teacher or an innovator in religious matters; in his plays the gods had a conventional role and he presented as normal their more appealing aspects. The real con-cern of Sophocles was the human fortunes of his characters. This inevitably grew out of his background, for as a man of wealth and education, who had been born in the fashionable Athenian suburb of Colonus, he served the state in various capacities and mingled with all classes of people. In the year 443 B.C., for example, Pericles appointed him chief treasurer during a reorganization of the Athe-nian empire; and three years later, having meanwhile produced the

Antigone, he was a general under Pericles in the Samian War. As a poet, Sophocles was chiefly interested in what effect life has upon a man's character and soul. The old legends were his framework, and his plays, which combine an exceptional harmony of beauty and reason and are almost perfect from the point of view of dramatic technique, show him to be not only a great artist, but also the most human of Greek tragedians. In the words of Matthew Arnold, he is the supreme example of a tragic poet "who saw life steadily and saw it whole."

Sophocles composed about one hundred and twenty plays, but only seven survive entire. Three of these deal with the Theban saga. The House of Cadmus, founder of Thebes, is doomed to misfortune because it has offended the gods. Oedipus, heir to the power and woes of this stock, is driven unwittingly to the commission of a dreadful sin, for he fulfills the awful prophecy that he will murder his father and marry his mother. He suffers unspeakable agony of mind, and his children inherit the curse. His two sons kill each other in a civil war, which legend calls "The Seven against Thebes"; his daughter, Antigone, is buried alive; the whole family is extinguished. Thus the cumulative crime, growing from generation to generation, brings its legitimate punishment.

Oedipus the King, the first of the Theban saga, is perhaps the greatest of the Sophoclean tragedies. As we discover in the course of the drama, Oedipus's parents, Laius and Jocasta, had exposed him at birth, but he had been rescued by a shepherd and reared by Polybus and Merope, the king and queen of Corinth. Years later Oedipus had met Laius on a lonely road; they had not known each other and there had been a quarrel, with the younger man killing the elder. Oedipus had continued his journey to Thebes, where a monster oppressed the city. He had guessed the riddle of the Sphinx, the city had been relieved, and the grateful people had made him king. He had then married Jocasta, the widow of the late king. They had had children, the years had passed, and a plague had fallen upon Thebes. At this point the play opens.

As he slowly learns the horrible truth about himself, Oedipus offers no plea of ignorance but accepts the responsibility for his acts. Yet we are overwhelmed by the tragedy of man powerless in the face of forces greater than himself. The well-known device of tragic irony—whereby a person makes a statement which means one thing to himself, and something quite different to the audience, and lives to find that his words have mocked him—is used with all its power by Sophocles; thus Oedipus curses the murderer of Laius, who, as the audience knows and he does not, is none other than himself.

Oedipus at Colonus, which continues the story, is the last play by Sophocles and was composed when he was almost ninety years of age. A tragedy of tremendous power and poetic beauty, it depicts the last hours and death of Oedipus. From the religious point of view the death of the aged and innocent Oedipus, who pleads the venial nature of an offense committed in ignorance although long since purified by his suffering, represents the highest achievement of paganism; the sheer beauty of the famous ode in praise of Attica and Sophocles's birthplace, Colonus, has seldom been equaled. In the *Antigone,* which deals with the last phase of the saga (though it was the first of the three to be written), two sons of Oedipus have fallen in single combat before Thebes, one of them a patriot, the other a rebel. Creon, the king, who represents cold logicality, orders that only the loyal brother may be buried. But Antigone, their sister, cannot draw this distinction, and takes her position first by instinct and then rationalizes it by an appeal to divine law. The play thus raises the eternal question of the relation between man's law and God's. Logicality, we learn, is wrong; instinct and tradition are right.

An age seems to separate Sophocles and his successor, the great exponent of the new spirit of individualism and the new humanism, Euripides (ca. 480–406 B.C.). In the older poet the spirit of Hellenism is strong. Euripides, who reputedly was of humble origin, is distinctly the first of the moderns. The apostle of humanism, Euripides issued his dramas as epistles to mankind. His message was a moral and spiritual interpretation of the utterance of Protagoras: man is the measure of all things. The keen intellect and the sensitive conscience, developed by a marvelous civilization, are the standards with which to judge truth and right on earth and in heaven. Casting off from traditional moorings, he pilots mankind over surging seas of thought and emotion, but his ship reaches no harbor. The poet of the submerged majority of humanity descends to the level of common folk, to sympathize with beggars and cripples, with women and slaves.

Skeptic and bitter realist though he was, and understanding human nature as few have done, Euripides nevertheless wrote some magical and brilliant verse; he had not only violent invective but tender pathos as well. The *Medea*, one of the eighteen plays that have survived from the original total of approximately ninety-two, is high tragedy, the story of a woman who is abandoned by the man she loves and for whom she has surrendered everything. Against tremendous odds Medea had helped Jason and the Argonauts to obtain the Golden Fleece and then, killing her brother to delay pursuit, had fled with them from her native land. On their return to Thessaly, Jason's wicked uncle refused to yield the throne he had usurped and was murdered by Medea. Again the couple was forced to flee, and at Corinth, the scene of the play, Jason finds that he can marry the daughter of the king and so dismisses Medea. Her love is turned to violent hatred, and she murders their children. Euripides gives us in Jason the picture of an egotist and a scoundrel; in Medea, a woman who is heartbroken, as anyone is when tragedy falls, but who, having the power to do as she wishes, reacts without the restraints that civilization imposes. There is no solution of the problem, and at the end Medea flees to Athens in a magic chariot drawn by winged dragons.

The poetical genius of Euripides is most evident in the *Hippolytus*. The play depicts the passionate love of Phaedra for her step-son, Hippolytus, who resists proudly—much too proudly—and thus prepares his own fall. The two goddesses, Aphrodite and Artemis, symbolize the struggle of passionate love and rigorous chastity, a conflict which in the end compels Hippolytus to consider whether in his scorn for the one and his devotion to the other he has not disobeyed the Greek precept, "Avoid excess."

Unlike the tragedians, the comic poets openly and vigorously sought to impress their views upon the audience. Much of the humor of Old Comedy, as it is called to differentiate it from the comedy of situation that developed later, derives from the fact that it violently attacked living persons, such as Socrates and Euripides or the demagogue Cleon, who as likely as not were seated in the theater; ancient democracy insisted on complete freedom of speech, and thought it well to mock the personalities and air the burning problems of the moment. Aristophanes (ca. 445–385 B.C.), the brilliant, creative poet of Old Comedy, was before all else a boisterous comedian, but he did not hesitate to ridicule his enemies and, if possible, to advance the interests of his own conservative class. Eleven of his forty plays have survived—the first was produced when he was eighteen years of age—and many of them are full of fierce attacks upon prominent persons, cruel caricatures, although they contain delicious humor and a high quality of true lyric genius. There is much bawdiness as well, which is to be explained partly by the origin of comedy in a fertility rite, partly by the fact that the ancients did not regard sex as sinful, and also by the simple truth that perhaps there was nothing Aristophanes loved more.

As might be expected of a conservative landowner who saw his farms destroyed by hostile armies, Aristophanes opposed the Peloponnesian War[2] and wrote several plays in favor of peace, a monument to Athenian tolerance and willingness to hear all points of view. By 411 B.C., however, peace would have been almost equivalent to Athenian defeat, and yet Aristophanes, in the Lysistrata, dared consider theoretical pacifism and appealed for Panhellenic peace. The theme is, of course, eternal, but the details of exactly how the women are to stop their men from fighting are fantastically Aristophanic.

[2] 431–404 B.C.; it was to culminate in Sparta's triumph over Athens

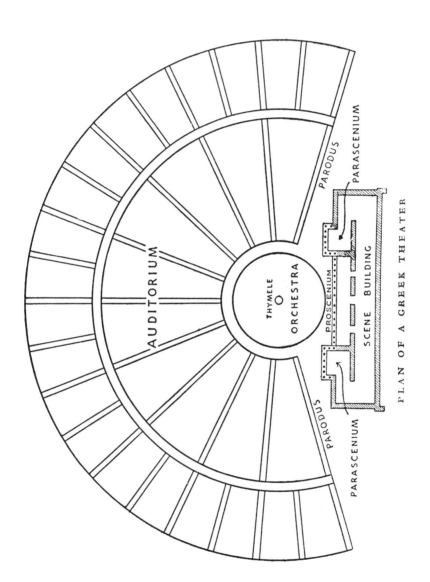

PLAN OF A GREEK THEATER

AUDITORIUM

THYMELE

ORCHESTRA

PARODUS

PARASCENIUM

PROSCENIUM

SCENE BUILDING

PARODUS

PARASCENIUM

NOTE ON THE PRODUCTION OF PLAYS

The Athenian audience which witnessed these plays was the most critical and outspoken in history (one unsatisfactory actor was almost stoned to death), for it had been educated by a succession of great dramatists, and many members of the audience had at one time or another taken part in dramatic exhibitions. Long before the date of the Greater or City Dionysia[3] a committee chose three tragic and five comic poets for the privilege of competing at this, the more important of the two festivals when Athenians could come together in their theater to witness the drama. Thus the atmosphere that surrounded the production of the plays was not only religious but also keenly intellectual, especially since the entire presentation was competitive. The playwrights generally oversaw the production of their plays. To each playwright was assigned a *choregos*, a wealthy citizen whose civic duty required him to assume the financial responsibility of supplying and training the chorus of amateurs. Since one character in a play usually far outshone the others, it became the custom to allot a protagonist, or leading actor, to each dramatist in order that the finest actors might each have a chance of winning the acting prize and to prevent a dramatist from obtaining the best talent for himself.[4] The actors, who were always men, were highly trained and were paid by the government. Admission was free till the end of the fifth century, when a small fee was charged those who could afford it; this change and others were necessitated by the Peloponnesian War.

A great procession normally occupied the first day of the festival; on the second day ten dithyrambic choruses of fifty each competed; and on the third, five comic poets each produced a play. The last three days were given over to the tragic poets, each of whom presented a tetralogy; that is, a trilogy, or group of three

[3] The March–April festival in celebration of spring and Dionysus, the god of fertility and patron of the theater. Another festival, that of the Wine-Press, or Lenaea, was held in January–February and was given over principally to comedy.

[4] The chief role was originally played by the dramatist himself, but Sophocles abandoned the custom on account of his weak voice.

plays often, though not always, on the same general theme, followed by a mock-heroic piece known as a satyr-play. The days were long, happy, and serious, and at the conclusion of the festival the judges, who had sat in the front row of the theater with the priest of Dionysus and other officials, rendered their verdict. The name of the winning dramatist, the titles of his plays, and the name of his protagonist were then carved on stone, while the fortunate *choregos* had the privilege of commemorating his service by erecting a small monument at his own expense. Aeschylus won first prize thirteen times; Sophocles, more than twenty; and Euripides, who was disliked for his advanced views, four, although after his death he was the most popular of the three. The number of Aristophanes's victories is unknown.

It should be remarked that a Greek tragedy ordinarily opened with a prologue—especially with Euripides—which gave the general situation. Then the chorus entered (*parodos*) and sang.[5] The importance of the chorus in its role as actor, a role which figured so largely at first, diminished with time, particularly in the hands of Euripides; but the chorus had the wonderful function of making the audience feel itself a part of the play, of joining with it in reflecting public opinion or perhaps in glimpsing the future. Moreover, the choral song always gave the poet the opportunity to write beautiful lyrics. The remainder of the play was devoted to an alternation of *episode* (act) and *stasimon* (choral ode), until the *exodos* (finale), when the chorus left the orchestra and the play ended. Occasionally a *kommos*, which was a passage sung by actors and chorus together, was substituted for a *stasimon*. The episodes were written in iambic trimeter, which resembles our blank verse; the *stasima,* in various meters, which presumably were governed structurally by the music that accompanied them. Because of the influence of tragedy, the form of a comedy was, broadly speaking, similar though more complex, but it was chiefly characterized by its division into two parts, the first developing the situation, the second giving the results.

[5] A pair of choral passages is known as *strophe* and *antistrophe*—"turn" and "counterturn"—for the chorus, while singing, performed various evolutions. Occasionally the pair was followed by an *epode* or "after song."

Normally there were three actors in a tragedy, though an actor might take more than one part; the number of actors in a comedy varied. During the fifth century there were fifteen members of the tragic chorus, one of whom acted as the leader. The comic chorus numbered twenty-four. Because of the large size of the theater, changes in facial expression, for example, could not be recognized by the audience. To compensate for this handicap the actors wore masks in order to set at least the general type of the character. The masks had an additional value in that they served as a megaphone, but the excellent acoustics of the theaters scattered across Greece are a source of constant amazement to modern visitors.

The open-air theater of Dionysus at Athens, where these plays were first produced, is situated on the southern slope of the Acropolis. Across the Attic Plain, to the left as one sits in the theater, is Mt. Hymettus, while to the right lie Homer's wine-dark sea and its islands. Behind the auditorium rises the pink rock of Athena's Hill, crowned by man's equally incredible additions that have been built with the famous Pentelic marble whose veins of iron are golden. Overhead is a peacock-blue sky; as the brilliance of the sun changes, the colors of mountains and plain turn from purple to russet and back again. Here stands the ancient theater. (See page xvi.) It had a long development, and eventually accommodated about 18,000 persons. Below the seats of the auditorium, as can be seen from the plan, was the orchestra, a level circular area of packed earth, and later of stone, where the chorus sang and danced; depending on the action, the actors stood either here or on a low platform beyond the orchestra. In the middle of the orchestra was the *thymele,* an altar dedicated to Dionysus; beside it sat the musicians, for an integral part of the drama was singing and dancing, all traces of which have long since vanished. In time, a long stone structure for the storage of costumes and other properties, known as the scene building or *skene* ("hut," whence our *scene*), was erected beyond the orchestra, and the actors emerged from it. Immediately in front of the *skene,* and connected with it by a high, narrow roof, was the *proscenium*—a line of columns almost tangent with the orchestra —which served as a background for actors and chorus. At either end of the proscenium was a projection forward (*parascenium*), and between it and the auditorium was the entrance passage (*parodus*) for chorus and audience.

Scenery was very simple and, according to tradition, was invented by Sophocles. It consisted chiefly of painted panels set between the columns of the proscenium. The action of a Greek play was perforce generally laid in the open, but an interior scene could be shown by means of the *eccyclema,* a sort of platform on wheels which was hauled from within the *skene.* A god who intervened miraculously in the course of a play was called "the god from the machine" (*deus ex machina*) and was presented by means of a crane placed on the roof above the proscenium.

Finally, we may remark that the *Agamemnon* was first produced in 458 B.C. and, with the *Choëphoroe* and the *Eumenides,* won first prize. The date of *Oedipus the King* is uncertain, but probably falls between 430 and 415 B.C.; it won second prize (the winning play is lost). The *Antigone* was probably first produced in 442 B.C. and won first prize. The *Medea* was first produced in 431 B.C., with the *Philoctetes,* the *Dictys,* and the *Harvesters,* the last a satyr-play, and won third prize. The *Hippolytus* won first prize when originally produced in 428 B.C. The first production of the *Lysistrata* took place in 411 B.C., but we lack information on the award of the prizes.

Charles Alexander Robinson, Jr.

Providence, Rhode Island
June, 1949

BIBLIOGRAPHICAL NOTE

There are excellent studies of the Greek theater in J. T. Allen, *Stage Antiquities of the Greeks and Romans and Their Influence,* New York, 1927; P. D. Arnott, *An Introduction to the Greek Theatre,* London, 1959; M. Bieber, *The History of the Greek and Roman Theater,* 2nd ed., Princeton, 1961; R. C. Flickinger, *The Greek Theater and Its Drama,* 4th ed., Chicago, 1936; A. W. Pickard-Cambridge, *The Theatre of Dionysus in Athens,* Oxford, 1946; A. W. Pickard-Cambridge, *The Dramatic Festivals of Athens,* Oxford, 1953. The drama is ably discussed by T. F. Driver, *The Sense of History in Greek and Shakespearean Drama,* New York, 1960; P. W. Harsh, *A Handbook of Classical Drama,* Stanford, 1944; H. D. F. Kitto, *Greek Tragedy,* 2nd ed., London, 1950; H. D. F. Kitto, *Form and Meaning in Drama,* London, 1956; R. Lattimore, *The Poetry of Greek Tragedy,* Baltimore, 1958; K. Lever, *The Art of Greek Comedy,* London, 1956; D. W. Lucas, *The Greek Tragic Poets,* London, 1950; G. Norwood, *Greek Tragedy,* Boston, 1928; G. Norwood, *Greek Comedy,* Boston, 1932; W. K. Prentice, *Those Ancient Dramas Called Tragedies,* Princeton, 1942.

Special works on Aeschylus: G. Murray, *Aeschylus, the Creator of Tragedy,* New York, 1940; E. T. Owen, *The Harmony of Aeschylus,* Toronto, 1952; J. T. Sheppard, *Aeschylus and Sophocles,* New York, 1927; H. W. Smyth, *Aeschylean Tragedy,* Berkeley, 1924; G. D. Thomson, *Aeschylus and Athens,* 2nd ed., London, 1946.

Special works on Sophocles: S. M. Adams, *Sophocles the Playwright,* Toronto, 1957; C. M. Bowra, *Sophoclean Tragedy,* New York, 1945; V. Ehrenberg, *Sophocles and Pericles,* Oxford, 1954; R. Goheen, *The Imagery of Sophocles' Antigone,* Princeton, 1951; G. M. Kirkwood, *A Study of Sophoclean Drama,* Ithaca, 1958; H. D. F. Kitto, *Sophocles, Dramatist and Philosopher,* London, 1958;

B. M. W. Knox, *Oedipus at Thebes,* New Haven, 1957; F. H. J. Letters, *Life and Works of Sophocles,* London, 1953; J. C. Opstelten, *Sophocles and Greek Pessimism,* Amsterdam, 1952; A. J. A. Waldock, *Sophocles the Dramatist,* Cambridge, 1951; T. B. L. Webster, *Introduction to Sophocles,* Oxford, 1936; C. H. Whitman, *Sophocles,* Cambridge, Massachusetts, 1951.

Special works on Euripides: E. M. Blaiklock, *The Male Characters of Euripides,* Wellington, 1952; L. H. G. Greenwood, *Aspects of Euripidean Tragedy,* Cambridge, 1953; G. M. A. Grube, *The Drama of Euripides,* London, 1941; F. L. Lucas, *Euripides and his Influence,* Boston, 1923; G. Murray, *Euripides and his Age,* 2nd ed., Oxford, 1946; G. Norwood, *Essays on Euripidean Drama,* Toronto, 1954.

Special works on Aristophanes: V. Ehrenberg, *The People of Aristophanes,* 2nd ed., Cambridge, Massachusetts, 1951; L. E. Lord, *Aristophanes,* Boston, 1925; G. Murray, *Aristophanes: A Study,* Oxford, 1933.

Those who wish to read additional plays might begin with Aeschylus's **Prometheus Bound, *Choëphoroe, *Eumenides, Persians;* Sophocles's *Electra, *Philoctetes, *Oedipus at Colonus;* Euripides's *Alcestis, Electra, Iphigenia in Tauris, *Trojan Women, *Bacchae;* Aristophanes's *Birds, Thesmophoriazusae, *Clouds, *Frogs* (the last two "attack," respectively, Socrates and Euripides). The starred plays are included in the second volume of this *Anthology.* Translations may also be found in W. Arrowsmith, D. Parker, and Others, *Complete Greek Comedy,* Ann Arbor, in progress; D. Grene and R. Lattimore, *Complete Greek Tragedy,* Chicago, 1959; *Loeb Classical Library,* Cambridge, Massachusetts, various dates; W. J. Oates and E. O'Neill, Jr., *The Complete Greek Drama,* New York, 1938.

ACKNOWLEDGMENTS

I AM INDEBTED to the following publishers for their permission to reprint certain of these plays, for which they hold the copyright: to The Macmillan Company for Arthur S. Way's translation of Euripides's *Hippolytus*, from his *The Tragedies of Euripides in English Verse*; to The Macmillan Company and The Cambridge University Press for George Thomson's translation of Aeschylus's *Agamemnon*, from his *The Oresteia*, 1938, and for R. C. Trevelyan's translation of Euripides's *Medea*, 1939; to The University of Chicago Press for David Grene's translation of Sophocles's *Oedipus the King*, from his *Three Greek Tragedies in Translation*, 1942; to Longmans, Green and Company for Charles T. Murphy's translation of Aristophanes's *Lysistrata*, from W. J. Oates and C. T. Murphy, *Greek Literature in Translation*, 1944. I am also indebted to The Macmillan Company for permission to base certain of my remarks in the Introduction on passages in G. W. Botsford and C. A. Robinson, Jr., *Hellenic History*, New York, 1948, and to The University of Chicago Press for permission to reproduce the plan of a Greek theater, from R. C. Flickinger, *The Greek Theater and Its Drama*, Chicago, 1936. For helpful suggestions I am especially grateful to Professors Rhys Carpenter, Harold Cherniss, H. N. Couch, J. H. Finley, Jr., David Grene, G. M. Harper, Jr., Richmond Lattimore, I. M. Linforth, C. A. Lynch, Thomas Means, W. J. Oates, L. A. Post, A. E. Raubitschek, A. C. Schlesinger, C. B. Welles, J. R. Workman; and, above all, to Celia Robinson, my wife.

C. A. R., Jr.

CONTENTS

AESCHYLUS

AGAMEMNON

TRANSLATED BY GEORGE THOMSON

CHARACTERS IN THE PLAY

A WATCHMAN
CHORUS of *Argive Elders*
CLYTEMNESTRA, *wife of Agamemnon*
A HERALD
AGAMEMNON, *King of Argos*
CASSANDRA, *daughter of Priam, King of Troy; now the slave of Agamemnon*
AEGISTHUS, *son of Thyestes; cousin of Agamemnon; lover of Clytemnestra*

AGAMEMNON

(SCENE: *The entrance to the palace of Agamemnon at Argos. Before the door stand sacred images. A* WATCHMAN *is stationed on the roof.*)

WATCHMAN: I've prayed God to deliver me from evil
Throughout a long year's vigil, couched like a dog
On the roof of the House of Atreus, where I scan
The pageant of Night's starry populace,
And in their midst, illustrious potentates,
The shining constellations that bring men
Summer and winter, as they rise and set.
And still I keep watch for the beacon-sign,
That radiant flame that shall flash out of Troy
The message of her capture. So strong in hope
A woman's heart, whose purpose is a man's.
Night after night, tossed on this restless bed,
With dew bedrenched, by no dreams visited,
Not mine—no sleep, but at my pillow fear
That keeps these eyes from slumber all too sound;
And when I start to sing or hum a tune,
And out of music cull sleep's antidote,
I always weep the state of this great house,
Not in high fettle as it used to be.
But now at last may good news in a flash
Scatter the darkness and deliver us! (*The beacon flashes.*)
Hail, lamp of joy, whose gleam turns night to day,
Hail, radiant sign of dances numberless
In Argos for our happy state! Ho there!
I summon Agamemnon's sleeping queen,
To leave her couch and lift the ringing voice
Of gracious alleluias through the house
To celebrate the beacon, if it be true
That Troy is taken, as this blaze portends.
And I will dance the overture myself. (*Dances.*)

My master's dice have fallen well, and I
For this night's work shall score a treble six.
Well, come what may, let it be mine to grasp
In this right hand my master's, home again!
The rest is secret: a heavy ox has trod
Across my tongue. These walls, if they had mouths,
Might tell tales all too plainly. I speak to those
Who know, to others—purposely forget.

(*He disappears into the palace. A woman's cry of joy is heard within. Enter* CHORUS OF ARGIVE ELDERS.)

CHORUS: Ten years is it since that plaintiff-at-arms
In the suit against Priam,
Menelaus, with lord Agamemnon his peer,
Twin-sceptred in sovranty ordered of Zeus,
Children of Atreus, strong brace of command,
Did embark with the fleet of a thousand ships
In a battle-array
And set out from the land of the Argives,
With a cry from the heart, with a clamour of war,
Like eagles bereft of their nestlings embowered
On a mountainous height, with a wheel and a whir
As of winged oars beating the waves of the wind,
Wasted the long watch
At the cradle and lost is their labour.
Yet aloft some God, maybe Apollo
Or Pan, or Zeus, giveth ear to the cry
Of the birds that have made
Their abode in the heavens, and lo, he doth send
On the head of the sinner a Fury!

(CLYTEMNESTRA *comes out of the palace and sacrifices before the sacred images.*)

Yea, so are the twin children of Atreus
By the mightier Zeus Hospitable sent
Unto Paris, to fight for a woman who knew
Many lovers, with many a knee bowed low

In the dust, spears bent, limbs locked in the sweat
Of the close-knit bridals of battle,
Bringing death to the Greek and the Trojan.
And howe'er it doth fare with them now, ordained
Is the end, unavailing the flesh and the wine
To appease God's fixed indignation.

As for us, in the frailty of age, unenrolled
In the martial array that is gathered and gone,
We are left, with the strength
Of a babe, no more, that doth lean on a staff.
For the youth of the marrow enthroned in the breast
Is at one with its age—
In neither the War-god stands at his post.
Old men, what are they? Fast fading the leaf,
Three-footed they walk, yet frail as a child,
As a dream set afloat in the daylight.

(*They see* CLYTEMNESTRA.)

O Queen, O daughter of Tyndareus,
Clytemnestra, declare
What news, what tidings have come to thine ears,
What message hath moved
Thee to offer these prayers at the altars?
O see, at the shrines of our guardian gods,
Of the sky, of the earth,
Of the threshold and market alike—yea, all
Are ablaze with thy gifts of entreaty.
One lamp from another is kindled and soars
High as the heavens,
All charmed into flame by the innocent spell,
Soft-spoken enchantment of incense drawn
From the inmost stores of the palace.
Speak, make known what is lawful to tell;
So heal these cares consuming the heart,
Which now sometimes frown heavy and dark,
Sometimes bright hope from an altar aflame
Gleams forth with a message of comfort.

(CLYTEMNESTRA *goes out to tend the other altars of the city*.)

Strophe 1

Strong am I yet to declare that sign which sped from the palace
Men in the fulness of power; for yet God-given
Prowess of song doth abide in the breast of the aged:
To sing of two kings
United in spirit and sovranty, marshals of Hellas,
Sped with avenging sword by the warlike
Eagle in ships to the land of the Trojans,
Monarch of birds to the monarchs of men, black-plumed was
        the first, white-tailed was his fellow—
Before the King's house
They appeared on the side of the spear-hand
Plainly for all to behold them,
Battening both on a hare still big with the burden of offspring,
Cut off before her course was run.
Ailinon, ailinon cry, but may well yet conquer!

Antistrophe 1

Then did the priest as he marked them, two and twain in their
        temper,
Feasting on hare's flesh, know them, the children of Atreus,
Lords of the host, and he spake in a prophecy saying:
"In time the great quest
Shall plunder the fortress of Priam and the herds of the people,
Teeming flocks at the gates, with a sudden
Judgment of Fate in the dust of destruction.
Only let no jealous eye from above fall blackening, blasting the
        host as it bridles
The mouth of high Troy. For the merciful Artemis hateth
Those twin hounds of the Father,
Slaying the cowering hare with her young unborn in the belly;
She loathes the eagles' feast of blood."
Ailinon, ailinon cry, but may well yet conquer!

Epode

"O Goddess, gentle to the weak and helpless suckling of the
        raging lion,

Gentle to all young life that is nursed by the beasts of the wild,
    so now we beseech thee
Bring what is fair in the sign to a happy
End, what is faulty amend and set upright.
And lo, I cry unto Apollo, Healer,
Let her not visit the fleet
With a contrary wind, with an idle, helpless, stormbound stay,
Driving them on to a feast unlike to the other, unholy,
Builder of inborn strife that doth fear no man. It abides yet,
Terrible wrath that departs not,
Treachery keeping the house, long-memoried, children-avenging!"
Thus did the prophet declare great blessings mingled with sorrows
Destined to be, as he saw that sign at the great kings' going.
So in the same strain:
Ailinon, ailinon cry, but may well yet conquer!

Strophe 2

Zeus, whoe'er he be, if so it best
Pleaseth him to be addressed,
So shall he be named by me.
All things have I measured, yet
Naught have found save him alone,
Zeus, if a man from a heart heavy-laden with sorrow
Care would truly cast aside.

Antistrophe 2

Long since lived a master of the world,
Puffed with martial pride, of whom
None shall tell, his day is done;
Yea, and he who followed him
Met his master and is gone.
Zeus the victorious, praise him and gladly acclaim him;
Perfect wisdom shalt thou find.

Strophe 3

He to wisdom leadeth man,
He hath stablished firm the law,
Man shall learn by suffering.

When deep slumber falls, remembered sins
Chafe the sore heart with fresh pain, and no
Welcome wisdom meets within.
Harsh the grace dispensed by powers immortal
On the awful bench enthroned.

Antistrophe 3

Even so the elder prince,
Marshal of the ships of Greece,
Never thought to doubt a priest;
Nay, his heart with swaying fortune swayed.
Harbour-locked, hunger-pinched, hard-oppressed,
Still the host of Hellas lay
Facing Chalcis, where the never-tiring
Tides of Aulis ebb and flow.

Strophe 4

And still the storm blew from out the cold north,
With moorings wind-swept and hungry crews pent
In idle ships,
With tackling unspared and rotting timbers,
Till Time's insistent, slow erosion
Had all but stripped bare the bloom of Greek manhood.
And then was found but one
Charm to allay the tempest—never a blast so bitter—
Cried in a loud voice by the priest, "Artemis!" whereat the
        Atreidae were afraid, each with his staff smiting the
        earth and weeping.

Antistrophe 4

And then the King spake, the elder, saying:
"A bitter thing surely not to hearken,
And bitter too
To slay my own child, my royal jewel,
With unclean hands before the altar
Myself, her father, to spill a girl's pure blood.
Whate'er the choice, 'tis ill.

How shall I fail my thousand ships and desert my comrades?
So shall the storm cease, and the host eager for war crieth for
      that virginal blood righteously! So pray for a happy
      issue!"

Strophe 5

And when he bowed down beneath the harness
Of dire compulsion, his spirit veering
With sudden sacrilegious change,
Regardless, reckless, he turned to foul sin.
For man is made bold with base-contriving
Impetuous madness, prime seed of much grief.
And so then he slew his own child
For a war to win a woman
And to speed the storm-bound ships from the shore to battle.

Antistrophe 5

She cried aloud "Father!", yet they heard not;
A maiden scarce flowered, yet they cared not,
The lords who gave the word for war.
Her father prayed, then he bade his servants
To seize her, where wrapt in robe and drooping
She lay, and lift her up, like a young kid,
With bold heart above the altar,
And her lovely lips to bridle
That they might not cry out, cursing the House of Atreus,

Strophe 6

With gags, her mouth sealed in mute violence.
And then she let fall her cloak of saffron,
And glanced at each face around her
With eyes that dumbly craved compassion;
And like a picture she would but could not speak;
For oft aforetime at home
Her father's guests, after they had feasted,
Their cups replenished, had sat while with sweet voice she sang
The hymn of thanksgiving, pure and spotless,
Standing beside her father.

Antistrophe 6

The end I saw not. It shall not be told.
The arts of Calchas were well accomplished.
But Justice leads man to wisdom
By suffering. Until the morrow
Appeareth, vex not thy heart; for vain it were
To weep before sorrow come.
It shall be soon known as clear as daybreak.
And so may all this at last end in good news, for which
The Queen doth pray, next of kin and single
Stay of the land of Argos.

(CLYTEMNESTRA *appears at the door of the palace.*)

All honour, Clytemnestra, unto thee!
For meet it is, while our great master's throne
Stands empty, to pay homage to his queen.
What means this glad expectant sacrifice?
Is it good news? Pray speak! I long to hear.
    CLYTEMNESTRA: Good news! So charged, as the old proverb says,
May Morning rise out of the womb of Night!
'Tis yours to hear of joy surpassing hope.
My news is this: the Greeks have taken Troy.
    CHORUS: What? No! I cannot grasp it, incredible!
    CLYTEMNESTRA: The Greeks hold Troy. Is that not plain
        enough?
    CHORUS: Joy steals upon me, such joy as calls forth tears.
    CLYTEMNESTRA: Indeed your looks betray your loyalty.
    CHORUS: What is the proof? Have you no evidence?
    CLYTEMNESTRA: Of course I have—unless the Gods have
        cheated.
    CHORUS: You have given ear to some beguiling dream?
    CLYTEMNESTRA: I would not scream the fancies of my sleep.
    CHORUS: Rumours have wings—on these your heart has fed.
    CLYTEMNESTRA: You mock my wits as though I were a girl.
    CHORUS: But when? How long is it since the city fell?
    CLYTEMNESTRA: The night that gave birth to this dawning
        day.
    CHORUS: What messenger could bring the news so fast?

CLYTEMNESTRA: The God of Fire from Ida sent forth light,
And beacon from beacon brought the trail of flame
To me. From Ida first to Hermes' cliff
On Lemnos, and from thence a third great lamp
Was flashed to Athos, lofty mount of Zeus;
Up, up it soared, and lured the dancing shoals
To skim the waves in rapture at the light;
A golden courier, like the sun, it sped
Post-haste its message to Macistus' rock,
Which vigilant and impatient bore it on
Across Euripus, till the flaming sign
Was marked by watchers on Messapium,
Who swift to answer kindled high the blaze
Of withered heath, whence with new strength the light
Undarkened yet rose like the radiant moon
Across the valley of Asopus, still
Relayed in glory, to Cithaeron's heights.
Onward it sped, not slow the sentinels
But burning more than was commanded them,
Till at one leap across Gorgopis' lake
To the peak of Aegiplanctus it passed the word
To burn and burn, and they unsparing flung
A flaming comet to the cape that looks
Over the gulf Saronian. Suddenly
It swooped, and pounced upon the Spider's Crag,
Next neighbour of this city, whence at last
It found its mark upon the roof of Atreus,
That beacon fathered by the fires of Ida.
Such were the stages of this torch-relay,
One from another snatching up the light,
And the last to run is victor in the race.
That is my evidence, the token which
My lord has signalled out of Troy to me.
  CHORUS: Lady, I will address the Gods anon,
But now with all my heart I long to hear
That tale again and take my fill of wonder.
  CLYTEMNESTRA: To-day the Greeks hold Troy; and I divine
That city rings with ill-assorted cries.
If oil and vinegar were to be poured

Into one vessel, you would not call them friends.
Even so the conquered and their conquerors,
Two voices have they for their fortunes twain.
For those, prostrate over their fallen kin,
Brother by brother, old men beside their sons,
Lament with lips no longer free the fate
Of those they loved most dearly; while again
These others, spent after the restless night
Of battle-rout, troop hungry to what meal
The town affords, undrilled, unbilleted,
But seizing each what luck apportions them.
Already in those captive Trojan homes
They take their lodging, free from the frosty sky,
From heaven's dew delivered—O how blest
Their sleep shall be, off guard the whole night long!
And if they honour the presiding Gods
And altars of the plundered territory,
Then those despoilers shall not be despoiled.
Only let no desire afflict the host
To lay rapacious hands on sanctities.
The homeward journey lies before them yet,
The last lap of the race is still to run.
And if they came guiltless before the Gods,
The grievance of the dead might then become
Fair-spoken—barring sudden accident.
Such is the message brought you by a woman.
May good prevail, inclined decisively!
Blessings abound, and I would reap their fruit.
    CHORUS: Woman, your gracious words are like a man's,
Most wise in judgment. I accept the sign
And now once more turn to address the Gods.
Long labour has been well repaid in joy.

    (CLYTEMNESTRA *retires into the palace.*)

O Zeus Almighty, O bountiful Night,
Housekeeper of heaven's embroidery, thou
Hast entangled the towers of the city of Troy
In a fine-spun net, which none could escape,
Not a man nor a child, nay all are entrapped

In the far-flung coils of destruction.
Great Zeus the Hospitable, him do I praise,
Who hath punished at last the transgressor; for long
Was his bow outstretched with unerring intent,
That the shaft might not fall short nor escape
Far out in the starry expanses.

Strophe 1

By Zeus struck down. 'Tis truly spoken,
With each step clear and plain to track out.
He willed, his will was done. It was declared once
That God regards not the man who hath trod
Beneath his feet holy sanctities. An unrighteous thought;
For lo, swift ruin worketh sure judgment on hearts
With pride puffed up and high presumption,
On all stored wealth that overpasseth
The bound of due measure. Far best to live
Free of want and griefless, rich in the gift of wisdom.
     Help is there none for him who,
     Glutted with gold, in wanton
     Pride from his sight has kicked the great
     Altar of watchful Justice.

Antistrophe 1

As fell Temptation drives him onward,
The dread fore-scheming child of Ruin,
What cure avails to heal? Behold, not darkly
His curse doth shine forth, a bright, baleful light.
And like to false bronze betrayed by touch of sure-testing stone,
His hue turns black and shows the truth time-tried; he seems
A fond child chasing birds that take wing;
And one crime brands a mighty city.
He prays to deaf heaven, none hears his cry;
Justice drags him down to death for his wicked converse.
     Thus did the sinner Paris
     Come to the House of Atreus,
     Leaving the table spread for him
     Shamed with theft of a woman.

Strophe 2

She left her own people shields massed for war,
And densely-thronged spears, a fleet manned and launched for
        battle;
She brought to Troy in lieu of dowry death.
On light foot through the gates she tripped—
A sin of sins! And long did they lament,
The seers, the King's prophets, saying darkly:
"Alas, the sad house and they that rule therein,
Alas, the bed tracked with print of love that fled!
Behold, in silence, unhonoured, without reproach,
They sit upon the ground and weep.
Beyond the sea lies their love,
Here a wraith seems to rule the palace."
    Shapely the grace of statues,
    Yet doth her lord abhor them;
    Love is there none in lifeless eyes,
    Aphrodite has vanished.

Antistrophe 2

Delusive dream-shapes that float through the night
Beguile and bring him delight sweet but unsubstantial;
For idly, even while he seems to see,
The arms clasp empty air, and soon
The passing vision turns and glides away
On silent wing down the paths of slumber.
At home the hearth lies in sorrow such as this,
And more; in each house throughout the land of Greece
That sent its dearest to make war beyond the sea,
The brave heart is called to school itself
In slow endurance against
Griefs that strike deep into the bosom:
    Those that were sent away they
    Knew, but now they receive back
    Not the faces they longed to see,
    Only a heap of ashes.

Strophe 3

The God of War holds the twin scales of strife,
Cruel gold-changer merchandising men,

Embarking homeward from Troy a heap of dust fire-refined,
Making up its weight in grief,
Shapely vessels laden each
With the ashes of a friend.
They mourn and praise them, saying, "*He*
Was practised well in feats of war,
And *he*, who died a noble death—
All to avenge another man's wife."
It is muttered in a whisper,
And it spreads with growling envy of the sons of Atreus.
    They lie still, the possessors
    Each of a strip of Trojan
    Soil, but the land that hides their fair
    Limbs is a foe and foreign.

Antistrophe 3

A people's wrath voiced abroad bringeth grave
Danger, no less than public curse pronounced.
It still abideth for me, a hidden fear wrapped in night.
Watchful are the Gods of all
Hands with slaughter stained. The black
Furies wait, and when a man
Has grown by luck, not justice, great,
With sudden overturn of chance
They wear him to a shade, and, cast
Down to perdition, who shall save him?
In excess of fame is danger.
With a jealous eye the Lord Zeus in a flash shall smite him.
    Mine be the life unenvied,
    Neither to plunder cities
    Nor myself a prisoner bow
    Down to the will of others.

—The tale of glad news afire
Throughout the town spreads its fleet
Rumour; yet if this be true,
Who knows? It is perhaps a trick played by God.
—Who is so childish or so maimed of wit
To let a mere fiery word

Inflame the heart, then with swiftly-changed import
Flicker out and fade to nought?
—A woman's heart ever thus
Accepteth joy ere the joy is brought to light.
—Too credulous a woman's longing flies
And spreading swiftly, swiftly dies,
An idle word noised abroad on woman's lips.

Soon shall we know what means this fleet exchange
Of lights relayed and beacon-messages—
Whether 'tis true, or like a dream it dawns,
This joyful daybreak, to beguile the mind.
Here is a herald running from the shore.
He wears a garland, and the thirsty dust,
Mire's brother and companion, testifies
That he shall not be dumb nor speak his news
With mountain pinewood flashing smoke and flame,
But either he shall bid us greater joy,
Or else—no, I abjure the contrary.
Glad shone the light, and gladly be it crowned!
Whoever prays that it be otherwise,
His be the harvest of his own offence!

(*Enter a* HERALD.)

HERALD: Joy, land of Argos, joy to my father's soil!
After ten years this dawn has brought me home.
Many the broken hopes, but this has held.
Little I thought here in this Argive earth
To die and in dear hands be laid to rest.
O Land, I bid thee joy, and thee, O Sun,
And Zeus the Highest, and the Pythian King,
Bending no more at us his bitter shafts—
Thy wrath beside Scamander was enough,
And now defend us, Saviour, Healer too,
Our Lord Apollo! All the public Gods
I greet, and most that messenger beloved,
My patron Hermes, to all heralds dear;
And those heroic dead who sent us forth,
Prepare to welcome those whom war has spared!

Hail, royal palace, roof most dear to me,
And holy shrines, whose faces catch the sun,
Now, as of old, with radiance in your eyes
Greet worthily your lord who comes at last
Bringing at night a lamp to lighten you
And all here present, Agamemnon, King.
O welcome gladly, for it is right and meet,
Him who with mattock of just-dealing Zeus
Has levelled Troy and laid her valleys waste
And all her seed uprooted from the earth.
Such is the yoke he set on her proud neck,
Great son of Atreus, master, sovran, blest,
Most worthy to be honoured over all
Men of his day. For Paris and his Troy
No longer boast to have suffered less than done.
Of rape convicted and of brigandage,
He lost his booty and in utter ruin
Brought down the ancient mansion of his sires.
The sons of Priam paid double for their sin.

CHORUS: Hail, Herald from the host, I bid you joy!
HERALD: 'Tis mine. Come, death! O God, I am content!
CHORUS: Love for your fatherland has worn you out.
HERALD: So much that joy has filled my eyes with tears.
CHORUS: Then bitterness was not unmixed with sweet.
HERALD: Sweetness? How so? Your wit eludes me there.
CHORUS: You loved in absence those who loved again.
HERALD: The country yearned for us, who yearned for her?
CHORUS: Even so, with many a groan of dark surmise.
HERALD: Whence came this sullen misgiving for our sake?
CHORUS: Let silence heal—I learnt that long ago.
HERALD: How? In our absence had you cause to fear?
CHORUS: As you have said, now it were joy to die.
HERALD: Yes, for the end is well. Our enterprise
At last is well concluded, though in part
The issue be found wanting. Who but a God
Might live unscathed by sorrow all his days?
If I should tell those labours, the rough lodging,
The hard thwart's scant repose, the weary groans

That were our lot through watches of the day;
And then ashore ills more insufferable,
In camp beneath the beetling walls of Troy,
The rains from heaven and the dews that dripped
From sodden soils with cruel insistence, breeding
A host of vermin in our woollen cloaks;
If I should tell those winters, when the birds
Dropped dead and Ida heaped on us her snows,
Those summers, when unstirred by wind or wave
The sea lay pillowed in the sleep of noon—
But why lament that now? The toil is past—
Yes, for the dead so past that, where they lie,
No care shall trouble them to rise again.
Ah, those are spent: why count our losses then
And vex the quick with grievance of the dead?
So to adversity I bid farewell:
For us, survivors of the Argive arms,
Misfortune sinks, our vantage turns the scale.
And hence 'tis meet before yon rising sun
To cry o'er land and sea on wings of fame,
"Long since the Argive host which plundered Troy
Set up these spoils, a time-worn ornament,
Before this palace to the Gods of Greece."
Whereto in answer should this land be praised
With those who led her, and to Zeus the giver
Shall thanks be given. That is all my news.
    CHORUS: Well said! Your say, I grant you, masters mine.
Old age is ever young enough to learn.
This news, although it shall enrich me too,
Concerns the palace, and most of all the Queen.

    (CLYTEMNESTRA *appears at the door of the palace.*)

    CLYTEMNESTRA: Long since I raised my joyful alleluias
When the first messenger flashed out of night
The tidings of the fall of Ilium,
And one rebuked me saying, "Has a beacon
Persuaded you that Troy has now been taken?
Truly a woman's heart is light as air."
Such was their gossip, and they called me mad;

But I still sacrificed, and through the town
The women's alleluia taken up
Was chanted gladly at the holy shrines,
Lulling to sleep the sacramental flame.
And now what need of further news from you?
I shall soon hear all from the King himself,
My honoured lord, for whom I shall prepare
A welcome home as fair as may be. What
Light could be sweeter in a woman's eyes
Than to fling wide the gates for her beloved
Whom God has saved from war? Go and command him
To hasten back, the darling of his people,
Where he shall find within his house a wife
As loyal as he left her, a faithful hound
Guarding his substance, to enemies unkind,
And in all else the same, his treasuries
Sealed all these years and still inviolate.
Delight from other men and ill-report
Are strange to me, as strange as tempered steel.

(She retires into the palace.)

HERALD: Such is her boast, and though 'tis big with truth,
Is it not unseemly on a lady's lips?
CHORUS: Such is her message, as you understand,
To the instructed fair—in outward show.
But tell me, messenger, what of Menelaus,
Co-regent of this kingdom? Has he too
Returned in safety to his fatherland?
HERALD: I cannot tell a falsehood fair to bring
Enduring comfort to the friends I love.
CHORUS: Can you not make your tale both fair and true?
It is vain to hide disunion of the pair.
HERALD: The man has vanished from the Grecian host,
Himself and ship together. 'Tis the truth.
CHORUS: Did he embark from Troy before your eyes,
Or was it a storm that struck the fleet at sea?
HERALD: A skilful archer, you have hit the mark
And told a long disaster in a word.

CHORUS: But what report did rumour spread of him
Among the other seamen—alive or dead?
HERALD: We know not; none has certain news of him
Unless the Sun, from whom this earth draws life.
CHORUS: But tell us of that tempest that came down
So suddenly, a bolt from angry heaven.
HERALD: It is not meet to mar a day of praise
With voice of evil tidings: such offices
Are not for Gods of Heaven. When a man
Drags sadly home defeat long prayed-against,
With twofold wound, one of the commonwealth,
And one of each man driven from his home
Beneath that double scourge, the curse of War,
Armed with twin spears and double-braced for blood,
Such dire event were fit to celebrate
With some fell hymn to the infernal Furies;
But when he brings deliverance and finds
A land rejoicing in prosperity,—
How should I mingle foul with fair, and tell
Of tempest stirred out of an angry sky?
Water and Fire, old enemies before,
Conspired together and made covenant
To overwhelm the fated ships of Greece.
When night had fallen, with a rising swell,
The fleet was battered by the winds of Thrace,
Hull against hull, till, gorged and buffeted
With blasts of hail and blinding hurricane,
An evil shepherd swept them out of sight.
And when at last the sun's pale light arose,
We saw the Aegean in blossom with the strewn
Flotsam of drowning men and shattered spars.
Our own ship went unscathed; it must have been
Some deity that touched the helm and snatched
Or begged us off, and then the saving spirit
Of Fortune took the wheel, our pilot, till
We passed between the rugged mountain-cliffs
And anchored where we shipped the foam no more;
And there, delivered from that watery hell,
We nursed in brooding hearts the sudden stroke

That had laid our great armada in the dust.
And now, if any of those others live,
Why, they must deem that we are dead and gone.
As they of us, so we surmise of them.
But pray still for the best. And Menelaus,
Though likeliest far that he is in distress,
Still, if some ray of sunlight from above
Marks him among the living, rescued by Zeus
Reluctant that his seed should wholly perish,
Then there is hope yet for his safe return.
In this, believe me, you have heard the truth.

(*The* HERALD *returns to the army.*)

Strophe 1

Who was he who named her name,
Justly called with perfect truth?
Surely one whom mortal eye may not see,
Prescient of her destiny,
Naming her with fatal chance
Bride of the lance and long dissension,
Helen—hell indeed she carried
Unto men and ships and a proud city, stealing
From the silk veils of her chamber, sailing seaward
With the Zephyr's breath behind her;
And the armed legions of men set out to hunt her
On the path that leaves no imprint
Till they beached on a leafy shore
Washed by Simois, bringing
War and the waste of bloodshed.

Antistrophe 1

Truly too for Ilium,
Turning into keeners kin,
Wrath, the instrument of God's will, at last
Claimed his payment for the spurned
Board of Zeus Hospitable,

Even from those who graced her nuptials
With the happy chant of Hymen
And acclaimed her coming with songs that soon were turned into
        weeping.
They have learned another music
In the length of time, and cry out
In a loud voice for the sin of Paris, naming
Him the groom of black betrothal,
Mourning the guilt that laid them low in the dust of battle,
Stricken and steeped in bloodshed.

Strophe 2

Of old, so it is said, an oxherd did rear at the hearth a young
Lion-cub, as a fosterling, in his infancy bringing
Smiles to the face of the aged,
Innocent sport of the children,
Often pampered and caressed,
Fondled like a babe with hands
Licked by the fawning tongue that craved
Meat from the master's table.

Antistrophe 2

But Time brought to the light his true nature, after his kind,
        and then
Years of care were repaid in slaughter of pasturing cattle,
Tearing the hand that had tended,
Blood in the house, and the inmates
Bowed in helpless anguish, struck
Down beneath the heaven-sent
Carnage which they had nursed, a fell
Priest of avenging bloodshed.

Strophe 3

And so it seemed once there came to Ilium
A sweet-smiling calm, without cloud, serene, beguiling,
A rare gem set in crown of riches,
Shaft of a softly-glancing eye,
Bloom of love that doth prick the bosom.

But a change carried her bridals
To a bitter consummation.
To the proud children of Priam,
With the guidance of the stern wrath
Of Zeus, she came as a fierce
Bridal-bewailing Fury.

(CLYTEMNESTRA *appears at the door of the palace.*)

Antistrophe 3

A tale of old time is told on mortal lips,
That when man hath brought to full growth abundant riches,
It dies not childless, nay it breedeth;
Whence from a happy life is reaped
Fruit of plenteous lamentation.
With a lone voice I deny it.
It is only deeds unholy
That increase, fruitful in offspring
Of the same breed as its fathers.
Where justice rules in the house,
Blest of God is the issue.

Strophe 4

But ancient pride loves to put forth a fresh bloom of sin out of
       human evil, soon or late.
Behold, whenever the time appointed come,
A cloud of deep night, spirit of vengeance irresistible,
Horror of dark disaster hung
Brooding within the palace,
True to the dam that bore it.

Antistrophe 4

But where is Justice? She lights up the smoke-darkened hut, yea
       she loves humility.
From gilded pinnacles of polluted hands
She turns her eyes back unto the dwelling of the pure in heart;
So, regarding not the false

Stamp on the face of wealth, leads
All to the end appointed.

(*Enter* AGAMEMNON *riding in a chariot and followed by another which carries Cassandra and other spoils of war.*)

All hail, son of Atreus, captor of Troy,
All hail to thee, King!
How shall I greet thee, how tune my address
So as neither to fall too short nor surpass
Due measure of joy?
  Full many are they who unjustly respect
Mere semblance of truth, and all men are quick
With a tear to the eye for a neighbour's distress,
But with hearts untouched by his trouble.
Just so they rejoice with him, forcing a smile
Like his on their laughterless faces.
Yet he that can read in the book of the eyes
Man's nature, will not be deluded by looks
Which fawn with dissembled fidelity, false
Like wine that is mingled with water.
So surely, I will not deny it, when thou
Didst marshal the host to recover
Helen, willingly wanton, with thousands of lives,
I accounted thee like to a picture deformed
Or a helm ill-turned by the pilot.
  But now from the depth of the heart it is mine
To salute thee with love:
Toil happily crowned
Brings sweetness at last to the toiler.
And in time thou shalt learn to distinguish apart
The unjust and the just housekeeper among
Those who are set over thy people.
  AGAMEMNON: First, it is just to greet this land of Argos
With her presiding Gods, my partners in
This homecoming, as in the just revenge
I brought to Priam's city. When the Gods
Heard that appeal unvoiced by mortal tongue,
They cast their votes decisive in the urn

Of blood with doom of death for Ilium
And uttermost destruction; and in the other
Hope hesitant still hovered on the brink.
The smoke of pillage marks that city yet,
The rites of ruin live. Her ashes breathe
Their last, with riches redolent, and die.
Wherefore 'tis right to render memorable
Thanks to the Gods. For that bold piracy
We have exacted payment; for a woman
That city lies in dust, struck by the fierce
Brood of the Horse, the Argive host in arms,
Which at the setting of the Pleiades
Leapt like a hungry lion across her towers
And slaked its thirst in streaming blood of kings.
   Such is my measured preface to the Gods.
I have marked well your loyal sentiments
At one with mine, and sealed with my assent.
Too few are they whose nature is to honour
A friend's good fortune without jealousy.
Malignant venom seated at the heart
Doubles the sick man's burden, as he groans
For his own case and grieves no less to see
His neighbour walking in prosperity.
Devotion seeming-full—an empty shadow
I call it, speaking from sure knowledge tried
In the true mirror of companionship.
Odysseus only, who sailed against his will,
Once harnessed, proved a trusty outrigger—
Alive or dead, I know not. What concerns
The city and the Gods we shall dispose
In public congress, and deliberate
How what is well may be continued so,
And where some sickness calls for remedy,
We shall with cautery or kindly knife
Of surgery essay to heal the sore.
   But now, returning to my royal hearth,
My first act shall be to salute the Gods
Who led me hence and lead me home again;
Victory attends me: may she rest secure!

CLYTEMNESTRA: People of Argos, elders assembled here,
I shall declare before you unashamed
My way with him I love; for diffidence
Dies in us all with time. I tell a tale
From my own heart of the unhappy life
I led while he fought under Ilium.
First, none can say how much a wife must bear,
Who sits at home, with no man's company,
And waits upon the train of evil news,
One messenger, then another with a tale
Of worse disaster shouted through the house;
And as for wounds, if he had met as many
As constant rumour poured into his home,
His limbs were like a net, pierced through and through.
If he had died, the prevalent report,
He was a second Geryon, with bodies three
And triple cloak of earth draped over them,
Three outstretched corpses and one death for each.
Beset with malignant rumours such as these,
Often the halter pressed my eager throat,
Released by others with no thanks from me.
    And hence it is our child is not here present,
As it were meet, pledge of our plighted vows,
Orestes. Marvel not at this. He lives
Safe in the charge of an old friend at arms,
Atrophius the Phocian, who admonished me
Of various dangers—your life in jeopardy,
A restive populace, and that fault of nature,
When man has been cast down, to trample on him.
In this excuse, believe me, lies the truth.
    As for myself, the fountains of my tears
Are drained away till not a drop is left.
The late night-vigils have outworn my eyes,
Weeping the light that was to burn for you,
With tears that went unheeded. Even in dreams
I would start up, roused by the tenuous beat
Of a gnat's wing from visions all of you,
Imagining more ills than credible
In the slow hours that kept me company.

But now, all griefs endured with patient heart,
I name this man the watchdog of the fold,
Forestay that saves the ship, upsoaring oak
That holds the roof, a longed-for only child,
A shore unhoped-for spied by sailors' eyes!
This is my greeting, this my homage to him,
And may no envy follow it! Enough
Our sorrows heretofore; and now, beloved,
Step from the chariot, but do not set
Upon the ground those feet that trampled Troy.
Make haste, my handmaids who have been appointed
To strew his path with outspread tapestry.
Prepare a road of purple coverlets
Where Justice leads to an unhoped-for home;
And there the rest our sleep-unvanquished care
Shall order justly, as the Gods ordain.

AGAMEMNON: Daughter of Leda, guardian of my home,
Your greeting was prolonged, proportionate
To my long absence; but tributes of due praise
Should come from other lips; and furthermore
Seek not to unman me with effeminate
Graces and barbarous salaams agape
In grovelling obeisance at my feet,
Nor with invidious purple pave my way.
Such honours are an appanage of God,
And I, being mortal, cannot but fear to tread
On this embroidered beauty, rich and rare.
Honour me as a man, not as a God.
Foot-mats and fine robes ring differently
In Rumour's ill-tongued music, and of all
God's gifts the chief is wisdom. Count him blest
Whose life has ended in felicity.
I shall act as I have told you, conscience-clear.
CLYTEMNESTRA: Yet tell me frankly, according to your judg-
ment—
AGAMEMNON: My judgment stands, make no mistake of that.
CLYTEMNESTRA: Would you in danger have vowed to God this
act?

AGAMEMNON: Yes, if the priesthood had commanded it.

CLYTEMNESTRA: And what, if Priam had conquered, would *hé* have done?

AGAMEMNON: He would have trod the purple, I do not doubt.

CLYTEMNESTRA: Then give no thought to mortal tongues that wag.

AGAMEMNON: The clamour of a populace counts for much.

CLYTEMNESTRA: Whom no man envies, no man shall admire.

AGAMEMNON: It is not for a woman to take part in strife.

CLYTEMNESTRA: Well may the victor yield a victory!

AGAMEMNON: Do *you* set store by such a victory?

CLYTEMNESTRA: Be tempted, freely vanquished, victor still!

AGAMEMNON: Well, if it be your will, let someone loose
The sandals bound in service to my feet;
And as they tread this ocean-purple, may
No far-off God cast on me envious eyes!
Deep shame there lies in prodigality
Which tramples robes woven of silver worth.
But be it so. And see this stranger here
Is treated gently. Kingship kindly used
Wins favour in the sight of God above;
For no man willingly endures the yoke
Of servitude, and she, the army's gift,
Is a blossom culled out of uncounted wealth.
And now, constrained to accept these honours from you,
Treading the purple I pass into my home.

CLYTEMNESTRA: There is still the sea, it shall not be dried up,
Renewing fresh from infinite abundance
Rich merchandise of purple-stained attire;
Wherein the Gods, my lord, have well endowed
A royal house that knows no penury.
How many robes would I have vowed to tread,
Had prophecy instructed, if thereby
I had contrived the ransom of one soul!
While the root lives, the foliage shall raise
Its shady arch against the burning Dog-star;
And, as your coming to your hearth and home
Signifies warmth that comes in wintry cold,

So, when Zeus from the bitter virgin-grape
Draws wine, then coolness fills the house at last,
As man made perfect moves about his home.

(AGAMEMNON *has gone into the palace.*)

Zeus, Zeus the Perfecter, perfect thou my prayer,
And perfect also that which is thy care!

(CLYTEMNESTRA *goes into the palace.*)

Strophe 1

What is this insistent fear
Which in my prophetic heart
Set and steady beats with evil omen,
Chanting unbidden a brooding, oracular music?
Why can I not cast it out
Like a dream of dark import,
Setting good courage firm
On my spirit's empty throne?
In time the day came
When the Greeks, with anchors plunged
Deep in that shingle strand,
Moored the sloops of war, and men
Thronged the beach of Ilium;

Antistrophe 1

So to-day my eyes have seen
Safe at last their homecoming.
Still I hear a strain of stringless music,
Dissonant dirge of the Furies, a chant uninstructed
Quired in this uneasy breast,
Desolate of hope and cheer.
Not for naught beats the heart
Stirred with ebb and flow of fate
In righteous men: soon
What is feared shall come to pass.
Yet against hope I pray,
May it prove of no import,
Unfulfilled and falsified!

Strophe 2

If a man's health be advanced over the due mean,
It will trespass soon upon sickness who stands
Close neighbour, between them a thin wall.
So doth the passage of life
Sped with a favouring breeze
Suddenly founder on reefs of destruction.
Caution seated at the helm
Casts a portion of the load
Overboard with measured throw.
So the ship shall come to shore;
So the house shall stand, if not
Overcharged with store of woe.
Plenty from Zeus and abundance that yieldeth a yearly return
        from the harvested furrows
Driveth hunger from the door.

Antistrophe 2

But if the red blood of a man ever be spilled on the ground, drip-
        ping and deadly, then who
Shall recall it again with his magic?
Even the healer who knew
Charms to recover the dead,
Zeus put an end to his wrongful powers.
Portions are there preordained,
Each supreme within its own
Bounds decreed eternally;
Else would heart outstripping tongue
Cast misgiving to the winds.
Now in darkness deep it groans,
Brooding in sickly despair, and no longer it hopes to resolve in
        an orderly web these
Mazes of a fevered mind.

(CLYTEMNESTRA *appears at the door of the palace.*)

CLYTEMNESTRA: You too, Cassandra, come within; for Zeus
Of his great mercy grants to you a part
In our domestic sacrifice, to stand

Among the slaves before his altar there.
Step from the chariot, put by your pride.
Even great Heracles submitted once
To toil and eat the bread of slavery;
And should compulsion bring a man to this,
Much comfort lies in service to a house
Of immemorial riches. Those who have reaped
A harvest never hoped-for out of hand
Are strict upon the rule and show no mercy.
What is customary shall here be yours.

CHORUS: To you she spoke, and made her meaning plain.
Caught in the casting-net of destiny,
'Twere best to yield; and yet perchance you will not.
 CLYTEMNESTRA: Nay, if she speak not, like the babbling
  swallow,
Some barbarous tongue which none can understand,
With mystic words I'll win the mind within.
 CHORUS: Go with her. Your plight affords no better choice.
Step from the chariot and do her will.
 CLYTEMNESTRA: I have no time to idle at the door.
The victims stand upon the palace hearth
Before the altar, ready for the knife
To render thanks for these unhoped-for joys.
If you too will take part, do not delay;
But, if you lack the wit to understand me,
Do *you* address her with barbarian hand.
 CHORUS: She needs, it seems, a clear interpreter.
Like some wild creature is she, newly-trapped.
 CLYTEMNESTRA: Nay, she is mad, and gives her ears to folly.
Her city newly-captured, hither brought
A slave, she knows not how to take the bit
Until her pride is foamed away in blood.
I'll waste no more words to demean myself.

(CLYTEMNESTRA *goes into the palace.*)

 CHORUS: *I* feel no anger, for I pity you.
Unhappy girl, dismount and follow her,
Yield to your fate and take its yoke upon you.

Strophe 1

CASSANDRA: Oh! Alas, Earth! Apollo, Apollo!
CHORUS: What is this cry in the name of Loxias?
He is not one to greet with lamentation.

Antistrophe 1

CASSANDRA: Oh! Alas, Earth! Apollo, Apollo!
CHORUS: Again she calls with blasphemous utterance
The God who stands aloof from mourning cries.

Strophe 2

CASSANDRA: Apollo, Apollo, the Wayfarer! Destroyed by thee!
Once more hast thou destroyed me wantonly!
CHORUS: Her own sad fate, it seems, she will prophesy.
She is now a slave, and yet God's gift abides.

Antistrophe 2

CASSANDRA: Apollo, Apollo, the Wayfarer! Destroyed by thee!
Ah, whither hast thou led me? What house is this?
CHORUS: The House of the Atreidae. Nay, if that
Thou knowest not, then hear the truth from me.

Strophe 3

CASSANDRA: Palace abhorred of God, conscious of hidden crime,
Sanguinary, sullied with slaughtered kin,
A charnel-house that streams with children's blood!
CHORUS: Keen as a hound upon the scent she seems,
This stranger, tracking down a murderous trail.

Antistrophe 3

CASSANDRA: I can declare a testimony plain to read.
Listen to them as they lament the foul
Repast of roasted flesh for father's mouth!
CHORUS: We know of thy prophetic fame already,
And have no need of an interpreter.

Strophe 4

CASSANDRA: Out, out, alas! What is it plotted now?
Horror unspeakable
Is plotted in this house, insufferable,
A hard cross for kinsfolk,
Without cure. The hoped-for succour is far away.
    CHORUS: This prophecy escapes me. Yet the first
I recognised—the country cries of it.

Antistrophe 4

CASSANDRA: Alas, O wicked! Is thy purpose *that?*
He who hath shared thy bed,
To bathe his limbs, to smile—how speak the end?
The end comes, and quickly:
A hand reaching out, followed by a hand again!
    CHORUS: Still at a loss am I; riddles before,
Now sightless oracles obscure my way.

Strophe 5

CASSANDRA: Ah, ah! O horrible!
What is appearing now? Some net of mesh infernal.
Mate of his bed and board, she is a snare
Of slaughter! Oh, murderous ministers,
Cry alleluia, cry,
Fat with blood, dance and sing!

Strophe 6

CHORUS: What is this Fury thou hast called to cry
In exultation? It brings no cheer to me.
Oh, to the heart it falls, saffron of hue, the drop
Of blood which doth sink with life's setting sun,
Smitten with edge of steel.
Nearer, yet nearer draws the swift judgment-stroke.

Antistrophe 5

CASSANDRA: Ah, ah! Beware, beware!
Let not the cow come near! See how the bull is captured!

She wraps him in the robe, the hornèd trap,
Then strikes. He falls into the bath, the foul
Treacherous bowl of blood. Such her skilled artistry.

Antistrophe 6

CHORUS: No gift I boast in reading prophecy,
But this must signify calamity.
When did a prophet's voice issue in happiness?
Amidst mortal stress his word-woven art,
Ever divining ill,
Teacheth mankind before the hour chants of fear.

Strophe 7

CASSANDRA: Alas, alas, unhappy, pitiful destiny!
Now I lament my own passion to fill the bowl.
Oh whither hast thou led me? O my grief,
Whither, unless that I with him must die?

Strophe 8

CHORUS: Spirit of frenzy borne on by the breath of God,
Thy own mournful dirge
Singest thou, like the red-brown bird
Who never-weary pours out her full heart in song;
Itys, Itys! she cries, sorrow hath filled her days,
The sad nightingale.

Antistrophe 7

CASSANDRA: Alas, alas, the sweet music of the nightingale!
Body of wings the Gods fashioned to cover her,
And gave her, free of weeping, happy days.
For me there waits the stroke of two-edged steel.

Antistrophe 8

CHORUS: Whence is this passionate madness inspired of God
That still streameth on?
Tales of fear told in uncouth cries,
Set to a strain of high-pitched and harsh harmonies?

Whither the path of wild prophecy evil-tongued?
O where must it end?

Strophe 9

CASSANDRA: O fatal bridal-day, Paris the curse of all his kin!
O swift Scamander, streaming past my home,
Once on the banks of those waters I dwelt, and they
Nourished me as a child.
But now, it seems, my cries shall soon resound
Beside Cocytus and sad Acheron.

Strophe 10

CHORUS: What is it now? A cry simple for all to read.
Even a child may understand.
With sharp anguish cleft, as though red with blood,
My heart breaks, as these pitiful plaintive cries
Shatter the listening soul.

Antistrophe 9

CASSANDRA: Alas the pain, the pain, agony of a plundered town!
Alas, the King's rich offerings at the gates,
Lavished from flocks and herds, little availed to bring
Help to the city, so
That she might not have been what she is now.
And I distraught shall dash into the snare.

Antistrophe 10

CHORUS: Like to the rest is this pitiful utterance.
What evil spirit hath possessed
Thy soul, cruelly bending those fevered lips
To give voice to such dolorous tunes of death?
Who shall divine the end?

CASSANDRA: Listen! No more my prophecy shall glance
As through a veil, like a new-wedded maid.
Nay, bright and fresh, I tell thee, it shall flow
Against the sunrise, and like a wave engulf
The daybreak in disaster greater far
Than this. No riddles now; I shall instruct,

And you shall bear me witness step by step,
As I track down the scent of crimes of old.
On yonder housetop ever abides a choir
Of minstrels unmelodious, singing of ill;
And deeply-drunk, to fortify their spirit,
In human blood, those revellers yet abide,
Whom none can banish, Furies congenital,
And settled on the roof they chant the tune
Of old primordial Ruin, each in turn
Spewing with horror at a brother's outraged bed.
Say, have I missed, or marked my quarry down?
Am I a false prophet babbling at the gates?
Bear me on oath your witness that I know
The story of this household's ancient crimes.

CHORUS: What could an oath, however truly sworn,
Avail to heal? Indeed I marvel at you,
Born far beyond the sea, speaking of this,
An alien country, as though you had been present.
   CASSANDRA: The seer Apollo bestowed that gift on me.
   CHORUS: Was he smitten with the shaft of love, a God?
   CASSANDRA: Time was, shame would not let me speak of this.
   CHORUS: Prosperity makes man fastidious.
   CASSANDRA: Oh, but he wrestled strenuously for my love.
   CHORUS: Did he bring you to the act of getting child?
   CASSANDRA: First I consented, then I cheated him.
   CHORUS: Already captive to his craft divine?
   CASSANDRA: Already I foretold my people's fate.
   CHORUS: How did you find refuge from his displeasure?
   CASSANDRA: The price I paid was that none gave me heed.
   CHORUS: Your prophecies have earned belief from us.

   CASSANDRA: Oh misery!
Again the travail of true prophecy
With prelude wild makes tumult in my soul!
Do you not see them, seated on the roof,
Those children, like the ghastly shapes of dreams,
Murdered, it seems, by their own kith and kin,
Meat in their hands from some familiar meal,

The inward parts and bowels, of which their father
Ate—what a pitiable load is theirs!
That is the sin for which is planned revenge
By the faint-hearted lion, stretched in the bed,
Who keeps house for my master—being his slave,
I must needs name him so—now home again.
Little he knows what that foul bitch, with ears
Laid back and lolling tongue, will bring to pass
With vicious snap of treacherous destruction.
So dead to shame! woman to murder man!
What beast abominable is her name?
Double-faced amphisbene, or skulking Scylla
Among the cliffs, waylaying mariners,
A hellish dam raging against her own,
In strife that gives no quarter! How loud she sang
Her alleluias over the routed foe,
While feigning gladness at his safe return!
Believe me not, what matter? 'Tis all one.
The future comes, and when your eyes have seen,
You shall cry out in pity, "She spoke true."
   CHORUS: Thyestes' banquet of the flesh of babes
I understood, and shuddered, terrified
To hear that tale told with unerring truth;
But for the rest I wander far astray.
   CASSANDRA: I say you shall see Agamemnon's death.
   CHORUS: Unhappy girl, hush those ill-omened lips!
   CASSANDRA: No healing god is here—there is no cure.
   CHORUS: None, if it be so; and yet may it not be!
   CASSANDRA: While you are praying, others prepare to kill.
   CHORUS: What man would plot so foul a villainy?
   CASSANDRA: Ah, you have missed my meaning utterly.
   CHORUS: But who shall do it? That escapes me still.
   CASSANDRA: And yet I know too well the speech of Greece.
   CHORUS: So does the Delphian, yet are his sayings dark.

   CASSANDRA: Ah, how it burns, the fire! It sweeps upon me!
Oh, oh, Apollo! Oh alas, my sorrow!
That lioness two-footed, lying with
The wolf in absence of the noble lion,

Shall kill me, O unhappy, and as though
Mixing a potion pours in the cup of wrath
My wages too, and while she sets an edge
Upon the steel for him, she vows to make
Murder the price of my conveyance hither.
   Why do I wear these tawdry mockeries,
This staff, this mantic wreath about my neck?
If I must die, then you shall perish first.
Down to perdition! Now you have your pay.
Bestow your fatal riches on another!
Behold Apollo stripping me himself
Of my prophetic raiment, regarding me,
Clad in his robes, a public laughing-stock
Of friend and enemy, one who has endured
The name of witch, waif, beggar, castaway.
So now the seer who made these eyes to see
Has led his servant to this mortal end.
No altar of my fathers waits for me,
But a block that drips blood at a dead man's grave.
   And yet we die not unavenged of heaven.
Another shall come to avenge us both,
Who for his father's sake shall kill his mother,
A wandering outcast, an exile far away,
He shall come back and set for his kin a crown
On this long tale of ruin. The Gods above
Have sworn a solemn covenant that his
Dead father's outstretched corpse shall call him home.
   Why do I weep for this so piteously?
Have I not seen the fall of Ilium?
And those who laid that city waste are thus
Discharged at last by heaven's arbitrament.
This door I name the gate of Hades: now
I will go and knock, I will endure to die.
My only prayer is that the blow be mortal,
To close these eyes in sleep without a struggle,
While my life's blood ebbs peacefully away.

CHORUS: O woman in whose wisdom is much grief,
Long have you spoken; and yet, if you know

The end, why like the consecrated ox
Walk with such patient step into the slaughter?
    CASSANDRA: Should the end linger, that is no escape.
    CHORUS: And yet the latest moment is the best.
    CASSANDRA: What should I gain by flight? My hour has come.
    CHORUS: You have the endurance of a valiant heart.
    CASSANDRA: Such words are common for those whom life has
        crossed.
    CHORUS: Yet there is comfort in honourable death.
    CASSANDRA: O father, father, and thy noble sons!

(CASSANDRA *approaches the door, then recoils.*)

    CHORUS: What is it? What terror has turned you back?
    CASSANDRA: Faugh!
    CHORUS: What means that cry? Some sickening at the heart?
    CASSANDRA: The palace reeks with fumes of dripping blood.
    CHORUS: No, 'tis the smell of fireside sacrifice.
    CASSANDRA: A vapour such as issues from a tomb.
    CHORUS: No scent of Araby have you marked in it.

    CASSANDRA: Nay, I will go to weep inside the house
Agamemnon's fate and mine. Enough of life!
O hear me, friends!
I am not scared like a bird once limed that takes
Fright at a bush. Witness, when I am dead,
The day when woman for this woman dies
And man mismarried for a man lies low.
I beg this of you at the point of death.
    CHORUS: Poor soul, foredoomed to death, I pity you.
    CASSANDRA: Yet one word more I have to speak, my own
Dirge for myself. I pray the Sun in heaven,
On whom I look my last, that he may grant
To him who shall come to avenge my master
From those who hate me payment of the price
For this dead slave-girl slain with so light a stroke.
Alas, mortality! when fortunate,
A painted image; in adversity,
The sponge's moist touch wipes it all away.
    CHORUS: And this to me is far more pitiable.

(CASSANDRA *goes into the palace.*)

Good fortune among mankind is a thing
Insatiable. Mansions of kings are marked
By the fingers of all, none warns her away,
None cries, O enter not hither!
Unto him the Immortals accorded the fall
Of the city of Troy,
And with honours divine he returns to his home.
But now, if the debt of the blood of the past
Is on him, if his death must crown it and pay
To the dead their price for the slaughtered of old,
Then who, when he hears these things, is assured
Of a life unwounded of sorrow?
    AGAMEMNON: Oh me, I am struck down!
    CHORUS: Hark, did you not hear that cry? The stroke of death!
    AGAMEMNON: Oh me, again!
    CHORUS: Ah, his voice it is, our King! The deed is done.
Come, take counsel how to meet this perilous hour.
1. I say, raise hue and cry—rally the people!
2. Break in at once upon their dripping blade.
3. Yes, let us act—no time for faltering now.
4. This bloody deed spells tyranny to come.
5. *They* spurn delay—*their* hands are not asleep.
6. What can we do, old men whose strength is gone?
7. No words of ours can raise the dead to life.
8. Must we wear out our age in slavery?
9. No, death is gentler than the tyrant's lash.
10. We heard his cries, but his death is still unproved.
11. Yes, we are only guessing—we must know.
12. Agreed, to find how is it with the King.

(*As the old men are about to enter the palace, the doors are thrown open:* CLYTEMNESTRA *is seen standing over the bodies of* AGAMEMNON *and* CASSANDRA, *which are laid out on a purple robe.*)

    CLYTEMNESTRA: Now I shall feel no shame to contradict
All that was said before to bide my time.
How else should one who pondered on revenge
Against a covert enemy, have strung the snare

Of death so high as to outsoar his leaping?
This duel, nurtured in my thoughts so long,
Is crowned at last with perfect victory.
I stand here, where I struck, over my work.
And it was so contrived, I'll not deny,
To leave no fissure, no escape from death.
With this vast net, as might be cast for fish,
I sieged him round in the fatal wealth of purple,
And twice I struck him, and with two cries of pain
He stretched his legs; then on his fallen body
I gave the third blow, my drink-offering
To the Zeus of Hell, Deliverer of the dead.
There he lay prostrate, gasping out his soul,
And pouring forth a sudden spurt of blood
Rained thick these drops of deathly dew upon me,
While I rejoiced like cornfields at the flow
Of heavenly moisture in birth-pangs of the bud.
So stands the case, elders of Argos, so
Rejoice, if so it please you—I glory in it.
For if due offerings were his to drink,
Then those were justly his, and more than just.
With bitter tears he filled the household bowl,
Now he himself has drained it and is gone.
     CHORUS: I marvel at your tongue so brazen-bold
That dares to speak so of your murdered king.
     CLYTEMNESTRA: You trifle with me as with a foolish woman,
While, nothing daunted, to such as understand
I say—commend or censure, as you will,
It is no matter—here is Agamemnon,
My husband, dead, the work of this right hand,
A just artificer. That is the truth.

   Strophe 1

   CHORUS: Woman, what evil charm bred out of earth or flowing
        sea,
Poison to eat or drink, hast thou devoured to take
On thee a crime that cries out for a public curse?
'Twas thine, the stroke, the blow—banishment shall be thine,
Hissed and hated of all men.

CLYTEMNESTRA: Your sentence now is banishment for me,
Abhorred of all, cursed and abominated;
But you did nothing then to contravene
His purpose, when, to exorcise the storms,
As though it were a ewe picked from his flocks
Whose wealth of snowy fleeces never fails
To multiply, unmoved, he killed his own
Child, born to me in pain, my well-beloved.
Why did you not drive *him* from hearth and home
For that foul crime, reserving your stern judgment
Until *I* acted? I bid you cast at me
Such menaces as will make for mastery
In combat match for match with one who stands
Prepared to meet them; and if with the help of God
The issue goes against you, suffering
Shall school those gray hairs in humility.

Antistrophe 1

CHORUS: Spirit of wickedness and haughty utterance! As now
Over the drops of red murder the mind doth rave,
So doth a fleck of red blood in the eyes appear.
Dishonoured and deserted of thy friends, for this
Stroke soon shalt thou be stricken.
CLYTEMNESTRA: Hark to the sanction of my solemn oath.
By perfect Justice who avenged my child,
By Ruin and the Fury unto whom
I slew this sacramental offering,
No thought of fear shall walk beneath this roof,
While on my hearth the fire is kindled by
Aegisthus, faithful to me from of old,
A shield and buckler strong in my defence.
Low lies the man that shamed his wedded wife,
Sweet solace of the Trojan Chryseids,
And stretched beside him this prisoner of war,
His paramour, this visionary seer,
His faithful bedfellow, who fondled him
On the ship's benches. Both have their deserts—
He as you see him; she like a swan has sung

Her last sad roundelay, and, lying there,
His leman, a side-dish for his nuptial bed,
She brings to me the spice that crowns my joy.

Strophe 2

CHORUS: Oh for the gift of death, speedy and free of pain,
Free from watch at the sick-bed,
To bring the long sleep that knows no waking,
Now that my lord and loyal protector
Lieth slain. For woman's sake
Long he warred far away while he lived,
Now at home dies beneath a woman's hand.
    O Helen, oh folly-beguiled,
    One woman to take those thousands of lives
    That were lost in the land of the Trojans,
    Now thou hast set on the curse of the household
    A crown of blood beyond ablution.
    Such the world has never known,
    Spirit of strife strong in man's destruction!
CLYTEMNESTRA: Pray not for the portion of death, though sore
Distressed is thy heart,
Nor turn upon Helen the edge of thy wrath,
Saying that she slew men without number,
One woman, a wound that shall close not.

Antistrophe 2

CHORUS: Demon of blood and tears, swooping upon the two
Tribes of Tantalus' children,
Enthroned in two women single-hearted,
Victor art thou, and my soul is stricken.
See on the palace-roof he stands,
Like the foul raven, evil-tongued,
Hear him croak, jubilant, his chant of joy!
    CLYTEMNESTRA: Ah, now is a true thought framed on thy lips,
Naming this demon
Thrice fed on the race, who, glutted with blood,
With the old wound smarting, is craving to lap
Fresh blood, still young in his hunger.

Strophe 3

CHORUS: Demon of sudden destruction,
Laying the house in the dust for ever!
Oh me, 'tis an evil tale of ruin that never resteth.
Alas, I weep the will of Zeus
Who causeth all and worketh all;
For what without his will befalleth mortals,
And what here was not sent from heaven?
    Oh me, I weep for my master and king.
    How shall I mourn thee?
    What words shall a fond heart speak thee?
    In the coils of the spider, the web of a death
    Ungodly, entangled thou diest.
    Oh me, I lament thy unkingly bed,
    With a sudden stroke of sharp
    Two-edged treachery felled and slaughtered.

CLYTEMNESTRA: Why dost thou declare that the murder was
    mine?
Name it not so, nor
Call me Agamemnon's wife. 'Tis not I
But a ghost in the likeness of woman, the vengeful
Shade of the banqueter whom Atreus fed,
Now crowneth his own
Firstfruits with a perfect oblation.

Antistrophe 3

CHORUS: How art thou guiltless of murder?
None is there, none that shall bear thee witness.
No, no, but perchance some ancient shade of wrath was abettor.
'Tis onward driven, stream on stream
Of slaughter sprung from common seed,
Murder red, that soon shall move to ransom
The dried gore of the flesh of children.
    Oh me, I weep for my master and king.
    How shall I mourn thee?
    What words shall a fond heart speak thee?
    In the coils of the spider, the web of a death

Ungodly, entangled thou diest.
Oh me, I lament thy unkingly bed,
With a sudden stroke of sharp
Two-edged treachery felled and slaughtered.

CLYTEMNESTRA: What of *him?* Did he not set ruin afoot
In the house when he slew
Iphigeneia, the child that I bore him?
And with long bitter tears have I mourned her.
So has he done, so is he done by.
Let him not speak proudly in darkness below.
With the death of the sword
For the sin of the sword he has perished.

Strophe 4

CHORUS: Alas, the mind strays disarmed, resourceless;
Weakly it drifts, and whither
To turn it knows not. The house is falling.
I fear the sharp beat of blood will soon have laid
The roof in ruins. The storm is growing.
Another mortal stroke for Justice' hand
Is now made sharp on other whetstones.
   Alas, Earth, Earth, would thou hadst taken
   This body before I had looked on my lord
   Laid low in the vessel of silver.
   Oh me, who shall bury him, who shall lament?
   Or wilt thou have the heart, having murdered thy own
   Master, to mourn at his tomb and to offer
   To his spirit a gift unacceptable, such
   Unholy return for his great deeds?
   Who shall intone at the tomb of a blessed spirit
   Tearful psalms of salutation,
   A tribute pure in heart and truthful?
CLYTEMNESTRA: That office is nothing to you—it is mine.
I struck him and killed him, I'll bury him too,
But not with mourners from home in his train,
No, Iphigeneia, his daughter shall come,
As is meet, to receive him, her father, beside

Those waters of wailing, and throwing her arms
On his neck with a kiss she shall greet him.

Antistrophe 4

CHORUS: The charge is answered with counter-charges.
Who shall be judge between them?
The spoiler spoiled, slaughtered he who slaughtered.
The law abides yet beside the throne of Zeus,
The sinner must suffer. So 'tis ordered.
The seed accurst, O who shall drive it out?
The whole house falleth, nailed to ruin.

CLYTEMNESTRA: So naming the law, truth hast thou spoken.
As for me, I consent
On my oath to the demon that haunteth the house
To endure ills present, though heavy to bear;
Let him now go hence
And inflict upon others the burden of blood
Outpoured by the hand of a kinsman.
Then would a scanty
Pittance content me better than plenty,
As the house is absolved
From the madness of murder for murder.

(*Enter* AEGISTHUS *with a bodyguard.*)

AEGISTHUS: O kindly light, O day of just reward,
Now have I proof there are avenging Gods
Who look down from above on human sin,
As I regard these purple snares of hell
Wherein to my delight this man doth lie,
Distrained by death for a father's treachery.
His father, Atreus, monarch of this realm,
Challenged in right of sovranty by mine,
Thyestes, his own brother, banished him
From hearth and home. A suppliant, he returned,
And found such safety for himself as not
To stain his native soil with his own blood;
But wicked Atreus, courteous more than kind,
Regaled him at a festive holiday

To a banquet of his children's flesh. The toes
And fingers set aside, the rest was laid
Disguised before him, where he sat apart.
My father unsuspecting took and ate—
A banquet prodigal in calamity
For this whole house. As soon as he divined
The monstrous crime, with a loud cry he fell
Back, spewing out the slaughtered flesh,
And cursed the House of Pelops—with a kick
That threw the table to the floor he cried,
"So perish all the seed of Pleisthenes!"
That is the sin for which this man lies here.
And that the plot should have been spun by me
Is also just; for, when I was a child
In swaddling-clothes, my father's third last hope,
I was condemned with him to banishment,
Till Justice reared me up and brought me home.
And so, though absent, still the blow was mine,
Mine were the threads of the conspiracy.
And now to die were sweet, since I have seen
My enemy caught by Justice in her snares.
   CHORUS: Aegisthus, insult in an evil hour
Wins no respect from me. If it be true
You killed with full intent, if you alone
Contrived this deed of bloodshed from afar,
Then be assured, your head shall not escape
The stones of an indignant people's curse.
   AEGISTHUS: Such talk from lower benches to the helm
Of high command! 'Tis hard, as you shall find,
For age to learn, and yet you shall be taught.
Even in dotage, dungeons and the pangs
Of hunger make an excellent physician
To school the spirit. Have you not eyes to see?
Kick not against the pricks, or smart for it!
   CHORUS: Woman! A man returned from feats of war,
While you kept house at home and fouled his bed,
A great commander—*you* contrived his death!
   AEGISTHUS: More talk that shall yet prove the seed of tears!
The tongue of Orpheus, contrary to yours,

Led all in listening rapture after him;
But you, a nuisance with your senseless bark,
Chains shall instruct you in docility.
   CHORUS: What? *you* my master, *you* tyrant of the land,
Who, though the plot was yours, yet lacked the courage
To raise a hand to execute the plot!
   AEGISTHUS: Plainly, temptation was the woman's part;
I, as his ancient enemy, was suspect.
But now, with his possessions, I shall try
My hand at monarchy. Who disobeys
Shall groan beneath the yoke—no trace-horse he
Pampered with corn; no, slow starvation walled
In noisome darkness shall see him humbled yet.
   CHORUS: O craven spirit, who had no heart to kill
But left it to a woman, who defiles
Her Gods and country! Oh, does Orestes yet
Behold the light of life, that he may come
Favoured of fortune home, and prove himself
The sovran executioner of both?
   AEGISTHUS: So? If you are bent on folly, you shall soon be
       taught.
Ho, my trusty guards, come forward, here is work to do.
   CAPTAIN OF THE GUARD: Ho, let each man draw and hold his
       sword in readiness!
   CHORUS: Be it so, we too are ready, unafraid to die.
   AEGISTHUS: Die! Well-spoken, we shall gladly take you at your
       word.
   CLYTEMNESTRA: Peace! my lord, forbear, and let no further ill
       be done.
Rich already is the harvest of calamity.
Grief is ours in plenty—draw no blood to make it more.
Go your ways, old men, and bow to destiny in due
Season, lest you suffer. What has been, it had to be.
Should this penance prove sufficient, though we bear the scars
Of an evil spirit's talons, we shall rest content.
Such the counsel of a woman; pray, be ruled by me.
   AEGISTHUS: Must I listen to their wanton threats of violence,
Flowers of insolence wherewith they trifle with their fate,
So bereft of sense they know not who is master here?

CHORUS: Men of Argos are not used to cringe before a knave.

AEGISTHUS: I shall overtake you yet—the reckoning is nigh.

CHORUS: Not if saving fortune guide Orestes home again.

AEGISTHUS: Yes, I know the only food of castaways is hope.

CHORUS: Gloat and grow fat, brag and blacken Justice while
you dare!

AEGISTHUS: Soon the hour shall come when foolish talk shall
cost you dear.

CHORUS: Flaunt your feathers, fluster like a cock beside his hen!

CLYTEMNESTRA: Do not heed their idle clamour. You and I,
the new
Masters of the house, henceforward shall direct it well.

SOPHOCLES

◫

OEDIPUS THE KING

TRANSLATED BY DAVID GRENE

CHARACTERS IN THE PLAY

OEDIPUS, *King of Thebes*
JOCASTA, *Queen of Thebes; wife of Oedipus; widow of Laius, the
 late King*
PRIEST OF ZEUS
CREON, *brother of Jocasta*
TEIRESIAS, *a blind prophet*
A MESSENGER, *from Corinth*
A HERDSMAN, *formerly in the service of Laius*
SECOND MESSENGER
CHORUS *of Theban Elders*
A CROWD *of Suppliants, men, women, and children*

OEDIPUS THE KING

(SCENE: *In front of the palace of* OEDIPUS *at* Thebes. *To the right of the stage near the altar stands the* PRIEST *with a crowd of suppliants of all ages.* OEDIPUS *emerges from the central door.*)

OEDIPUS: Children, young sons and daughters of old Cadmus,
why do you sit here with your suppliant crowns?
The town is heavy with a mingled burden
of sounds and smells, of groans and hymns and incense;
I did not think it fit that I should hear
of this from messengers but came myself,—
I Oedipus whom all men call the Great.

(*He turns to the* PRIEST.)

You're old and they are young; come, speak for them.
What do you fear or want, that you sit here
suppliant? Indeed I'm willing to give all
that you may need; I would be very hard
should I not pity suppliants like these.
PRIEST: O ruler of my country, Oedipus,
you see our company around the altar;
you see our ages; some of us, like these,
who cannot yet fly far, and some of us
heavy with age; these children are the chosen
among the young, and I the priest of Zeus.
Within the market place sit others crowned
with suppliant garlands, at the double shrine
of Pallas and the temple where Ismenus
gives oracles by fire. King, you yourself
have seen our city reeling like a wreck
already; it can scarcely lift its prow
out of the depths, out of the bloody surf.
A blight is on the fruitful plants of the earth,
a blight is on the cattle in the fields,
a blight is on our women that no children

are born to them; a God that carries fire,
a deadly pestilence, is on our town,
strikes us and spares not, and the house of Cadmus
is emptied of its people while black Death
grows rich in groaning and in lamentation.
We have not come as suppliants to this altar
because we thought of you as of a God,
but rather judging you the first of men
in all the chances of this life and when
we mortals have to do with more than man.
You came and by your coming saved our city,
freed us from tribute which we paid of old
to the Sphinx, cruel singer. This you did
in virtue of no knowledge we could give you,
in virtue of no teaching; it was God
that aided you, men say, and you are held
with God's assistance to have saved our lives.
Now Oedipus, whom all men call the Greatest,
here falling at your feet we all entreat you,
find us some strength for rescue.
Perhaps you'll hear a wise word from some God,
perhaps you will learn something from a man
(for I have seen that for the skilled of practice
the outcome of their counsels live the most).
Noblest of men, go, and raise up our city,
go,—and give heed. For now this land of ours
calls you its savior since you saved it once.
So, let us never speak about your reign
as of a time when first our feet were set
secure on high, but later fell to ruin.
Raise up our city, save it and raise it up.
Once you have brought us luck with happy omen;
be no less now in fortune.
If you will rule this land, as now you rule it,
better to rule it full of men than empty.
For neither town nor ship is anything
when empty, and none live in it together.

    OEDIPUS: Poor children! You have come to me entreating,
but I have known the story before you told it

only too well. I know you are all sick,
yet there is not one of you, sick though you are,
that is as sick as I myself.
Your several sorrows each have single scope
and touch but one of you. My spirit groans
for city and myself and you at once.
You have not roused me like a man from sleep;
know that I have given many tears to this,
gone many ways wandering in thought,
but as I thought I found only one remedy
and that I took. I sent Menoeceus' son
Creon, Jocasta's brother, to Apollo,
to his Pythian temple,
that he might learn there by what act or word
I could save this city. As I count the days,
it vexes me what ails him; he is gone
far longer than he needed for the journey.
But when he comes, then, may I prove a villain,
if I shall not do all the God commands.

   PRIEST: Thanks for your gracious words. Your servants here
signal that Creon is this moment coming.

   OEDIPUS: His face is bright. O holy Lord Apollo,
grant that his news too may be bright for us
and bring us safety.

   PRIEST: It is happy news,
I think, for else his head would not be crowned
with sprigs of fruitful laurel.

   OEDIPUS: We will know soon,
he's within hail. Lord Creon, my good brother,
what is the word you bring us from the God?

(CREON *enters.*)

   CREON: A good word,—for things hard to bear themselves
if in the final issue all is well
I count complete good fortune.

   OEDIPUS: What do you mean?
What you have said so far
leaves me uncertain whether to trust or fear.

   CREON: If you will hear my news before these others

I am ready to speak, or else to go within.

OEDIPUS: Speak it to all;
the grief I bear, I bear it more for these
than for my own heart.

CREON: I will tell you, then,
what I heard from the God.
King Phoebus in plain words commanded us
to drive out a pollution from our land,
pollution grown ingrained within the land;
drive it out, said the God, not cherish it,
till it's past cure.

OEDIPUS: What is the rite
of purification? How shall it be done?

CREON: By banishing a man, or expiation
of blood by blood, since it is murder guilt
which holds our city in this storm of death.

OEDIPUS: Who is this man whose fate the God pronounces?

CREON: My Lord, before you piloted the state
we had a king called Laius.

OEDIPUS: I know of him by hearsay. I have not seen him.

CREON: The God commanded clearly: let some one
punish with force this dead man's murderers.

OEDIPUS: Where are they in the world? Where would a trace
of this old crime be found? It would be hard
to guess where.

CREON: The clue is in this land;
that which is sought is found;
the unheeded thing escapes:
so said the God.

OEDIPUS: Was it at home,
or in the country that death came upon him,
or in another country travelling?

CREON: He went, he said himself, upon an embassy,
but never returned when he set out from home.

OEDIPUS: Was there no messenger, no fellow traveller
who knew what happened? Such a one might tell
something of use.

CREON: They were all killed save one. He fled in terror
and he could tell us nothing in clear terms

of what he knew, nothing, but one thing only.
    OEDIPUS: What was it?
If we could even find a slim beginning
in which to hope, we might discover much.
    CREON: This man said that the robbers they encountered
were many and the hands that did the murder
were many; it was no man's single power.
    OEDIPUS: How could a robber dare a deed like this
were he not helped with money from the city,
money and treachery?
    CREON: That indeed was thought.
But Laius was dead and in our trouble
there was none to help.
    OEDIPUS: What trouble was so great to hinder you
inquiring out the murder of your king?
    CREON: The riddling Sphinx induced us to neglect
mysterious crimes and rather seek solution
of troubles at our feet.
    OEDIPUS: I will bring this to light again. King Phoebus
fittingly took this care about the dead,
and you too fittingly.
And justly you will see in me an ally,
a champion of my country and the God.
For when I drive pollution from the land
I will not serve a distant friend's advantage,
but act in my own interest. Whoever
he was that killed the king may readily
wish to dispatch me with his murderous hand;
so helping the dead king I help myself.

Come children, take your suppliant boughs and go;
up from the altars now. Call the assembly
and let it meet upon the understanding
that I'll do everything. God will decide
whether we prosper or remain in sorrow.
    PRIEST: Rise, children—it was this we came to seek,
which of himself the king now offers us.
May Phoebus who gave us the oracle
come to our rescue and stay the plague.

(*Exeunt. Enter* CHORUS OF THEBAN ELDERS.)

Strophe 1

CHORUS: What is the sweet spoken word of God from the
            shrine of Pytho rich in gold
that has come to glorious Thebes?
I am stretched on the rack of doubt, and terror and trembling
            hold
my heart, O Delian Healer, and I worship full of fears
for what doom you will bring to pass, new or renewed in the
            revolving years.
Speak to me, immortal voice,
child of golden Hope.

Antistrophe 1

First I call on you, Athene, deathless daughter of Zeus,
and Artemis, Earth Upholder,
who sits in the midst of the market place in the throne which
            men call Fame,
and Phoebus, the Far Shooter, three averters of Fate,
come to us now, if ever before, when ruin rushed upon the state,
you drove destruction's flame away
out of our land.

Strophe 2

Our sorrows defy number;
all the ship's timbers are rotten;
taking of thought is no spear for the driving away of the plague.
There are no growing children in this famous land;
there are no women staunchly bearing the pangs of childbirth.
You may see them one with another, like birds swift on the wing,
quicker than fire unmastered,
speeding away to the coast of the Western God.

Antistrophe 2

In the unnumbered deaths
of its people the city dies;
those children that are born lie dead on the naked earth

unpitied, spreading contagion of death; and grey haired mothers
     and wives
everywhere stand at the altar's edge, suppliant, moaning;
the hymn to the healing God rings out but with it the wailing
     voices are blended.
From these our sufferings grant us, O golden Daughter of Zeus,
glad faced deliverance.

Strophe 3

There is no clash of brazen shields but our fight is with the War
     God,
a War God ringed with the cries of men, a savage God who burns
     us;
grant that he turn in racing course backwards out of our country's
     bounds
to the great palace of Amphitrite or where the waves of the
     Thracian sea
deny the stranger safe anchorage.
Whatsoever escapes the night
at last the light of day revisits;
so smite the War God, Father Zeus,
beneath your thunderbolt,
for you are the Lord of the lightning, the lightning that
carries fire.

Antistrophe 3

And your unconquered arrow shafts, winged by the golden corded
     bow,
Lycean King, I beg to be at our side for help;
and the gleaming torches of Artemis with which she scours the
     Lycean hills,
and I call on the God with the turban of gold, who gave his name
     to this country of ours,
the Bacchic God with the wine flushed face,
Evian One, who travel
with the Maenad company,
combat the God that burns us
with your torch of pine;

for the God that is our enemy is a God unhonoured among the
    Gods.

·(OEDIPUS *returns.*)

OEDIPUS: For what you ask me—if you will hear my words,
and hearing welcome them and fight the plague,
you will find strength and lightening of your load.

Hark to me; what I say to you, I say
as one that is a stranger to the story
as stranger to the deed. For I would not
be far upon the track if I alone
were tracing it without a clue. But now,
since after all was finished, I became
a citizen among you, citizens—
now I proclaim to all the men of Thebes:
who so among you knows the murderer
by whose hand Laius, son of Labdacus,
died—I command him to tell everything
to me,—yes, though he fears himself to take the blame
on his own head; for bitter punishment
he shall have none, but leave this land unharmed.
Or if he knows the murderer, another,
a foreigner, still let him speak the truth.
For I will pay him and be grateful, too.
But if you shall keep silence, if perhaps
some one of you, to shield a guilty friend,
or for his own sake shall reject my words—
hear what I shall do then:
I forbid that man, whoever he be, my land,
my land where I hold sovereignty and throne;
and I forbid any to welcome him
or cry him greeting or make him a sharer
in sacrifice or offering to the Gods,
or give him water for his hands to wash.
I command all to drive him from their homes,
since he is our pollution, as the oracle
of Pytho's God proclaimed him now to me.
So I stand forth a champion of the God

and of the man who died.
Upon the murderer I invoke this curse—
whether he is one man and all unknown,
or one of many—may he wear out his life
in misery to miserable doom!
If with my knowledge he lives at my hearth
I pray that I myself may feel my curse.

Even were this no matter of God's ordinance
it would not fit you so to leave it lie,
unpurified, since a good man is dead
and one that was a king. Search it out.
Since I am now the holder of his office,
and have his bed and wife that once was his,
and had his line not been unfortunate
we would have common children—(fortune leaped
upon his head)—because of all these things,
I fight in his defence as for my father,
and I shall try all means to take the murderer
of Laius the son of Labdacus
the son of Polydorus and before him
of Cadmus and before him of Agenor.
Those who do not obey me, may the Gods
grant no crops springing from the ground they plough
nor children to their women! May a fate
like this, or one still worse than this consume them!
For you whom these words please, the other Thebans,
may Justice as your ally and all the Gods
live with you, blessing you now and for ever!
    CHORUS: As you have held me to my oath, I speak:
I neither killed the king nor can declare
the killer; but since Phoebus set the quest
it is his part to tell who the man is.
    OEDIPUS: Right; but to put compulsion on the Gods
against their will—no man has strength for that.
    CHORUS: May I then say what I think second best?
    OEDIPUS: If there's a third best, too, spare not to tell it.
    CHORUS: I know that what the Lord Teiresias
sees, is most often what the Lord Apollo

sees. If you should inquire of this from him
you might find out most clearly.

oedipus: Even in this my actions have not been sluggard.
On Creon's word I have sent two messengers
and why the prophet is not here already
I have been wondering.

chorus: His skill apart
there is besides only an old faint story.

oedipus: What is it?
I seize on every story.

chorus: It was said
that he was killed by certain wayfarers.

oedipus: I heard that, too, but no one saw the killer.

chorus: Yet if he has a share of fear at all,
his courage will not stand firm, hearing your curse.

oedipus: The man who in the doing did not shrink
will fear no word.

chorus: Here comes his prosecutor:
led by your men the godly prophet comes
in whom alone of mankind truth is native.

(*Enter* teiresias, *led by a little boy.*)

oedipus: Teiresias, you are versed in everything,
things teachable and things not to be spoken,
things of the heaven and earth-creeping things.
You have no eyes but in your mind you know
with what a plague our city is afflicted.
My lord, in you alone we find a champion,
in you alone one that can rescue us.
Perhaps you have not heard the messengers,
but Phoebus sent in answer to our sending
an oracle declaring that our freedom
from this disease would only come when we
should learn the names of those who killed King Laius,
and kill them or expel from our country.
Do not begrudge us oracles from birds,
or any other way of prophecy
within your skill; save yourself and the city,

save me; redeem the debt of our pollution
that lies on us because of this dead man.
We are in your hands; it is the finest task
to help another when you have means and power.

TEIRESIAS: Alas, how terrible is wisdom when
it brings no profit to the man that's wise!
This I knew well, but had forgotten it,
else I would not have come here.

OEDIPUS: What is this?
How sad you are now you have come!

TEIRESIAS: Let me
go home. It will be easiest for us both
to bear our several destinies to the end
if you will follow my advice.

OEDIPUS: You'd rob us
of this your gift of prophecy? You talk
as one who had no care for law nor love
for Thebes who reared you.

TEIRESIAS: Yes, but I see that even your own words
miss the mark; therefore I must fear for mine.

OEDIPUS: For God's sake if you know of anything,
do not turn from us; all of us kneel to you,
all of us here, your suppliants.

TEIRESIAS: All of you here know nothing. I will not
bring to the light of day my troubles, mine—
rather than call them yours.

OEDIPUS: What do you mean?
You know of something but refuse to speak.
Would you betray us and destroy the city?

TEIRESIAS: I will not bring this pain upon us both,
neither on you nor on myself. Why is it
you question me and waste your labour? I
will tell you nothing.

OEDIPUS: You would provoke a stone! Tell us, you villain,
tell us, and do not stand there quietly
unmoved and balking at the final issue.

TEIRESIAS: You blame my temper but you do not see
your own that lives within you; it is me
you chide.

OEDIPUS: Who would not feel his temper rise
at words like these with which you shame our city?
 TEIRESIAS: Of themselves things will come, although I hide
          them
and breathe no word of them.
 OEDIPUS: Since they will come
tell them to me.
 TEIRESIAS: I will say nothing further.
Against this answer let your temper rage
as wildly as you will.
 OEDIPUS: Indeed I am
so angry I shall not hold back a jot
of what I think. For I would have you know
I think you were complotter of the deed
and doer of the deed save in so far
as for the actual killing. Had you had eyes
I would have said alone you murdered him.
 TEIRESIAS: Yes? Then I warn you faithfully to keep
the letter of your proclamation and
from this day forth to speak no word of greeting
to these nor me; you are the land's pollution.
 OEDIPUS: How shamelessly you started up this taunt!
How do you think you will escape?
 TEIRESIAS: I have.
I have escaped; the truth is what I cherish
and that's my strength.
 OEDIPUS: And who has taught you truth?
Not your profession surely!
 TEIRESIAS: You have taught me,
for you have made me speak against my will.
 OEDIPUS: Speak what? Tell me again that I may learn it better.
 TEIRESIAS: Did you not understand before or would you
provoke me into speaking?
 OEDIPUS: I did not grasp it,
not so to call it known. Say it again.
 TEIRESIAS: I say you are the murderer of the king
whose murderer you seek.
 OEDIPUS: Not twice you shall not
say calumnies like this and stay unpunished.

TEIRESIAS: Shall I say more to tempt your anger more?

OEDIPUS: As much as you desire; it will be said
in vain.

TEIRESIAS: I say that with those you love best
you live in foulest shame unconsciously
and do not see where you are in calamity.

OEDIPUS: Do you imagine you can always talk
like this, and live to laugh at it hereafter?

TEIRESIAS: Yes, if the truth has anything of strength.

OEDIPUS: It has, but not for you; it has no strength
for you because you are blind in mind and ears
as well as in your eyes.

TEIRESIAS: You are a poor wretch
to taunt me with the very insults which
every one soon will heap upon yourself.

OEDIPUS: Your life is one long night so that you cannot
hurt me or any other who sees the light.

TEIRESIAS: It is not fate that I should be your ruin,
Apollo is enough; it is his care
to work this out.

OEDIPUS: Was this your own design
or Creon's?

TEIRESIAS: Creon is no hurt to you,
but you are to yourself.

OEDIPUS: Wealth, sovereignty and skill outmatching skill
for the contrivance of an envied life,
great store of jealousy fill your treasury chests,
if my friend Creon, friend from the first and loyal,
thus secretly attacks me, secretly
desires to drive me out and secretly
suborns this juggling, trick devising quack,
this wily beggar who has only eyes
for his own gains, but blindness in his skill.
For, tell me, where have you seen clear, Teiresias,
with your prophetic eyes? When the dark singer,
the Sphinx, was in your country, did you speak
word of deliverance to its citizens?
And yet the riddle's answer was not the province
of a chance comer. It was a prophet's task

and plainly you had no such gift of prophecy
from birds nor otherwise from any God
to glean a word of knowledge. But I came,
Oedipus, who knew nothing, and I stopped her.
I solved the riddle by my wit alone.
Mine was no knowledge got from birds. And now
you would expel me,
because you think that you will find a place
by Creon's throne. I think you will be sorry,
both you and your accomplice, for your plot
to drive me out. And did I not regard you
as an old man, some suffering would have taught you
that what was in your heart was treason.

CHORUS: We look at this man's words and yours, my king,
and we find both have spoken them in anger.
We need no angry words but only thought
how we may best hit the God's meaning for us.

TEIRESIAS: If you are king, at least I have the right
no less to speak in my defence against you.
Of that much I am master. I am no slave
of yours, but Loxias', and so I shall not
enroll myself with Creon for my patron.
Since you have taunted me with being blind,
here is my word for you.
You have your eyes but see not where you are
in sin, nor where you live, nor whom you live with.
Do you know who your parents are? Unknowing
you are an enemy to kith and kin
in death, beneath the earth, and in this life.
A deadly footed, double striking curse,
from father and mother both, shall drive you forth
out of this land, with darkness on your eyes,
that now have such straight vision. Shall there be
a place will not be harbour to your cries,
a corner of Cithaeron will not ring
in echo to your cries, soon, soon,—
when you shall learn the secret of your marriage,
which steered you to a haven in this house,—
haven no haven, after lucky voyage?

And of the multitude of other evils
establishing a grim equality
between you and your children, you know nothing.
So, muddy with contempt my words and Creon's!
there is no man shall perish as you shall.

OEDIPUS: Is it endurable that I should hear
such words from him? Go and a curse go with you!
Quick, home with you! Out of my house at once!

TEIRESIAS: I would not have come either had you not called me.

OEDIPUS: I did not know then you would talk like a fool—
or it would have been long before I called you.

TEIRESIAS: I am a fool then, as it seems to you—
but to the parents who have bred you, wise.

OEDIPUS: What parents? Stop! Who are they of all the world?

TEIRESIAS: This day will show your birth and bring your ruin.

OEDIPUS: How needlessly your riddles darken everything.

TEIRESIAS: But it's in riddle answering you are strongest.

OEDIPUS: Yes. Taunt me where you will find me great.

TEIRESIAS: It is this very luck that has destroyed you.

OEDIPUS: I do not care, if it has served this city.

TEIRESIAS: Well, I will go. Come, boy, lead me away.

OEDIPUS: Yes, lead him off. So long as you are here,
you'll be a stumbling block and a vexation;
once gone, you will not trouble me again.

TEIRESIAS: I have said
what I came here to say not fearing your
countenance: there is no way you can hurt me.
I tell you, king, this man, this murderer
(whom you have long declared you are in search of,
indicting him in threatening proclamation
as murderer of Laius)—he is here.
In name he is a stranger among citizens
but soon he will be shown to be a citizen
true native Theban, and he'll have no joy
of the discovery: blindness for sight
and beggary for riches his exchange,
he shall go journeying to a foreign country
tapping his way before him with a stick.
He shall be proved father and brother both

to his own children in his house; to her
that gave him birth, a son and husband both;
a fellow sower in his father's bed
with that same father that he murdered.
Go within, reckon that out, and if you find me
mistaken, say I have no skill in prophecy.

(*Exeunt separately* TEIRESIAS *and* OEDIPUS.)

Strophe 1

CHORUS: Who is the man proclaimèd
by Delphi's prophetic rock
as the bloody handed murderer,
the doer of deeds that none dare name?
Now is the time for him to run
with a stronger foot
than Pegasus
for the child of Zeus leaps in arms upon him
with fire and the lightning bolt,
and terribly close on his heels
are the Fates that never miss.

Antistrophe 1

Lately from snowy Parnassus
clearly the voice flashed forth,
bidding each Theban track him down,
the unknown murderer.
In the savage forests he lurks and in
the caverns like
the mountain bull.
He is sad and lonely, and lonely his feet
that carry him far from the navel of earth;
but its prophecies, ever living,
flutter around his head.

Strophe 2

The augur has spread confusion
terrible confusion;
I do not approve what was said

nor can I deny it.
I do not know what to say;
I am in a flutter of foreboding;
I never heard in the present
nor past of a quarrel between
the sons of Labdacus and Polybus,
that I might bring as proof,
in attacking the popular fame
of Oedipus, seeking
to take vengeance for undiscovered
death in the line of Labdacus.

Antistrophe 2

Truly Zeus and Apollo are wise
and in human things all knowing;
but amongst men there is no
distinct judgment, between the prophet
and me—which of us is right.
One man may pass another in wisdom
but I would never agree
with those that find fault with the king
till I should see the word
proved right beyond doubt. For once
in visible form the Sphinx
came on him and all of us
saw his wisdom and in that test
he saved the city. So he will not be condemned by my mind.

(*Enter* CREON.)

CREON: Citizens, I have come because I heard
deadly words spread about me, that the king
accuses me. I cannot take that from him.
If he believes that in these present troubles
he has been wronged by me in word or deed
I do not want to live on with the burden
of such a scandal on me. The report
injures me doubly and most vitally—
for I'll be called a traitor to my city
and traitor also to my friends and you.

CHORUS: Perhaps it was a sudden gust of anger
that forced that insult from him, and no judgment.
CREON: But did he say that it was in compliance
with schemes of mine that the seer told him lies?
CHORUS: Yes, he said that, but why, I do not know.
CREON: Were his eyes straight in his head? Was his mind right
when he accused me in this fashion?
CHORUS: I do not know; I have no eyes to see
what princes do. Here comes the king himself.

(*Enter* OEDIPUS.)

OEDIPUS: You, sir, how is it you come here? Have you so much
brazen-faced daring that you venture in
my house although you are proved manifestly
the murderer of that man, and though you tried,
openly, highway robbery of my crown?
For God's sake, tell me what you saw in me,
what cowardice or what stupidity,
that made you lay a plot like this against me?
Did you imagine I should not observe
the crafty scheme that stole upon me or
seeing it, take no means to counter it?
Was it not stupid of you to make the attempt,
to try to hunt down royal power without
the people at your back or friends? For only
with the people at your back or money can
the hunt end in the capture of a crown.
CREON: Do you know what you're doing? Will you listen
to words to answer yours, and then pass judgment?
OEDIPUS: You're quick to speak, but I am slow to grasp you,
for I have found you dangerous,—and my foe.
CREON: First of all hear what I shall say to that.
OEDIPUS: At least don't tell me that you are not guilty.
CREON: If you believe you cherish something fine
in obstinacy without brains, you're wrong.
OEDIPUS: And you are wrong if you believe that one,
a criminal, will not be punished only
because he is my kinsman.

CREON: This is but just—
but tell me, then, of what offense I'm guilty?
    OEDIPUS: Did you or did you not urge me to send
to this prophetic mumbler?
    CREON: I did indeed,
and I shall stand by what I told you.
    OEDIPUS: How long ago is it since Laius . . . .
    CREON: What about Laius? I don't understand.
    OEDIPUS: Vanished—died—was murdered?
    CREON: It is long,
a long, long time to reckon.
    OEDIPUS: Was this prophet
in the profession then?
    CREON: He was, and honoured
as highly as he is today.
    OEDIPUS: At that time did he say a word about me?
    CREON: Never, at least when I was near him.
    OEDIPUS: You never made a search for the dead man?
    CREON: We searched, indeed, but never learned of anything.
    OEDIPUS: Why did our wise old friend not say this then?
    CREON: I don't know; and when I know nothing, I
usually hold my tongue.
    OEDIPUS: You know this much,
and can declare this much if you are loyal.
    CREON: What is it? If I know I'll not deny it.
    OEDIPUS: That he would not have said that I killed Laius
had he not met you first.
    CREON: You know yourself
whether he said this, but I demand that I
should hear as much from you as you from me.
    OEDIPUS: Then hear,—I'll not be proved a murderer.
    CREON: Well, then. You're married to my sister.
    OEDIPUS: Yes,
that I am not disposed to deny.
    CREON: You rule
this country giving her an equal share
in the government?
    OEDIPUS: Yes, everything she wants
she has from me.

CREON: And I, as thirdsman to you,
am rated as the equal of you two?
    OEDIPUS: Yes, and it's there you've proved yourself false friend.
    CREON: Not if you will reflect on it as I do.
Consider, first, if you think any one
would choose to rule and fear rather than rule
and sleep untroubled by a fear if power
were equal in both cases. I, at least,
I was not born with such a frantic yearning
to be a king—but to do what kings do.
And so it is with every one who has learned
wisdom and self-control. As it stands now,
the prizes are all mine—and without fear.
But if I were the king myself, I must
do much that went against the grain.
How should despotic rule seem sweeter to me
than painless power and an assured authority?
I am not so besotted yet that I
want other honours than those that come with profit.
Now every man's my pleasure; every man greets me;
now those who are your suitors fawn on me,—
success for them depends upon my favour.
Why should I let all this go to win that?
My mind would not be traitor if it's wise;
I am no treason lover, of my nature,
nor would I ever dare to join a plot.
Prove what I say. Go to the oracle
at Pytho and inquire about the answers,
if they are as I told you. For the rest,
if you discover I laid any plot
together with the seer, kill me, I say,
not only by your vote but by my own.
But do not charge me on obscure opinion
without some proof to back it. It's not just
lightly to count your knaves as honest men,
nor honest men as knaves. To throw away
an honest friend is, as it were, to throw
your life away, which a man loves the best.
In time you will know all with certainty;

time is the only test of honest men,
one day is space enough to know a rogue.
    CHORUS: His words are wise, king, if one fears to fall.
Those who are quick of temper are not safe.
    OEDIPUS: When he that plots against me secretly
moves quickly, I must quickly counterplot.
If I wait taking no decisive measure
his business will be done, and mine be spoiled.
    CREON: What do you want to do then? Banish me?
    OEDIPUS: No, certainly; kill you, not banish you.
    CREON: I do not think that you've your wits about you.
    OEDIPUS: For my own interests, yes.
    CREON: But for mine, too,
you should think equally.
    OEDIPUS: You are a rogue.
    CREON: Suppose you do not understand?
    OEDIPUS: But yet
I must be ruler.
    CREON: Not if you rule badly.
    OEDIPUS: O, city, city!
    CREON: I too have some share
in the city; it is not yours alone.
    CHORUS: Stop, my lords! Here—and in the nick of time
I see Jocasta coming from the house;
with her help lay the quarrel that now stirs you.

(Enter JOCASTA.)

    JOCASTA: For shame! Why have you raised this foolish squab-
        bling
brawl? Are you not ashamed to air your private
griefs when the country's sick? Go in, you, Oedipus,
and you, too, Creon, into the house. Don't magnify
your nothing troubles.
    CREON: Sister, Oedipus,
your husband, thinks he has the right to do
terrible wrongs—he has but to choose between
two terrors: banishing or killing me.
    OEDIPUS: He's right, Jocasta; for I find him plotting
with knavish tricks against my person.

CREON: That God may never bless me! May I die
accursed, if I have been guilty of
one tittle of the charge you bring against me!

JOCASTA: I beg you, Oedipus, trust him in this,
spare him for the sake of this his oath to God,
for my sake, and the sake of those who stand here.

CHORUS: Be gracious, be merciful,
we beg of you.

OEDIPUS: In what would you have me yield?

CHORUS: He has been no silly child in the past.
He is strong in his oath now.
Spare him.

OEDIPUS: Do you know what you ask?

CHORUS: Yes.

OEDIPUS: Tell me then.

CHORUS: He has been your friend before all men's eyes; do not
cast
him away dishonoured on an obscure conjecture.

OEDIPUS: I would have you know that this request of yours
really requests my death or banishment.

CHORUS: May the Sun God, king of Gods, forbid! May I die
without
God's blessing, without friends' help, if I had any such
thought. But my spirit is broken by my unhappiness for my
wasting country; and this would but add troubles amongst
ourselves to the other troubles.

OEDIPUS: Well, let him go then—if I must die ten times for it,
or be sent out dishonoured into exile.
It is your lips that prayed for him I pitied,
not his; wherever he is, I shall hate him.

CREON: I see you sulk in yielding and you're dangerous
when you are out of temper; natures like yours
are justly heaviest for themselves to bear.

OEDIPUS: Leave me alone! Take yourself off, I tell you.

CREON: I'll go, you have not known me, but they have,
and they have known my innocence.

(*Exit.*)

CHORUS: Won't you take him inside, lady?

JOCASTA: Yes, when I've found out what was the matter.

CHORUS: There was some misconceived suspicion of a story, and on
the other side the sting of injustice.

JOCASTA: So, on both sides?

CHORUS: Yes.

JOCASTA: What was the story?

CHORUS: I think it best, in the interests of the country, to leave it
where it ended.

OEDIPUS: You see where you have ended, straight of judgment
although you are, by softening my anger.

CHORUS: Sir, I have said before and I say again—be sure that I would
have been proved a madman, bankrupt in sane council, if I
should put you away, you who steered the country I love
safely when she was crazed with troubles. God grant that
now, too, you may prove a fortunate guide for us.

JOCASTA: Tell me, my lord, I beg of you, what was it
that roused your anger so?

OEDIPUS: Yes, I will tell you.
I honour you more than I honour them.
It was Creon and the plots he laid against me.

JOCASTA: Tell me—if you can clearly tell the quarrel—

OEDIPUS: Creon says
that I'm the murderer of Laius.

JOCASTA: Of his own knowledge or on information?

OEDIPUS: He sent this rascal prophet to me, since
he keeps his own mouth clean of any guilt.

JOCASTA: Do not concern yourself about this matter;
listen to me and learn that human beings
have no part in the craft of prophecy.
Of that I'll show you a short proof.
There was an oracle once that came to Laius,—
I will not say that it was Phoebus' own,
but it was from his servants—and it told him
that it was fate that he should die a victim
at the hands of his own son, a son to be born
of Laius and me. But, see now, he,
the king, was killed by foreign highway robbers

at a place where three roads meet—so goes the story;
and for the son—before three days were out
after his birth King Laius pierced his ankles
and by the hands of others cast him forth
upon a pathless hillside. So Apollo
failed to fulfill his oracle to the son,
that he should kill his father, and to Laius
also proved false in that the thing he feared,
death at his son's hands, never came to pass.
So clear in this case were the oracles,
so clear and false. Give them no heed, I say;
what God discovers need of, easily
he shows to us himself.

OEDIPUS: O dear Jocasta,
as I hear this from you, there comes upon me
a wandering of the soul—I could run mad.

JOCASTA: What trouble is it, that you turn again
and speak like this?

OEDIPUS: I thought I heard you say
that Laius was killed at a crossroads.

JOCASTA: Yes, that was how the story went and still
that word goes round.

OEDIPUS: Where is this place, Jocasta,
where he was murdered?

JOCASTA: Phocis is the country
and the road splits there, one of two roads from Delphi,
another comes from Daulia.

OEDIPUS: How long ago is this?

JOCASTA: The news came to the city just before
you became king and all men's eyes looked to you.
What is it, Oedipus, that's in your mind?

OEDIPUS: Don't ask me yet—tell me of Laius—
how did he look? How old or young was he?

JOCASTA: He was a tall man and his hair was grizzled
already—nearly white—and in his form
not unlike you.

OEDIPUS: O God, I think I have
called curses on myself in ignorance.

JOCASTA: What do you mean? I am terrified

when I look at you.

OEDIPUS: I have a deadly fear
that the old seer had eyes. You'll show me more
if you can tell me one more thing.

JOCASTA: I will.
I'm frightened,—but if I can understand,
I'll tell you all you ask.

OEDIPUS: How was his company?
Had he few with him when he went this journey,
or many servants, as would suit a prince?

JOCASTA: In all there were but five, and among them
a herald; and one carriage for the king.

OEDIPUS: It's plain—it's plain—who was it told you this?

JOCASTA: The only servant that escaped safe home.

OEDIPUS: Is he at home now?

JOCASTA: No, when he came home again
and saw you king and Laius was dead,
he came to me and touched my hand and begged
that I should send him to the fields to be
my shepherd and so he might see the city
as far off as he might. So I
sent him away. He was an honest man,
as slaves go, and was worthy of far more
than what he asked of me.

OEDIPUS: O, how I wish that he could come back quickly!

JOCASTA: He can. Why is your heart so set on this?

OEDIPUS: O dear Jocasta, I am full of fears
that I have spoken far too much; and therefore
I wish to see this shepherd.

JOCASTA: He will come;
but, Oedipus, I think I'm worthy too
to know what is it that disquiets you.

OEDIPUS: It shall not be kept from you, since my mind
has gone so far with its forebodings. Whom
should I confide in rather than you, who is there
of more importance to me who have passed
through such a fortune?
Polybus was my father, king of Corinth,
and Merope, the Dorian, my mother.

I was held greatest of the citizens
in Corinth till a curious chance befell me
as I shall tell you—curious, indeed,
but hardly worth the store I set upon it.
There was a dinner and at it a man,
a drunken man, accused me in his drink
of being bastard. I was furious
but held my temper under for that day.
Next day I went and taxed my parents with it;
they took the insult very ill from him,
the drunken fellow who had uttered it.
So I was comforted for their part, but
still this thing rankled always, for the story
crept about widely. And I went at last
to Pytho, though my parents did not know.
But Phoebus sent me home again unhonoured
in what I came to learn, but he foretold
other and desperate horrors to befall me,
that I was fated to lie with my mother,
and show to daylight an accursed breed
which men would not endure, and I was doomed
to be murderer of the father that begot me.
When I heard this I fled, and in the days
that followed I would measure from the stars
the whereabouts of Corinth—yes, I fled
to somewhere where I should not see fulfilled
the infamies told in that dreadful oracle.
And as I journeyed I came to the place
where, as you say, this king met with his death.
Jocasta, I will tell you the whole truth.
When I was near the branching of the crossroads,
going on foot, I was encountered by
a herald and a carriage with a man in it,
just as you tell me. He that led the way
and the old man himself wanted to thrust me
out of the road by force. I became angry
and struck the coachman who was pushing me.
When the old man saw this he watched his moment,
and as I passed he struck me from his carriage,

full on the head with his two pointed goad.
But he was paid in full and presently
my stick had struck him backwards from the car
and he rolled out of it. And then I killed them
all. If it happened there was any tie
of kinship twixt this man and Laius,
who is then now more miserable than I,
what man on earth so hated by the Gods,
since neither citizen nor foreigner
may welcome me at home or even greet me,
but drive me out of doors? And it is I,
I and no other have so cursed myself.
And I pollute the bed of him I killed
by the hands that killed him. Was I not born evil?
Am I not utterly unclean? I had to fly
and in my banishment not even see
my kindred nor set foot in my own country,
or otherwise my fate was to be yoked
in marriage with my mother and kill my father,
Polybus who begot me and had reared me.
Would not one rightly judge and say that on me
these things were sent by some malignant God?
O no, no, no—O holy majesty
of God on high, may I not see that day!
May I be gone out of men's sight before
I see the deadly taint of this disaster
come upon me.

CHORUS: Sir, we too fear these things. But until you see this
man face to face and hear his story, hope.

OEDIPUS: Yes, I have just this much of hope—to wait until the
herdsman comes.

JOCASTA: And when he comes, what do you want with him?

OEDIPUS: I'll tell you; if I find that his story is the same as yours,
I at least will be clear of this guilt.

JOCASTA: Why what so particularly did you learn from my
story?

OEDIPUS: You said that he spoke of highway *robbers* who killed
Laius. Now if he uses the same number, it was not I who killed
him. One man cannot be the same as many. But if he speaks of a

man travelling alone, then clearly the burden of the guilt inclines towards me.

JOCASTA: Be sure, at least, that this was how he told the story. He cannot unsay it now, for every one in the city heard it—not I alone. But, Oedipus, even if he diverges from what he said then, he shall never prove that the murder of Laius squares rightly with the prophecy—for Loxias declared that the king should be killed by his own son. And that poor creature did not kill him surely,—for he died himself first. So as far as prophecy goes, henceforward I shall not look to the right hand or the left.

OEDIPUS: Right. But yet, send some one for the peasant to bring him here; do not neglect it.

JOCASTA: I will send quickly. Now let me go indoors. I will do nothing except what pleases you.

(*Exeunt.*)

Strophe 1

CHORUS: May destiny ever find me
pious in word and deed
prescribed by the laws that live on high:
laws begotten in the clear air of heaven,
whose only father is Olympus;
no mortal nature brought them to birth,
no forgetfulness shall lull them to sleep;
for God is great in them and grows not old.

Antistrophe 1

Insolence breeds the tyrant, insolence
if it is glutted with a surfeit, unseasonable, unprofitable,
climbs to the roof-top and plunges
sheer down to the ruin that must be,
and there its feet are no service.
But I pray that the God may never
abolish the eager ambition that profits the state.
  or I shall never cease to hold the God as our protector.

Strophe 2

If a man walks with haughtiness
of hand or word and gives no heed

to Justice and the shrines of Gods
despises—may an evil doom
smite him for his ill-starred pride of heart!—
if he reaps gains without justice
and will not hold from impiety
and his fingers itch for untouchable things.
When such things are done, what man shall contrive
to shield his soul from the shafts of the God?
When such deeds are held in honour,
why should I honour the Gods in the dance?

    Antistrophe 2

No longer to the holy place,
to the navel of earth I'll go
to worship, nor to Abae
nor to Olympia,
unless the oracles are proved to fit,
for all men's hands to point at.
O Zeus, if you are rightly called
the sovereign lord, all-mastering,
let this not escape you nor your ever-living power!
The oracles concerning Laius
are old and dim and men regard them not.
Apollo is nowhere clear in honour; God's service perishes.

    (*Enter* JOCASTA, *carrying garlands.*)

    JOCASTA: Princes of the land, I have had the thought to go
to the Gods' temples, bringing in my hand
garlands and gifts of incense, as you see.
For Oedipus excites himself too much
at every sort of trouble, not conjecturing,
like a man of sense, what will be from what was,
but he is always at the speaker's mercy,
when he speaks terrors. I can do no good
by my advice, and so I came as suppliant
to you, Lycaean Apollo, who are nearest.
These are the symbols of my prayer and this
my prayer: grant us escape free of the curse.

Now when we look to him we are all afraid;
he's pilot of our ship and he is frightened.

(*Enter a* MESSENGER.)

MESSENGER: Might I learn from you, sirs, where is the house of
Oedipus? Or best of all, if you know, where is the king himself?
CHORUS: This is his house and he is within doors. This lady
is his wife and mother of his children.
MESSENGER: God bless you, lady, and God bless your household!
God bless Oedipus' noble wife!
JOCASTA: God bless you, sir, for your kind greeting! What do
you want of us that you have come here? What have you to tell
us?
MESSENGER: Good news, lady. Good for your house and for
your husband.
JOCASTA: What is your news? Who sent you to us?
MESSENGER: I come from Corinth and the news I bring will
give you pleasure. Perhaps a little pain too.
JOCASTA: What is this news of double meaning?
MESSENGER: The people of the Isthmus will choose Oedipus to
be their king. That is the rumour there.
JOCASTA: But isn't their king still old Polybus?
MESSENGER: No. He is in his grave. Death has got him.
JOCASTA: Is that the truth? Is Oedipus' father dead?
MESSENGER: May I die myself if it be otherwise!
JOCASTA (*to a servant*): Be quick and run to the King with the
news! O oracles of the Gods, where are you now? It was from this
man Oedipus fled, lest he should be his murderer! And now he is
dead, in the course of nature, and not killed by Oedipus.

(*Enter* OEDIPUS.)

OEDIPUS: Dearest Jocasta, why have you sent for me?
JOCASTA: Listen to this man and when you hear reflect what is
the outcome of the holy oracles of the Gods.
OEDIPUS: Who is he? What is his message for me?
JOCASTA: He is from Corinth and he tells us that your father
Polybus is dead and gone.

OEDIPUS: What's this you say, sir? Tell me yourself.

MESSENGER: Since this is the first matter you want clearly told:
Polybus has gone down to death. You may be sure of it.

OEDIPUS: By treachery or sickness?

MESSENGER: A small thing will put old bodies asleep.

OEDIPUS: So he died of sickness, it seems,—poor old man!

MESSENGER: Yes, and of age—the long years he had measured.

OEDIPUS: Ha! Ha! O dear Jocasta, why should one
look to the Pythian hearth? Why should one look
to the birds screaming overhead? They prophesied
that I should kill my father! But he's dead,
and hidden deep in earth, and I stand here
who never laid a hand on spear against him,—
unless perhaps he died of longing for me,
and thus I am his murderer. But they,
the oracles, as they stand—he's taken them
away with him, they're dead as he himself is,
and worthless.

JOCASTA: That I told you before now.

OEDIPUS: You did, but I was misled by my fear.

JOCASTA: Then lay no more of them to heart, not one.

OEDIPUS: But surely I must fear my mother's bed?

JOCASTA: Why should man fear since chance is all in all
for him, and he can clearly foreknow nothing?
Best to live lightly, as one can, unthinkingly.
As to your mother's marriage bed,—don't fear it.
Before this, in dreams too, as well as oracles,
many a man has lain with his own mother.
But he to whom such things are nothing bears
his life most easily.

OEDIPUS: All that you say would be said perfectly
if she were dead; but since she lives I must
still fear, although you talk so well, Jocasta.

JOCASTA: Still in your father's death there's light of comfort?

OEDIPUS: Great light of comfort; but I fear the living.

MESSENGER: Who is the woman that makes you afraid?

OEDIPUS: Merope, old man, Polybus' wife.

MESSENGER: What about her frightens the queen and you?

OEDIPUS: A terrible oracle, stranger, from the Gods.

MESSENGER: Can it be told? Or does the sacred law
forbid another to have knowledge of it?

OEDIPUS: O no! Once on a time Loxias said
that I should lie with my own mother and
take on my hands the blood of my own father.
And so for these long years I've lived away
from Corinth; it has been to my great happiness;
but yet it's sweet to see the face of parents.

MESSENGER: This was the fear which drove you out of Corinth?

OEDIPUS: Old man, I did not wish to kill my father.

MESSENGER: Why should I not free you from this fear, sir,
since I have come to you in all goodwill?

OEDIPUS: You would not find me thankless if you did.

MESSENGER: Why, it was just for this I brought the news,—
to earn your thanks when you had come safe home.

OEDIPUS: No, I will never come near my parents.

MESSENGER: Son,
it's very plain you don't know what you're doing.

OEDIPUS: What do you mean, old man? For God's sake, tell
me.

MESSENGER: If your homecoming is checked by fears like these.

OEDIPUS: Yes, I'm afraid that Phoebus may prove right.

MESSENGER: The murder and the incest?

OEDIPUS: Yes, old man;
that is my constant terror.

MESSENGER: Do you know
that all your fears are empty?

OEDIPUS: How is that,
if they are father and mother and I their son?

MESSENGER: Because Polybus was no kin to you in blood.

OEDIPUS: What, was not Polybus my father?

MESSENGER: No more than I but just so much.

OEDIPUS: How can
my father be my father as much as one
that's nothing to me?

MESSENGER: Neither he nor I
begat you.

OEDIPUS: Why then did he call me son?

MESSENGER: A gift he took you from these hands of mine.

OEDIPUS: Did he love so much what he took from another's hand?

MESSENGER: His childlessness before persuaded him.

OEDIPUS: Was I a child you bought or found when I was given to him?

MESSENGER: On Cithaeron's slopes in the twisting thickets you were found.

OEDIPUS: And why were you a traveller in those parts?

MESSENGER: I was in charge of mountain flocks.

OEDIPUS: You were a shepherd? A hireling vagrant?

MESSENGER: Yes, but at least at that time the man that saved your life, son.

OEDIPUS: What ailed me when you took me in your arms?

MESSENGER: In that your ankles should be witnesses.

OEDIPUS: Why do you speak of that old pain?

MESSENGER: I loosed you; the tendons of your feet were pierced and fettered,—

OEDIPUS: My swaddling clothes brought me a rare disgrace.

MESSENGER: So that from this you're called your present name.

OEDIPUS: Was this my father's doing or my mother's? For God's sake, tell me.

MESSENGER: I don't know, but he who gave you to me has more knowledge than I.

OEDIPUS: You yourself did not find me then? You took me from someone else?

MESSENGER: Yes, from another shepherd.

OEDIPUS: Who was he? Do you know him well enough to tell?

MESSENGER: He was called Laius' man.

OEDIPUS: You mean the king who reigned here in the old days?

MESSENGER: Yes, he was that man's shepherd.

OEDIPUS: Is he alive still, so that I could see him?

MESSENGER: You who live here would know that best.

OEDIPUS: Do any of you here
know of this shepherd whom he speaks about
in town or in the fields? Tell me. It's time
that this was found out once for all.

CHORUS: I think he is none other than the peasant
whom you have sought to see already; but
Jocasta here can tell us best of that.

OEDIPUS: Jocasta, do you know about this man
whom we have sent for? Is he the man he mentions?

JOCASTA: Why ask of whom he spoke? Don't give it heed;
nor try to keep in mind what has been said.
It will be wasted labour.

OEDIPUS: With such clues
I could not fail to bring my birth to light.

JOCASTA: I beg you—do not hunt this out—I beg you,
if you have any care for your own life.
What I am suffering is enough.

OEDIPUS: Keep up
your heart, Jocasta. Though I'm proved a slave,
thrice slave, and though my mother is thrice slave,
you'll not be shown to be of lowly lineage.

JOCASTA: O be persuaded by me, I entreat you;
do not do this.

OEDIPUS: I will not be persuaded to let be
the chance of finding out the whole thing clearly.

JOCASTA: It is because I wish you well that I
give you this counsel—and it's the best counsel.

OEDIPUS: Then the best counsel vexes me, and has
for some while since.

JOCASTA: O Oedipus, God help you!
God keep you from the knowledge of who you are!

OEDIPUS: Here, some one, go and fetch the shepherd for me;
and let her find her joy in her rich family!

JOCASTA: O Oedipus, unhappy Oedipus!
that is all I can call you, and the last thing
that I shall ever call you.

(*Exit.*)

CHORUS: Why has the queen gone, Oedipus, in wild

grief rushing from us? I am afraid that trouble
will break out of this silence.
    OEDIPUS: Break out what will! I at least shall be
willing to see my ancestry, though humble.
Perhaps she is ashamed of my low birth,
for she has all a woman's high-flown pride.
But I account myself a child of Fortune,
beneficent Fortune, and I shall not be
dishonoured. She's the mother from whom I spring;
the months, my brothers, marked me, now as small,
and now again as mighty. Such is my breeding,
and I shall never prove so false to it,
as not to find the secret of my birth.

    Strophe

    CHORUS: If I am a prophet and wise of heart
you shall not fail, Cithaeron,
by the limitless sky, you shall not!—
to know at tomorrow's full moon that Oedipus honours
        you as native to him and mother and nurse at once;
and that you are honoured in dancing by us, as finding
        favour in sight of our king.
Apollo, to whom we cry, find these things pleasing!

    Antistrophe

Who was it bore you, child? One of
the long-lived nymphs who lay with Pan—
the father who treads the hills?
Or was she a bride of Loxias, your mother? The grassy slopes
are all of them dear to him. Or perhaps Cyllene's king
or the Bacchants' God that lives on the tops
of the hills received you a gift from some
one of the Helicon Nymphs, with whom he mostly plays?

    (*Enter an old man, led by* OEDIPUS' *servants.*)

    OEDIPUS: If some one like myself who never met him
may make a guess,—I think this is the herdsman,
whom we were seeking. His old age is consonant
with the other. And besides, the men who bring him

I recognize as my own servants. You
perhaps may better me in knowledge since
you've seen the man before.

CHORUS: You can be sure
I recognize him. For if Laius
had ever an honest shepherd, this was he.

OEDIPUS: You, sir, from Corinth, I must ask you first,
is this the man you spoke of?

MESSENGER: This is he
before your eyes.

OEDIPUS: Old man, look here at me
and tell me what I ask you. Were you ever
a servant of King Laius?

HERDSMAN: I was,—
no slave he bought but reared in his own house.

OEDIPUS: What did you do as work? How did you live?

HERDSMAN: Most of my life was spent among the flocks.

OEDIPUS: In what part of the country did you live?

HERDSMAN: Cithaeron and the places near to it.

OEDIPUS: And somewhere there perhaps you knew this man?

HERDSMAN: What was his occupation? Who?

OEDIPUS: This man here,
have you had any dealings with him?

HERDSMAN: No—
not such that I can quickly call to mind.

MESSENGER: That is no wonder, master. But I'll make him
remember what he does not know. For I know, that he well knows
the country of Cithaeron, how he with two flocks, I with one
kept company for three years—each year half a year—from spring
till autumn time and then when winter came I drove my flocks
to our fold home again and he to Laius' steadings. Well—am I
right or not in what I said we did?

HERDSMAN: You're right—although it's a long time ago.

MESSENGER: Do you remember giving me a child
to bring up as my foster child?

HERDSMAN: What's this?
Why do you ask this question?

MESSENGER: Look, old man,
here he is—here's the man who was that child!

HERDSMAN: Death take you! Won't you hold your tongue?
OEDIPUS: No, no,
do not find fault with him, old man. Your words
are more at fault than his.
HERDSMAN: O best of masters,
how do I give offense?
OEDIPUS: When you refuse
to speak about the child of whom he asks you.
HERDSMAN: He speaks out of his ignorance, without meaning.
OEDIPUS: If you'll not talk to gratify me, you
will talk with pain to urge you.
HERDSMAN: O please, sir,
don't hurt an old man, sir.
OEDIPUS (to the servants): Here, one of you,
twist his hands behind him.
HERDSMAN: Why, God help me, why?
What do you want to know?
OEDIPUS: You gave a child
to him,—the child he asked you of?
HERDSMAN: '   I did.
I wish I'd died the day I did.
OEDIPUS: You will
unless you tell me truly.
HERDSMAN: And I'll die
far worse if I should tell you.
OEDIPUS: This fellow
is bent on more delays, as it would seem.
HERDSMAN: O no, no! I have told you that I gave it.
OEDIPUS: Where did you get this child from? Was it your own
or did you get it from another?
HERDSMAN: Not
my own at all; I had it from some one.
OEDIPUS: One of these citizens? or from what house?
HERDSMAN: O master, please—I beg you, master, please
don't ask me more.
OEDIPUS: You're a dead man if I
ask you again.
HERDSMAN: It was one of the children
of Laius.

OEDIPUS: A slave? Or born in wedlock?

HERDSMAN: O God, I am on the brink of frightful speech.

OEDIPUS: And I of frightful hearing. But I must hear.

HERDSMAN: The child was called his child; but she within,
your wife would tell you best how all this was.

OEDIPUS: *She* gave it to you?

HERDSMAN: Yes, she did, my lord.

OEDIPUS: To do what with it?

HERDSMAN: Make away with it.

OEDIPUS: She was so hard—its mother?

HERDSMAN: Aye, through fear
of evil oracles.

OEDIPUS: Which?

HERDSMAN: They said that he
should kill his parents.

OEDIPUS: How was it that you
gave it away to this old man?

HERDSMAN: O master,
I pitied it, and thought that I could send it
off to another country and this man
was from another country. But he saved it
for the most terrible troubles. If you are
the man he says you are, you're bred to misery

OEDIPUS: O, O, O, they will all come,
all come out clearly! Light of the sun, let me
look upon you no more after today!
I who first saw the light bred of a match
accursed, and accursed in my living
with them I lived with, cursed in my killing.

(*Exeunt all but the* CHORUS.)

Strophe 1

CHORUS: O generations of men, how I
count you as equal with those who live
not at all!
what man, what man on earth wins more
of happiness than a seeming
and after that turning away?

Oedipus, you are my pattern of this,
Oedipus, you and your fate!
Luckless Oedipus, whom of all men
I envy not at all.

Antistrophe 1

In as much as he shot his bolt
beyond the others and won the prize
of happiness complete—
O Zeus—and killed and reduced to nought
the hooked taloned maid of the riddling speech,
standing a tower against death for my land:
hence he was called my king and hence
was honoured the highest of all
honours; and hence he ruled
in the great city of Thebes.

Strophe 2

But now whose tale is more miserable?
Who is there lives with a savager fate?
Whose troubles so reverse his life as his?

O Oedipus, the famous prince
for whom a great haven
the same both as father and son
sufficed for generation,
how, O how, have the furrows ploughed
by your father endured to bear you, poor wretch,
and hold their peace so long?

Antistrophe 2

Time who sees all has found you out
against your will; judges your marriage accursed,
begetter and begot at one in it.

O child of Laius,
would I had never seen you,
I weep for you and cry
a dirge of lamentation.

To speak directly, I drew my breath
from you at the first and so now I lull
my mouth to sleep with your name.

(*Enter a* SECOND MESSENGER.)

SECOND MESSENGER: O Princes always honoured by our country,
what deeds you'll hear of and what horrors see
what grief you'll feel, if you as true born Thebans
care for the house of Labdacus's sons.
Phasis nor Ister cannot purge this house,
I think, with all their streams, such things
it hides, such evils shortly will bring forth
into the light, whether they will or not;
and troubles hurt the most
when they prove self-inflicted.
CHORUS: What we had known before did not fall short
of bitter groaning's worth; what's more to tell?
SECOND MESSENGER: Shortest to hear and tell—our glorious
        queen
Jocasta's dead.
CHORUS: Unhappy woman! How?
SECOND MESSENGER: By her own hand. The worst of what was
        done
you cannot know. You did not see the sight.
Yet in so far as I remember it
you'll hear the end of our unlucky queen.
When she came raging into the house she went
straight to her marriage bed, tearing her hair
with both her hands, and crying upon Laius
long dead—Do you remember, Laius,
that night long past which bred a child for us
to send you to your death and leave
a mother making children with her son?
And then she groaned and cursed the bed in which
she brought forth husband by her husband, children
by her own child, an infamous double bond.
How after that she died I do not know,—
for Oedipus distracted us from seeing.
He burst upon us shouting and we looked

to him as he paced frantically around,
begging us always: Give me a sword, I say,
to find this wife no wife, this mother's womb,
this field of double sowing whence I sprang
and where I sowed my children! As he raved
some god showed him the way—none of us there.
Bellowing terribly and led by some
invisible guide he rushed on the two doors,—
wrenching the hollow bolts out of their sockets,
he charged inside. There, there, we saw his wife
hanging, the twisted rope around her neck.
When he saw her, he cried out fearfully
and cut the dangling noose. Then, as she lay,
poor woman, on the ground, what happened after,
was terrible to see. He tore the brooches—
the gold chased brooches fastening her robe—
away from her and lifting them up high
dashed them on his own eyeballs, shrieking out
such things as: they will never see the crime
I have committed or had done upon me!
Dark eyes, now in the days to come look on
forbidden faces, do not recognize
those whom you long for—with such imprecations
he struck his eyes again and yet again
with the brooches. And the bleeding eyeballs gushed
and stained his beard—no sluggish oozing drops
but a black rain and bloody hail poured down.

So it has broken—and not on one head
but troubles mixed for husband and for wife.
The fortune of the days gone by was true
good fortune—but today groans and destruction
and death and shame—of all ills can be named
not one is missing.
    CHORUS: Is he now in any ease from pain?
    SECOND MESSENGER: He shouts
for some one to unbar the doors and show him
to all the men of Thebes, his father's killer,
his mother's—no I cannot say the word,

it is unholy—for he'll cast himself,
out of the land, he says, and not remain
to bring a curse upon his house, the curse
he called upon it in his proclamation. But
he wants for strength, aye, and some one to guide him;
his sickness is too great to bear. You, too,
will be shown that. The bolts are opening.
Soon you will see a sight to waken pity
even in the horror of it.

(*Enter the blinded* OEDIPUS.)

CHORUS: This is a terrible sight for men to see!
I never found a worse!
Poor wretch, what madness came upon you!
What evil spirit leaped upon your life
to your ill-luck—a leap beyond man's strength!
Indeed I pity you, but I cannot
look at you, though there's much I want to ask
and much to learn and much to see.
I shudder at the sight of you.
OEDIPUS: O, O,
where am I going? Where is my voice
borne on the wind to and fro?
Spirit, how far have you sprung?
CHORUS: To a terrible place whereof men's ears
may not hear, nor their eyes behold it.
OEDIPUS: Darkness!
Horror of darkness enfolding, resistless, unspeakable visitant sped
        by an ill wind in haste!
madness and stabbing pain and memory
of evil deeds I have done!
CHORUS: In such misfortunes it's no wonder
if double weighs the burden of your grief.
OEDIPUS: My friend,
you are the only one steadfast, the only one that attends on me;
you still stay nursing the blind man.
Your care is not unnoticed. I can know
your voice, although this darkness is my world.

CHORUS: Doer of dreadful deeds, how did you dare
so far to do despite to your own eyes?
what spirit urged you to it?
OEDIPUS: It was Apollo, friends, Apollo,
that brought this bitter bitterness, my sorrows to completion.
But the hand that struck me
was none but my own.
Why should I see
whose vision showed me nothing sweet to see?
CHORUS: These things are as you say.
OEDIPUS: What can I see to love?
What greeting can touch my ears with joy?
Take me away, and haste—to a place out of the way!
Take me away, my friends, the greatly miserable,
the most accursed, whom God too hates
above all men on earth!
CHORUS: Unhappy in your mind and your misfortune,
would I had never known you!
OEDIPUS: Curse on the man who took
the cruel bonds from off my legs, as I lay in the field.
He stole me from death and saved me,
no kindly service.
Had I died then
I would not be so burdensome to friends.
CHORUS: I, too, could have wished it had been so.
OEDIPUS: Then I would not have come
to kill my father and marry my mother infamously.
Now I am godless and child of impurity,
begetter in the same seed that created my wretched self.
If there is any ill worse than ill,
that is the lot of Oedipus.
CHORUS: I cannot say your remedy was good;
you would be better dead than blind and living.
OEDIPUS: What I have done here was best done—don't tell me
otherwise, do not give me further counsel.
I do not know with what eyes I could look
upon my father when I die and go
under the earth, nor yet my wretched mother—
those two to whom I have done things deserving

worse punishment than hanging. Would the sight
of children, bred as mine are, gladden me?
No, not these eyes, never. And my city,
its towers and sacred places of the Gods,
of these I robbed my miserable self
when I commanded all to drive *him* out,
the criminal since proved by God impure
and of the race of Laius.
To this guilt I bore witness against myself—
with what eyes shall I look upon my people?
No. If there were a means to choke the fountain
of hearing I would not have stayed my hand
from locking up my miserable carcase,
seeing and hearing nothing; it is sweet
to keep our thoughts out of the range of hurt.

Cithaeron, why did you receive me? why
having received me did you not kill me straight?
And so I had not shown to men my birth.

O Polybus and Corinth and the house,
the old house that I used to call my father's—
what fairness you were nurse to, and what foulness
festered beneath! Now I am found to be
a sinner and a son of sinners. Crossroads,
and hidden glade, oak and the narrow way
at the crossroads, that drank my father's blood
offered you by my hands, do you remember
still what I did as you looked on, and what
I did when I came here? O marriage, marriage!
you bred me and again when you had bred
bred children of your child and showed to men
brides, wives and mothers and the foulest deeds
that can be in this world of ours.

Come—it's unfit to say what is unfit
to do.—I beg of you in God's name hide me
somewhere outside your country, yes, or kill me,
or throw me into the sea, to be forever

out of your sight. Approach and deign to touch me
for all my wretchedness, and do not fear.
No man but I can bear my evil doom.

CHORUS: Here Creon comes in fit time to perform
or give advice in what you ask of us.
Creon is left sole ruler in your stead.

OEDIPUS: Creon! Creon! What shall I say to him?
How can I justly hope that he will trust me?
In what is past I have been proved towards him
an utter liar.

(Enter CREON.*)*

CREON: Oedipus, I've come
not so that I might laugh at you nor taunt you
with evil of the past. But if you still
are without shame before the face of men
reverence at least the flame that gives all life,
our Lord the Sun, and do not show unveiled
to him pollution such that neither land
nor holy rain nor light of day can welcome.

(To a servant.)

Be quick and take him in. It is most decent
that only kin should see and hear the troubles
of kin.

OEDIPUS: I beg you, since you've torn me from
my dreadful expectations and have come
in a most noble spirit to a man
that has used you vilely—do a thing for me.
I shall speak for your own good, not for my own.

CREON: What do you need that you would ask of me?

OEDIPUS: Drive me from here with all the speed you can
to where I may not hear a human voice.

CREON: Be sure, I would have done this had not I
wished first of all to learn from the God the course
of action I should follow.

OEDIPUS: But his word
has been quite clear to let the parricide,
the sinner, die.

CREON: Yes, that indeed was said.
But in the present need we had best discover
what we should do.
    OEDIPUS: And will you ask about
a man so wretched?
    CREON: Now even you will trust
the God.
    OEDIPUS: So. I command you—and will beseech you—
to her that lies inside that house give burial
as you would have it; she is yours and rightly
you will perform the rites for her. For me—
never let this my father's city have me
living a dweller in it. Leave me live
in the mountains where Cithaeron is, that's called
my mountain, which my mother and my father
while they were living would have made my tomb.
So I may die by their decree who sought
indeed to kill me. Yet I know this much:
no sickness and no other thing will kill me.
I would not have been saved from death if not
for some strange evil fate. Well, let my fate
go where it will.
                        Creon, you need not care
about my sons; they're men and so wherever
they are, they will not lack a livelihood.
But my two girls—so sad and pitiful—
whose table never stood apart from mine,
and everything I touchèd they always shared—
O Creon, have a thought for them! And most
I wish that you might suffer me to touch them
and sorrow with them.

(*Enter* ANTIGONE *and* ISMENE, OEDIPUS' *two daughters.*)

O my lord! O true noble Creon! Can I
really be touching them, as when I saw?
What shall I say?
Yes, I can hear them sobbing—my two darlings!
and Creon has had pity and has sent me

what I loved most?
Am I right?
    CREON: You're right: it was I gave you this
because I knew from old days how you loved them
as I see now.
    OEDIPUS: God bless you for it, Creon,
and may God guard you better on your road
than he did me!
                 O children,
where are you? Come here, come to my hands,
a brother's hands which turned your father's eyes,
those bright eyes you knew once, to what you see,
a father seeing nothing, knowing nothing,
begetting you from his own source of life.
I weep for you—I cannot see your faces—
I weep when I think of the bitterness
there will be in your lives, how you must live
before the world. At what assemblages
of citizens will you make one? to what
gay company will you go and not come home
in tears instead of sharing in the holiday?
And when you're ripe for marriage, who will he be,
the man who'll risk to take such infamy
as shall cling to my children, to bring hurt
on them and those that marry with them? What
curse is not there? "Your father killed his father
and sowed the seed where he had sprung himself
and begot you out of the womb that held him."
These insults you will hear. Then who will marry you?
No one, my children; clearly you are doomed
to waste away in barrenness unmarried.
Son of Menoeceus, since you are all the father
left these two girls, and we, their parents, both
are dead to them—do not allow them wander
like beggars, poor and husbandless.
They are of your own blood.
And do not make them equal with myself
in wretchedness; for you can see them now
so young, so utterly alone, save for you only.

Touch my hand, noble Creon, and say yes.
If you were older, children, and were wiser,
there's much advice I'd give you. But as it is,
let this be what you pray: give me a life
wherever there is opportunity
to live, and better life than was my father's.

CREON: Your tears have had enough of scope; now go within
the house.

OEDIPUS: I must obey, though bitter of heart.

CREON: In season, all is good.

OEDIPUS: Do you know on what conditions I obey?

CREON: You tell me them,
and I shall know them when I hear.

OEDIPUS: That you shall send me out
to live away from Thebes.

CREON: That gift you must ask of the God.

OEDIPUS: But I'm now hated by the Gods.

CREON: So quickly you'll obtain your prayer.

OEDIPUS: You consent then?

CREON: What I do not mean, I do not use to say.

OEDIPUS: Now lead me away from here.

CREON: Let go the children, then, and come.

OEDIPUS: Do not take them from me.

CREON: Do not seek to be master in everything,
for the things you mastered did not follow you throughout your
life.

(*As* CREON *and* OEDIPUS *go out.*)

CHORUS: You that live in my ancestral Thebes, behold this
Oedipus,—
him who knew the famous riddles and was a man most masterful;
not a citizen who did not look with envy on his lot—
See him now and see the breakers of misfortune swallow him!
Look upon that last day always. Count no mortal happy till
he has passed the final limit of his life secure from pain.

SOPHOCLES

ANTIGONE

TRANSLATED BY ROBERT WHITELAW

CHARACTERS IN THE PLAY

ANTIGONE ⎫ *daughters of Oedipus*
ISMENE ⎭
CREON, *King of Thebes*
A SENTINEL
HAEMON, *son of Creon*
TEIRESIAS, *a blind prophet*
A MESSENGER
EURYDICE, *the wife of Creon*
SECOND MESSENGER
CHORUS *of Theban Elders*

ANTIGONE

(SCENE: *An open space before the palace at Thebes. Enter* ANTIGONE *and* ISMENE.)

ANTIGONE: O Sister-Life, Ismene's, twin with mine,
Knowest thou of the burden of our race
Aught that from us yet living Zeus holds back?
Nay, for nought grievous and nought ruinous,
No shame and no dishonour, have I not seen
Poured on our hapless heads, both thine and mine.
And even now what edict hath the prince
Uttered, men say, to all this Theban folk?
Thou knowest it and hast heard? or 'scapes thy sense,
Aimed at thy friends, the mischief of thy foes?
   ISMENE: To me of friends, Antigone, no word
Hath come, or sweet or bitter, since that we
Two sisters of two brothers were bereaved,
Both on a day slain by a twofold blow:
And, now that vanished is the Argive host
Ev'n with the night fled hence, I know no more,
If that I fare the better or the worse.
   ANTIGONE: I knew full well, and therefore from the gates
O' the court I led thee hither, alone to hear.
   ISMENE: There's trouble in thy looks: thy tidings tell.
   ANTIGONE: Yea, hath not Creon, of our two brothers slain,
Honoured with burial one, disdained the other?
For Eteocles, they say, he in the earth
With all fair rites and ceremony hath laid,
Nor lacks he honour in the world below;
But the poor dust of Polyneices dead
Through Thebes, 'tis said, the edict has gone forth
That none may bury, none make moan for him,
But leave unwept, untombed, a dainty prize
For ravening birds that gloat upon their prey.
So hath our good lord Creon to thee and me

Published, men say, his pleasure—ay, to *me*—
And hither comes, to all who know it not
Its purport to make plain, nor deems the thing
Of slight account, but, whoso does this deed,
A public death by stoning is his doom.
Thou hast it now; and quickly shall be proved
If thou art noble, or base from noble strain.
   ISMENE: O rash of heart, if this indeed be so,
What help in me, to loosen or to bind?
    ANTIGONE: Consider, toil and pain if thou wilt share.
    ISMENE: On what adventure bound? What wouldst thou do?
    ANTIGONE: To lift his body, wilt thou join with me?
    ISMENE: Wouldst thou indeed rebel, and bury him?
    ANTIGONE: My brother I will bury, and thine no less,
Whether thou wilt or no: no traitress I.
    ISMENE: O all too bold—when Creon hath forbid?
    ANTIGONE: My rights to hinder is no right of his.
    ISMENE: Ah, sister, yet think how our father died,
Wrapt in what cloud of hate and ignominy
By his own sins, self-proved, and both his eyes
With suicidal hand himself he stabbed:
Then too his mother-wife, two names in one,
Fordid with twisted noose her woful life:
Last, our two brothers in one fatal day
Drew sword, O miserable, and each to each
Dealt mutual slaughter with unnatural hands:
And now shall we twain, who alone are left,
Fall like the rest, and worse—in spite of law,
And scorning kings, their edicts and their power?
Oh rather let us think, 'tis not for us,
Who are but women, to contend with men:
And the king's word is mighty, and to this,
And harsher words than this, we needs must bow.
Therefore will I, imploring of the dead
Forgiveness, that I yield but as I must,
Obey the king's commandment: for with things
Beyond our reach 'twere foolishness to meddle.
    ANTIGONE: I'll neither urge thee, nor, if now thou'dst help
My doing, should I thank thee for thine aid.

Do thou after thy kind: thy choice is made:
I'll bury him; doing this, so let me die.
So with my loved one loved shall I abide,
My crime a deed most holy: for the dead
Longer have I to please than these on earth.
There I shall dwell for ever: be it thine
To have scorned what gods have hallowed, if thou wilt.
ISMENE: Nay, nothing do I scorn: but, how to break
My country's law—I am witless of the way.
ANTIGONE: Be this thy better part: I go to heap
The earth upon my brother, whom I love.
ISMENE: Alas, unhappy, how I fear for thee!
ANTIGONE: Fear not for me: guide thine own fate aright.
ISMENE: Yet breathe this purpose to no ear but mine:
Keep thou thy counsel well—and so will I.
ANTIGONE: Oh speak: for much more hatred thou wilt get,
Concealing, than proclaiming it to all.
ISMENE: This fever at thy heart by frost is fed.
ANTIGONE: But, whom I most should please, they most are
    pleased.
ISMENE: So wouldst thou: but thou canst not as thou wouldst.
ANTIGONE: Why, then, when strength shall fail me, I will cease.
ISMENE: Not to attempt the impossible is best.
ANTIGONE: Hated by me, and hated by the dead—
To him a hateful presence evermore—
Thou shouldst be, and thou shalt be, speaking thus.
But leave me, and the folly that is mine,
This worst to suffer—not the worst—since still
A worse remains, no noble death to die.
ISMENE: Go if thou wilt: but going know thyself
Senseless, yet to thy friends a friend indeed.

(*Exeunt. Enter* CHORUS OF THEBAN ELDERS.)

Strophe 1

CHORUS: Lo, the sun upspringing!
Fairest light we hail thee
Of all dawns that on Thebes the seven-gated
Ever broke! Eye of golden day!

Over Dirce's fount appearing,
Hence the Argive host white-shielded,
That in complete arms came hither,
Headlong homeward thou didst urge
Faster still with shaken rein.
At call of Polyneices, stirred
By bitter heat of wrangling claims,
Against our land they gathered, and they swooped
Down on us—like an eagle, screaming hoarse,
White-clad, with wings of snow—
With shields a many and with waving crests.

Antistrophe 1

But above our dwellings,
With his spears that thirsted
For our blood, at each gate's mouth of the seven
Gaping round, paused the foe—and went,
Ere his jaws with blood were sated,
Or our circling towers the torch-flame
Caught and kindled: so behind him
Raged intense the battle-din—
While for life the Serpent fought.
For Zeus the tongue of vaunting pride
Hates with exceeding hate; he marked
That torrent army's onward flood, superb
With clank of gold, and with his brandished fire
Smote down who foremost climbed
To shout his triumph on our ramparts' heights.

Strophe 2

Hurled from that height with swift reverse,
The unpitying earth received him as he fell,
And quenched the brand he fain had flung,
And quelled the mad endeavour,
The frantic storm-gusts of his windy hate.
So fared it then with him;
Nor less elsewhere great Ares dealt
Against the foemen thunderous blows—
Our trace-horse on the right.

For seven chieftains at our seven gates
Met each his equal foe: and Zeus,
Who foiled their onset, claims from all his due,
The brazen arms, which on the field they left:
Save that infuriate pair,
Who, from one father and one mother sprung,
Against each other laid in rest
Their spears, victorious both,
And each by other share one equal death.

Antistrophe 2

But now of Victory be glad:
She meets our gladness with an answering smile,
And Thebes, the many-charioted,
Hears far resound her praises:
Now then with war have done, and strife forget!
All temples of the gods
Fill we with song and night-long dance;
And, Theban Bacchus, this our mirth
Lead thou, and shake the earth!
But lo the ruler of this Theban land,
Son of Menoeceus, Creon comes,
Crowned by these new and strange events, he comes—
By will of heav'n our new-created king,
What counsel pondering?
Who by his sovereign will hath now convoked,
In solemn conference to meet,
The elders of the state;
Obedient to whose summons, we are here.

(*Enter* CREON.)

CREON: Sirs, it hath pleased the gods to right again
Our Theban fortunes, by sore tempest tossed:
And by my messenger I summoned hither
You out of all the state; first, as I knew you
To the might o' the throne of Laius loyal ever:
Also, when Oedipus upheld the state,
And when he perished, to their children still

Ye with a constant mind were faithful found:
Now they are gone: both on one fatal field
An equal guilt atoned with equal doom,
Slayers of each other, by each other slain:
And I am left, the nearest to their blood,
To wield alone the sceptre and the realm.
There is no way to know of any man
The spirit and the wisdom and the will,
Till he stands proved, ruler and lawgiver.
For who, with a whole city to direct,
Yet cleaves not to those counsels that are best,
But locks his lips in silence, being afraid,
I held and hold him ever of men most base:
And whoso greater than his country's cause
Esteems a friend, I count him nothing worth.
For, Zeus who seeth all be witness now,
Nor for the safety's sake would I keep silence,
And see the ruin on my country fall,
Nor would I deem an enemy to the state
Friend to myself; remembering still that she,
She only brings us safe; her deck we pace,
Unfoundered 'mid the storm, our friends and we.
So for the good of Thebes her laws I'll frame:
And such the proclamation I set forth,
Touching the sons of Oedipus, ev'n now—
Eteocles, who fighting for this land
In battle has fall'n, more valiant none than he,
To bury, and no funeral rite omit,
To brave men paid—their solace in the grave:
Not so his brother, Polyneices: he,
From exile back returning, utterly
With fire his country and his fathers' gods
Would fain have burnt, fain would with kinsmen's blood
Have slaked his thirst, or dragged us captive hence:
Therefore to all this city it is proclaimed
That none may bury, none make moan for him,
But leave him lying all ghastly where he fell,
Till fowls o' the air and dogs have picked his bones.
So am I purposed: not at least by me

Shall traitors be preferred to honest men:
But, whoso loves this city, him indeed
I shall not cease to honour, alive or dead.
   CHORUS: Creon, son of Menoeceus, 'tis thy pleasure
The friend and foe of Thebes so to requite:
And, whatso pleases thee, that same is law,
Both for our Theban dead and us who live.
   CREON: Look to it, then, my bidding is performed.
   CHORUS: Upon some younger man impose this burden.
   CREON: To watch the body, sentinels are set.
   CHORUS: What service more then wouldst thou lay on us?
   CREON: That ye resist whoever disobeys.
   CHORUS: Who is so senseless that desires to die?
   CREON: The penalty is death: yet hopes deceive,
And men wax foolish oft through greed of gain.

   (*Enter a* SENTINEL.)

   SENTINEL: That I come hither, king, nimble of foot,
And breathless with my haste, I'll not profess:
For many a doubtful halt upon the way,
And many a wheel to the right-about, I had,
Oft as my prating heart gave counsel, "Fool,
What ails thee going into the lion's mouth?"
Then, "Blockhead, wilt thou tarry? if Creon learns
This from another man, shalt thou not smart?"
So doubtfully I fared—much haste, scant speed—
And, if the way was short, 'twas long to me.
But to come hither to thee prevailed at last,
And, though the speech be nought, yet I will speak.
For I have come fast clutching at the hope
That nought's to suffer but what fate decrees.
   CREON: What is it that hath troubled thus thy mind
   SENTINEL: First for myself this let me say: the deed
I neither did, nor saw who was the doer,
And 'twere not just that I should suffer harm.
   CREON: Wisely, thyself in covert, at the mark
Thou aimest: some shrewd news, methinks, thou'lt tell.
   SENTINEL: Danger to face, well may a man be cautious.
   CREON: Speak then, and go thy way, and make an end.

SENTINEL: Now I will speak. Some one ev'n now hath buried
The body and is gone; with thirsty dust
Sprinkling it o'er, and paying observance due.
CREON: How? By what man was dared a deed so rash?
SENTINEL: I cannot tell. No mattock's stroke indeed,
Nor spade's upcast was there: hard was the ground,
Baked dry, unbroken: track of chariot-wheels
Was none, nor any sign who did this thing.
But he who kept the watch at earliest dawn
Showed to us all—a mystery, hard to clear.
Not buried was the dead man, but concealed,
With dust besprinkled, as for fear of sin:
And neither of dog, nor any beast of prey,
That came, that tore the body, found we trace.
Then bitter words we bandied to and fro,
Denouncing each the other; and soon to blows
Our strife had grown—was none would keep the peace—
For every one was guilty of the deed,
And none confessed, but all denied they knew.
And we were fain to handle red-hot iron,
Or walk through fire barefoot, or swear by heaven,
That neither had we done it, nor had shared
His secret with who planned it or who wrought.
So all in vain we questioned: and at last
One spake, and all who heard him, bowed by fear,
Bent to the earth their faces, knowing not
How to gainsay, nor doing what he said
How we might 'scape mischance. This deed to thee
He urged that we should show, and hide it not.
And his advice prevailed; and by the lot
To luckless me this privilege befell.
Unwilling and unwelcome is my errand,
A bearer of ill news, whom no man loves.
CHORUS: O king, my thought hath counselled me long since,
Haply this deed is ordered by the gods.
CREON: Cease, ere my wrath is kindled at thy speech,
Lest thou be found an old man and a fool.
Intolerably thou pratest of the gods,
That they to yonder dead man have respect.

Yea, for what service with exceeding honour
Sought they his burial, who came here to burn
Their pillared shrines and temple-offerings,
And of their land and of their laws make havoc?
Or seest thou that the gods allow the wicked?
Not so: but some impatient of my will
Among my people made a murmuring,
Shaking their heads in secret, to the yoke
With stubborn necks unbent, and hearts disloyal.
Full certainly I know that they with bribes
Have on these men prevailed to do this deed.
Of all the evils current in this world
Most mischievous is gold. This hath laid waste
Fair cities, and unpeopled homes of men:
Many an honest heart hath the false lure
Of gold seduced to walk in ways of shame;
And hence mankind are versed in villanies,
And of all godless acts have learnt the lore.
But, who took hire to execute this work,
Wrought to their own undoing at the last.
Since, if the dread of Zeus I still revere,
Be well assured—and what I speak I swear—
Unless the author of this burial
Ye find, and in my sight produce him here,
For you mere death shall not suffice, until
Gibbeted alive this outrage ye disclose,
That ye may know what gains are worth the winning,
And henceforth clutch the wiselier, having learnt
That to seek gain in all things is not well.
For from ill-gotten pelf the lives of men
Ruined than saved more often shall ye see.

SENTINEL: May I speak a word, or thus am I dismissed?
CREON: Know'st thou not that ev'n now thy voice offends?
SENTINEL: Do I afflict thy hearing or thy heart?
CREON: Where I am pained, it skills not to define.
SENTINEL: The doer grieves thy mind, but I thine ears.
CREON: That thou wast born to chatter, 'tis too plain.
SENTINEL: And therefore not the doer of this deed.
CREON: At thy life's cost thou didst it, bought with gold.

SENTINEL: Alas!
'Tis pity, men should judge, yet judge amiss.
    CREON: Talk you of "judging" glibly as you may—
Who did this deed, I'll know, or ye shall own
That all your wondrous winnings end in loss.
    SENTINEL: With all my heart I wish he may be found:
But found or no—for that's as fortune will—
I shall not show my face to you again.
Great cause I have to thank the gracious gods,
Saved past all hope and reckoning even now.

(*Exeunt* CREON *and the* SENTINEL.)

Strophe 1

CHORUS: Many are the wonders of the world,
And none so wonderful as Man.
Over the waters wan
His storm-vext bark he steers,
While the fierce billows break
Round his path, and o'er his head:
And the Earth-mother, first of gods,
The ageless, the indomitable,
With his ploughing to and fro
He wearieth, year by year:
In the deep furrow toil the patient mules.

Antistrophe 1

The birds o' the air he snares and takes,
All the light-hearted fluttering race:
And tribes of savage beasts,
And creatures of the deep,
Meshed in his woven toils,
Own the master-mind of man.
Free lives of upland and of wild
By human arts are curbed and tamed:
See the horse's shaggy neck
Submissive to the yoke—
And strength untired of mountain-roaming bulls.

Strophe 2

Language withal he learnt,
And Thought that as the wind is free,
And aptitudes of civic life:
Ill-lodged no more he lies,
His roof the sky, the earth his bed,
Screened now from piercing frost and pelting rain;
All-fertile in resource, resourceless never
Meets he the morrow; only death
He wants the skill to shun:
But many a fell disease the healer's art hath foiled.

Antistrophe 2

So soaring far past hope,
The wise inventiveness of man
Finds diverse issues, good and ill:
If from their course he wrests
The firm foundations of the state,
Laws, and the justice he is sworn to keep,
High in the city, citiless I deem him,
Dealing with baseness: overbold,
May he my hearth avoid,
Nor let my thoughts with his, who does such deeds, agree!

(*Enter the* SENTINEL *with* ANTIGONE.)

What strange portentous sight is this,
I doubt my eyes, beholding? This—
How shall I gainsay what I know?—
This maiden *is*—Antigone!
Daughter of Oedipus,
Hapless child of a hapless sire,
What hast thou done? It cannot be
That thou hast transgressed the king's command—
That, taken in folly, *thee* they bring!
   SENTINEL: This same is she that did the burial:
We caught her in the act. But where's the king?
   CHORUS: Back from the palace in good time he comes.

(*Enter* CREON.)

CREON: What chance is this, to which my steps are timed?
SENTINEL: Nothing, sir king, should men swear not to do;
For second thoughts to first thoughts give the lie.
Hither, I made full sure, I scarce should come
Back, by your threats beruffled as I was.
Yet here, surprised by most unlooked-for joy,
That trifles all delights that e'er I knew,
I bring you—though my coming breaks my oath—
This maiden, whom, busied about the corpse,
We captured. This time were no lots to throw:
My own good fortune this, and none but mine.
Now therefore, king, take her yourself and try her,
And question as you will: but I have earned
Full clearance and acquittal of this coil.
   CREON: Where, on what manner, was your captive taken?
   SENTINEL: Burying the man, we took her: all is told.
   CREON: Art thou advised of this? Is it the truth?
   SENTINEL: I say I saw her burying the body,
That you forbade. Is that distinct and clear?
   CREON: How was she seen, and taken in the act?
   SENTINEL: So it fell out. When I had gone from hence,
With thy loud threats yet sounding in my ears,
We swept off all the dust that hid the limbs,
And to the light stripped bare the clammy corpse,
And on the hill's brow sat, and faced the wind,
Choosing a spot clear of the body's stench.
Roundly we chid each other to the work;
"No sleeping at your post there" was our word.
So did we keep the watch, till in mid-heaven
The sun's bright-burning orb above us hung,
With fierce noon-heat: and now a sudden blast
Swept, and a storm of dust, that vexed the sky
And choked the plain, and all the leaves o' the trees
O' the plain were marred, and the wide heaven it filled:
We with shut eyes the heaven-sent plague endured.
And, when after long time its force was spent,
We saw this maiden, and a bitter cry

She poured, as of a wailing bird that sees
Her empty nest dismantled of its brood:
So she, when she espied the body bare,
Cried out and wept, and many a grievous curse
Upon their heads invoked by whom 'twas done.
And thirsty dust she sprinkled with her hands,
And lifted up an urn, fair-wrought of brass,
And with thrice-poured libations crowned the dead.
We saw it and we hasted, and at once,
All undismayed, our captive, hemmed her round,
And with the two offences charged her there,
Both first and last. Nothing did she deny,
But made me glad and sorry, owning all.
For to have slipped one's own neck from the noose
Is sweet, yet no one likes to get his friends
In trouble: but my nature is to make
All else of small account, so I am safe.
 CREON: Speak thou, who bendest on the earth thy gaze,
Are these things, which are witnessed, true or false?
 ANTIGONE: Not false, but true: that which he saw, he speaks.
 CREON: So, sirrah, thou art free; go where thou wilt,
Loosed from the burden of this heavy charge.

(*Exit the* SENTINEL.)

But tell me thou—and let thy speech be brief—
The edict hadst thou heard, which this forbade?
 ANTIGONE: I could not choose but hear what all men heard.
 CREON: And didst thou dare to disobey the law?
 ANTIGONE: Nowise from Zeus, methought, this edict came,
Nor Justice, that abides among the gods
In Hades, who ordained these laws for men.
Nor did I deem *thine* edicts of such force
That they, a mortal's bidding, should o'erride
Unwritten laws, eternal in the heavens.
Not of to-day or yesterday are these,
But live from everlasting, and from whence
They sprang, none knoweth. I would not, for the breach
Of these, through fear of any human pride,

To heaven atone. I knew that I must die:
How else? Without thine edict, that were so.
And if before my time, why, this were gain.
Compassed about with ills, who lives, as I,
Death, to such life as his, must needs be gain.
So is it to me to undergo this doom
No grief at all: but had I left my brother,
My mother's child, unburied where he lay,
Then I had grieved; but now this grieves me not.
Senseless I seem to thee, so doing? Belike
A senseless judgment finds me void of sense.
   CHORUS: How in the child the sternness of the sire
Shows stern, before the storm untaught to bend!
   CREON: Yet know full well that such o'er-stubborn wills
Are broken most of all, as sturdiest steel,
Of an untempered hardness, fresh from forge,
Most surely snapped and shivered should ye see.
Lo how a little curb has strength enough
To tame the restive horse: for to a slave
His masters give no license to be proud.
Insult on insult heaped! Was't not enough
My promulgated laws to have transgressed,
But, having done it, face to face with me
She boasts of this and glories in the deed?
I surely am the woman, she the man,
If she defies my power, and I submit.
Be she my sister's child, or sprung from one
More near of blood than all my house to me,
Not so shall they escape my direst doom—
She and her sister: for I count her too
Guilty no less of having planned this work.
Go, call her hither: in the house I saw her
Raving ev'n now, nor mistress of her thoughts.
So oft the mind, revolving secret crime,
Makes premature disclosure of its guilt.
But this is hateful, when the guilty one,
Detected, thinks to glorify his fault.
   ANTIGONE: To kill me—wouldst thou more with me than this?
   CREON: This is enough: I do desire no more.

ANTIGONE: Why dost thou then delay? I have no pleasure
To hear thee speak—have not and would not have:
Nor less distasteful is my speech to thee.
Yet how could I have won myself a praise
More honourable than this, of burying
My brother? This from every voice should win
Approval, might but fear men's lips unseal.
But kings are fortunate—not least in this,
That they may do and speak what things they will.
    CREON: All Thebes sees this with other eyes than thine.
    ANTIGONE: They see as I, but bate their breath to thee.
    CREON: And art thou not ashamed, from them to differ?
    ANTIGONE: To reverence a brother is not shameful.
    CREON: And was not he who died for Thebes thy brother?
    ANTIGONE: One mother bore us, and one sire begat.
    CREON: Yet, honouring both, thou dost dishonour him.
    ANTIGONE: He in the grave will not subscribe to this.
    CREON: How, if no less thou dost revere the guilty?
    ANTIGONE: 'Twas not his slave that perished, but his brother.
    CREON: The enemy of this land: its champion, he.
    ANTIGONE: Yet Death of due observance must not fail.
    CREON: Just and unjust urge not an equal claim.
    ANTIGONE: Perchance in Hades 'tis a holy deed.
    CREON: Hatred, not ev'n in death, converts to love.
    ANTIGONE: Not in your hates, but in your loves, I'd share.
    CREON: Go to the shades, and, if thou'lt love, love there:
No woman, while I live, shall master me.

    (*Enter* ISMENE.)

    CHORUS: See, from the palace comes Ismene—
Sisterly drops from her eyes down-shedding:
Clouded her brows droop, heavy with sorrow;
And the blood-red tinge of a burning blush
Covers her beautiful downcast face.
    CREON: Thou, who hast crept, a serpent in my home,
Draining my blood, unseen; and I knew not
Rearing two pests, to overset my throne;
Speak—wilt thou too confess that in this work
Thou hadst a hand, or swear thou didst not know?

ISMENE: I'll say the deed was mine, if she consents:
My share of the blame I bear, and do not shrink.

ANTIGONE: Justice forbids thy claim; neither didst thou
Agree, nor I admit thee to my counsels.

ISMENE: I am not ashamed, in thine extremity,
To make myself companion of thy fate.

ANTIGONE: Whose was the deed, know Hades and the dead:
I love not friends, who talk of friendliness.

ISMENE: Sister, disdain me not, but let me pour
My blood with thine, an offering to the dead.

ANTIGONE: Leave me to die alone, nor claim the work
Thou wouldst not help. My death will be enough.

ISMENE: What joy have I to live, when thou art gone?

ANTIGONE: Ask Creon that: thou art of kin to him.

ISMENE: Why wilt thou grieve me with thy needless taunts?

ANTIGONE: If I mock thee, 'tis with a heavy heart.

ISMENE: What may I do to serve thee even now?

ANTIGONE: Look to thyself: I grudge thee not thy safety.

ISMENE: And may I not, unhappy, share thy death?

ANTIGONE: Thou didst make choice to live, but I to die.

ISMENE: Might I unsay my words, this were not so.

ANTIGONE: Wise seemed we—thou to these, and I to those.

ISMENE: But now our fault is equal, thine and mine.

ANTIGONE: Take heart to live: for so thou dost: but I—
Dead is my life long since—to help the dead.

CREON: One of these two, methinks, proves foolish now;
The other's folly with her life began.

ISMENE: Nay, for, O king, misfortunes of the wise
To madness turn the wisdom that they have.

CREON: 'Tis so with thee, choosing to share her guilt.

ISMENE: How should I live alone, without my sister?

CREON: Call her not thine: thou hast no sister now.

ISMENE: But wilt thou tear her from thy son's embrace?

CREON: Are there no women in the world but she?

ISMENE: Not as their faith was plighted, each to each.

CREON: An evil wife I like not for my son.

ANTIGONE: Haemon! beloved! hear not thy father's scorn.

CREON: Thou and thy love to me are wearisome.

CHORUS: Wilt thou indeed snatch from thy son his bride?

CREON: 'Tis death that will unloose their marriage-bond.
CHORUS: It seems thou art resolved that she must die?
CREON: Of that we are agreed. Delay no more:
Ye, servants, lead them in. For from this time
Women they needs must be, and range no more:
Since ev'n the bold may play the runaway,
When death he sees close-creeping on his life.

(*Exeunt* ANTIGONE *and* ISMENE.)

Strophe 1

CHORUS: Happy indeed is the life of the man who tastes not of
      trouble!
For when from the gods a house is shaken,
Fails nevermore the curse,
On most and on least of the race descending:
Like to a rolling wave,
By furious blasts from the Thraceward driven—
Out of the nethermost deeps, out of the fathomless gloom,
Casting up mire and blackness and storm-vext wrack of the sea—
And back, with a moan like thunder, from the cliffs the surf is
      hurled.

Antistrophe 1

So from of old to the Labdacid race comes sorrow on sorrow:
And, ev'n as the dead, so fare the living:
Respite from ills is none,
Nor one generation redeems another—
All will some god bring low.
Now o'er the last root of the house, fate-stricken,
Woe for the light that had shined, woe for the lingering hope!
Smooth over all is lying the blood-stained dust they have spread—
Rash speech, and a frantic purpose, and the gods who reign below.

Strophe 2

What human trespass, Zeus,
May circumscribe thy power,
Which neither sleep o'ercomes,
That saps the strength of all things else,

Nor months that run their tireless course
But thou for ever with an ageless sway
The dazzling splendour dost possess
Of thine Olympian home?
'Tis now as it hath ever been,
And still in years to come
The old order will not change:
Never from human life departs
The universal scourge of man,
His own presumptuous pride.

Antistrophe 2

Hope wings her daring flight,
By strong winds borne afar—
And some are blessed; and some
Are cheated of their vain desires,
That learn their folly all too late,
When in the fire they tread with scorchèd feet.
'Twas said of old—and time approves
The wisdom of the saw—
That, when in foolish ways, that end
In ruin, gods would lead
A mortal's mind astray,
Evil that man miscalls his good:
A brief while then he holds his course
By fatuous pride unscathed.
See, thy son Haemon comes hither, of all
Thy children the last. Comes he lamenting
The doom of the maiden, his bride Antigone—
And the frustrated hope of his marriage?

(*Enter* HAEMON.)

CREON: Soon we shall know, better than seers could say.
My son, in anger art thou come to me,
Hearing the sentence, not to be reversed,
Which on thy destined bride I have pronounced?
Or am I still thy friend, do what I may?
HAEMON: Father, I am in thy hand: with thy wise counsels
Thou dost direct me; these I shall obey.

Not rightly should I deem of more account
The winning of a wife than thy good guidance.
   CREON: Be this thy dearest wish and next thy heart,
In all things to uphold thy father's will.
For to this end men crave to see grow up
Obedient children round them in their homes,
Both to requite their enemies with hate,
And render equal honour to their friends.
Whoso begets unprofitable children,
What shall be said of him, but that he gets
Grief for himself, loud laughter for his foes?
Never, my son, let for a woman's sake
Reason give way to sense, but know full well
Cold is the pleasure that he clasps, who woos
An evil woman to his board and bed.
What wounds so deeply as an evil friend?
Count then this maiden as thine enemy,
Loathe her, and give her leave, in that dark world
To which she goes, to marry with another.
For out of all the city since I found
Her only, and her openly, rebellious,
I shall not to the city break my word,
But she shall die. Let her appeal to Zeus,
And sing the sanctity of kindred blood—
What then? If in my own house I shall nurse
Rebellion, how shall strangers not rebel?
He who to his own kith and kin does right,
Will in the state deal righteously with all.
Of such a man I shall not fear to boast,
Well he can rule, and well he would obey,
And in the storm of battle at his post
Firm he would stand, a comrade staunch and true.
But praise from me that man shall never have,
Who either boldly thrusts aside the law
Or takes upon him to instruct his rulers,
Whom, by the state empowered, he should obey,
In little and in much, in right and wrong.
The worst of evils is to disobey.
Cities by this are ruined, homes of men

Made desolate by this; this in the battle
Breaks into headlong rout the wavering line;
The steadfast ranks, the many lives unhurt,
Are to obedience due. We must defend
The government and order of the state,
And not be governed by a wilful girl.
We'll yield our place up, if we must, to men;
To women that we stooped, shall not be said.

CHORUS: Unless an old man's judgment is at fault,
These words of thine, we deem, are words of wisdom.

HAEMON: Reason, my father, in the mind of man,
Noblest of all their gifts, the gods implant,
And how to find thy reasoning at fault,
I know not, and to learn I should be loth;
Yet for another it might not be amiss.
But I for thee am vigilant to mark
All that men say, or do, or find to blame.
Thy presence awes the simple citizen
From speaking words that shall not please thine ear,
But I hear what they whisper in the dark,
And how the city for this maid laments,
That of all women she the least deserving
Dies for most glorious deeds a death most cruel,
Who her own brother, fall'n among the slain,
Left not unburied there, to be devoured
By ravening dogs or any bird o' the air:—
"Should not her deed be blazoned all in gold?"
Upon the darkness still such whisper grows.
But I of all possessions that I have
Prize most, my father, thy prosperity.
Welldoing and fair fame of sire to son,
Of son to sire, is noblest ornament.
Cleave not, I pray thee, to this constant mind,
That what thou sayest, and nought beside, is truth.
For men who think that only they are wise,
None eloquent, right-minded none, but they,
Often, when searched, prove empty. 'Tis no shame,
Ev'n if a man be wise, that he should yet
Learn many things, and not hold out too stiffly.

Beside the torrent's course, of trees that bend
Each bough, thou seest, and every twig is safe;
Those that resist are by the roots uptorn.
And ships, that brace with stubborn hardihood
Their mainsheet to the gale, pursue their voyage
Keel-uppermost, their sailors' thwarts reversed.
Cease from thy wrath; be not inexorable:
For if despite my youth I too may think
My thought, I'll say that best it is by far
That men should be all-knowing if they may,
But if—as oft the scale inclines not so—
Why then, by good advice 'tis good to learn.
    CHORUS: What in thy son's speech, king, is seasonable
'Tis fit thou shouldst receive: and thou in his:
For there is reason in the words of both.
    CREON: Shall I, grown grey with age, be taught indeed—
And by this boy—to think what he thinks right?
    HAEMON: Nothing that is not right: though I am young,
Consider not my years, but how I act.
    CREON: Is this thine act—to honour the unruly?
    HAEMON: Wrongdoers, dishonour—outrage, if thou wilt!
    CREON: Hath not this maiden caught this malady?
    HAEMON: The general voice of Thebes says no to that.
    CREON: Shall Thebes prescribe to me how I must govern?
    HAEMON: How all too young art thou in speaking thus!
    CREON: Whose business is't but mine how Thebes is governed?
    HAEMON: A city is none, that to one man belongs.
    CREON: Is it not held, the city is the king's?
    HAEMON: Finely thou'dst rule, alone, a land dispeopled!
    CREON: It seems this boy will plead the woman's cause.
    HAEMON: Woman art thou? my care is all for thee.
    CREON: Shameless—is't right to wrangle with thy father?
    HAEMON: I see that wrong for right thou dost mistake.
    CREON: Do I mistake, to reverence my office?
    HAEMON: What reverence, heaven's honours to contemn?
    CREON: O hateful spirit, ruled by a woman's will!
    HAEMON: To no base service shalt thou prove me bound.
    CREON: Art thou not pleading all the time for her?
    HAEMON: For thee and me, and for the gods below.

CREON: Thou shalt not marry her, this side the grave.
HAEMON: If she must die, she shall: but not alone.
CREON: Art grown so bold, thou dost fly out in threats?
HAEMON: What threats, to argue with a foolish purpose?
CREON: Thou'lt rue—unwise—thy wisdom spent on me.
HAEMON: Thou art my father; or wise I scarce had called thee.
CREON: Slave—to thy mistress babble, not to me.
HAEMON: Wouldst thou have all the talking for thine own?
CREON: Is't come to this? But, by Olympus yonder,
Know well, thou shalt be sorry for these taunts,
Wherewith thou dost upbraid me. Slaves, what ho!
Bring that abhorence hither, that she may die,
Now, in her bridegroom's sight, whilst here he stands.
HAEMON: Neither in my sight—imagine no such thing—
Shall she be slain; nor shalt thou from this hour
Look with thine eyes upon my face again:
To friends who love thy madness I commit thee.

(*Exit* HAEMON.)

CHORUS: Suddenly, sire, in anger he is gone:
Young minds grow desperate, by grief distemper'd.
CREON: More than a man let him conceive and do;
He shall not save these maidens from their doom.
CHORUS: Both sisters art thou purposed to destroy?
CREON: Not her whose hands sinned not; thou askest well.
CHORUS: What of the other? how shall she be slain?
CREON: By paths untrodden of men I will conduct her,
And shut her, living in a vault, rock-hewn,
And there, with food, no more than shall suffice
To avert the guilt of murder from the city,
To Hades, the one god whom she reveres,
She, praying not to die, either shall have
Her asking, or shall learn, albeit too late,
That to revere the dead is fruitless toil.

(*Exit* CREON.)

Strophe

CHORUS: O Love, our conqueror, matchless in might,
Thou prevailest, O Love, thou dividest the prey:

In damask cheeks of a maiden
Thy watch through the night is set.
Thou roamest over the sea;
On the hills, in the shepherds' huts, thou art;
Nor of deathless gods, nor of short-lived men,
From thy madness any escapeth.

   Antistrophe

Unjust, through thee, are the thoughts of the just,
Thou dost bend them, O Love, to thy will, to thy spite.
Unkindly strife thou hast kindled,
This wrangling of son with sire.
For great laws, throned in the heart,
To the sway of a rival power give place,
To the love-light flashed from a fair bride's eyes:
In her triumph laughs Aphrodite.
Me, even now, me also,
Seeing these things, a sudden pity
Beyond all governance transports:
The fountains of my tears
I can refrain no more,
Seeing Antigone here to the bridal chamber
Come, to the all-receiving chamber of Death.

   (ANTIGONE *is led out of the palace by guards.*)

   ANTIGONE: Friends and my countrymen, ye see me
Upon the last of all my ways
Set forth, the Sun-god's latest light
Beholding, now and never more:
But Death, who giveth sleep to all,
Yet living leads me hence
To the Acherontian shore,
Of marriage rites amerced,
And me no bridal song hath ever sung,
But Acheron will make of me his bride.
   CHORUS: Therefore renowned, with praise of men,
To yonder vault o' the dead thou goest,
By no slow-wasting sickness stricken,
Nor doomed to fall with those who win

The wages of the swords they drew,
But, being to thyself a law,
Alone of mortals the dark road
To deathward, living, thou shalt tread.

ANTIGONE: I heard of one, most piteous in her ending,
That stranger, child of Phrygian Tantalus,
On heights of Sipylus enclasped,
And ivy-like enchained,
By clinging tendrils of the branching rock,
Who day and night unceasingly
'Mid drizzle of rain and drift of snow
Slow-wasting in her place
Stands, as the tale is told,
Her lids surcharged with weeping, and her neck
And bosom drenched with falling of her tears:—
A fate most like to hers
Seals up with sleep these eyes of mine.

CHORUS: She was a goddess, sprung from gods:
Mortals, of mortal birth, are we.
But for one dead to win with those
Who rank no lower than the gods—
In life and afterwards in death—
An equal lot, were much to hear.

ANTIGONE: Ah, I am mocked! Nay, by our fathers' gods,
Withhold thy taunts till I am gone—
Gone and evanished from thy sight.
O Thebes, my city!
O wealthy men of Thebes!
But *ye* will witness—yes, to you I turn—
O fount Dircaean, and this sacred grove
Of Thebè the fair-charioted,
By what stern law, and how of friends unwept,
To that strange grave I go,
The massy dungeon for my burial heaped.
O luckless wight,
Exiled from earth nor housed below,
Both by the living and the dead disowned!

CHORUS: To furthest brink of boldness thou didst stray,
And stumbling there, at foot of Justice' throne,

Full heavily, my daughter, hast thou fallen:
Yet of thy father's fault belike
This suffering pays the price.
  ANTIGONE: Thou hast touched, ev'n there, my bitterest\pang of
      all,
A thrice-told tale, my father's grief—
And all our grievous doom that clung
About the famed Labdacidae.
O that incestuous bed
Of horror, and my father's sin—
The hapless mother who bore him to the light,
By him enclasped—wherefrom I luckless sprang:
With whom, accurst, unwedded,
I must go hence to dwell.
O brother, a bride ·ill-starred
Who to thy couch didst win,
How, being dead, me living thou hast slain!
  CHORUS: Religion prompts the reverent deed:
But power, to whomso power belongs,
Must nowise be transgressed; and thee
A self-willed temper hath o'erthrown.
  ANTIGONE: Unwept and unfriended,
Cheered by no song Hymenaeal—
Lo, I am led, heavy-hearted,
This road that awaits me.
The sacred light-giving eye in heaven
Now no more must I see, unhappy:
But for my fate not a tear falls,
Not a friend makes moan.

  (*Enter* CREON.)

  CREON: Know ye not, songs and weepings before death
That none would pretermit, were he allowed?
Hence with her, hence, and tarry not, but deep
In her tomb-prison, even as I have said,
Leave her alone, forsaken: to die, or else
Live, in that vault entombed, if so she will:
Since of this maiden's blood our hands are clean,
Only we ban her sojourn in the light.

ANTIGONE: O tomb! O nuptial chamber! O house deep-delved
In earth, safe-guarded ever! To thee I come,
And to my kin in thee, who many an one
Are with Persephone, dead among the dead:
And last of all, most miserably by far,
I thither am going, ere my life's term be done.
But a good hope I cherish, that, come there,
My father's love will greet me, yea and thine,
My mother—and thy welcome, brother dear:
Since, when ye died, I with mine own hands laved
And dressed your limbs, and poured upon your graves
Libations; and like service done to thee
Hath brought me, Polyneices, now to this.
Yet well I honoured thee, the wise will say:
Since not for children's sake would I, their mother,
Nor for my husband, slain, and mouldering there,
Have travailed thus, doing despite to Thebes.
According to what law, do I speak this?
One husband slain, another might have been,
And children from another, losing these;
But, father and mother buried out of sight,
There can be born no brother any more.
Such was the law whereby I held thee first
In honour; but to Creon all mistaken,
O dear my brother, I seemed, and overbold—
And now, made captive thus, he leads me hence
No wife, no bride for ever—of marriage-joy
And nursery of children quite bereft:
So by my friends forsaken I depart,
Living, unhappy, to dim vaults of death.
Yet I transgressed—what ordinance of heaven?
Why to the gods, ill-fated, any more
Should I look up—whom call to succour—since
Impiety my piety is named?
But, if these things are pleasing to the gods,
I'll freely own I suffered for my fault;
If theirs the fault, who doomed me, may to them
No worse befall than they unjustly do!
  CHORUS: Stormily still o'er the soul of the maiden

The selfsame gusts of passion sweep.
CREON: Therefore, I warn them, ruth for their lingering,
To those who lead her, this shall cause.
ANTIGONE: Short shrift, swift death—ah! woe is me—
This speech portends.
CREON: Lay to thy soul no flattering hope,
That unfulfilled this doom may be.
ANTIGONE: O country of Thebes and my father's city,
And gods my progenitors,
Lo, how they lead me—now, and delay not.
O all ye princes of Thebes, behold me—
Of the race of your kings, me, sole surviving—
What things at the hands of what men I suffer,
For the fear of the gods I feared.

(*Exit* ANTIGONE.)

Strophe 1

CHORUS: Out of the sunlight so,
In brass-bound prison-courts,
Were pent the limbs of Danaë,
And in a living tomb sealed up from sight;
Albeit, O daughter, she as thou
Came of a noble line,
And that life-quickening treasure of his golden rain
She had in charge from Zeus to keep.
O dread mysterious power of fate,
That neither wealth nor war can quell,
Nor walls shut out, nor ships escape,
Dark-fleeing o'er the foam!

Antistrophe 1

And that Edonian king
Was bound, the choleric son
Of Dryas, splenetive and hot,
Fast in the rock by Dionysus chained.
Such fierce and fevered issue streams
From madness at the height.
With splenetive rash speech what madness had assailed

The vengeful god, too late he learned.
To women-worshippers inspired
Their torchlit revels he forbade,
And flutings that the Muses loved
Had silenced with his scorn.

Strophe 2

From the dark rock-portals of the divided sea
Here go the cliffs of Bosporus, and there
The savage Thracian coast
Of Salmydessus, where the neighbour-worshipped God
Of Battle saw the blinding blow accurst,
Dealt by that fierce stepdame,
Darkling descend on both the sons
Of Phineus—on their sightless orbs
That plead for vengeance, stricken through and stabbed
By the sharp shuttle in her murderous hands.

Antistrophe 2

Wasted with their sorrow, their mother's hapless fate
They hapless wept, and in their mother's shame
Had part, as those base-born:
Yet she from the old Erechtheid blood her birth derived,
And in deep caverns of the hills was nursed,
Amid her father's storms,
Child of the North-wind—up the steep
Hillsides no bounding foal so fleet,
A daughter of the gods: but her, O child,
Fate's everlasting hands availed to reach.

(*Enter* TEIRESIAS, *led by a boy.*)

TEIRESIAS: Prince of Thebes, we come—one sight for both
Our common road descrying, as behoves
Blind men to find their way by help of others.
    CREON: What tidings, old Teiresias, dost thou bring?
    TEIRESIAS: Hear then the prophet, and attend his speech.
    CREON: Have I aforetime from thy wisdom swerved?
    TEIRESIAS: So, clear of shoals, thou pilotest the state.
    CREON: The service thou hast rendered I attest.

TEIRESIAS: Once more on razor's edge thy fortunes stand.
CREON: Hearing thy speech, I shudder: tell me more.
TEIRESIAS: My art's prognostications hear and judge.
For in my ancient seat, to watch the birds
In that their general gathering-place, I sat,
And heard an unintelligible noise,
A cry and clangour of birds, confused with rage;
And what fierce fray they waged with murderous claws
I guessed too surely by the whirr of wings.
Scared by that sound, burnt-offerings I then
Essayed on blazing altars; but no flame
Leapt from the sacrifice; a clammy ooze
Reeked from the thighs, and 'mid the ashes dripped,
Smoking and sputtering; the gall disparted,
And on the air was spent; and the thigh-bones
Of the enfolding fat fell stripped and bare.
This from this boy I heard, whose eyes beheld
The failing signs of sacrifice obscure:
Others by me are guided, I by him.
And by thy will we are afflicted thus.
For now our hearths and altars every one
Have ravening dogs and birds fouled with the flesh
Of this poor fallen son of Oedipus;
And so no flame of victims burnt may move
Gods any more to hearken to our prayers,
And birds obscene flap forth a bodeful cry,
With fat of human carrion newly gorged.
Slight not, my son, such warning. For all men,
Both great and small, are liable to err:
But he who errs no more unfortunate
Or all unwise shall be, if having tripped
He rights the wrong nor stubbornly persists.
He who persists in folly is the fool.
Give death his due: stab not the fallen foe:
What valour is in this, to slay the slain?
Wisely I speak and well; and sweet it is
To hear good counsel, when it counsels gain.
CREON: Old man, ye all, as bowmen at a mark,
Shoot at this man, and with your prophecies

Ye practise on me too, and mine own kin
Mere merchandise and salework make of me.
Go to, get gain, and barter, if ye will,
Amber ye buy from Sardis, and fine gold
Of Ind: but him, I say, ye shall not bury:
No, not if eagles, ministers of Zeus,
Should bear him piecemeal to their Master's throne,
Will I, for fear of such pollution, grant
Leave for his burial; knowing well that men
Soil not the stainless majesty of heaven.
But, aged seer, the wisest of mankind
Dishonourably may fall, who fairly speak
Dishonourable words, and all for gain.
   TEIRESIAS: Alas!
Who knows, or who considers, in this world—
   CREON: What wilt thou say? What commonplace is this?
   TEIRESIAS: How prudence is the best of all our wealth?
   CREON: As folly, I suppose, our deadliest hurt.
   TEIRESIAS: Yet with this malady art thou possest.
   CREON: Reproaches I'll not bandy with the prophet.
   TEIRESIAS: Saying that I falsely prophesy, thou dost.
   CREON: So are all prophets; 'tis a covetous race.
   TEIRESIAS: Greed of base gain marks still the tyrant-sort.
   CREON: Knowest thou that of thy rulers this is said?
   TEIRESIAS: I know; for thou through me didst save the state.
   CREON: Wise in thy craft art thou, but false at heart.
   TEIRESIAS: Secrets, fast-locked, thou'lt move me to disclose.
   CREON: Unlock them, only speaking not for gain.
   TEIRESIAS: So, for thy part indeed, methinks I shall.
   CREON: Think not that in my purpose thou shalt trade.
   TEIRESIAS: But surely know that thou not many more
Revolving courses of the sun shalt pass,
Ere of thine own blood one, to make amends,
Dead for the dead, thou shalt have rendered up,
For that a living soul thou hast sent below,
And with dishonour in the grave hast lodged,
And that one dead thou holdest here cut off
From presence of the gods who reign below,
All rites of death, all obsequies denied—

With whom thou shouldst not meddle, nor the gods
In heaven, but of their due thou robb'st the dead.
Therefore of Hades and the gods for thee
The Avengers wait, with ruin slow yet sure,
To take thee in the pit which thou hast dug.
Do I speak this for gold? Thyself shalt judge:
For, yet a little while, and wailings loud
Of men and women in thy house shall show.
Think, of each city too what gathering rage,
That sees its mangled dead entombed in maws
Of dogs and all fierce beasts, or borne by kites
With stench unhallowed to its hearth-crowned heights.
So like a bowman have I launched at thee
In wrath, for thou provok'st me, shafts indeed
To pierce thy heart, and fail not, from whose smart
Thou'lt not escape. But now, boy, lead me home,
That he may vent his spleen on younger men,
And learn to keep a tongue more temperate,
And in his breast a better mind than now.

(*Exit* TEIRESIAS.)

CHORUS: The man has prophesied dread things, O king,
And gone: and never have I known—not since
These temples changed their raven locks to snow—
That aught of false this city heard from him.
CREON: Yea, this I know, and much am I perplexed:
For hard it is to yield, but standing firm
I fear to pluck swift ruin on my pride.
CHORUS: Son of Menoeceus, be advised in time.
CREON: Say then, what must I do? and I'll obey.
CHORUS: Go, from her prison in the rock release
The maiden, and the unburied corpse inter.
CREON: Dost thou think this, and wouldst thou have me yield?
CHORUS: Yea, king, and quickly; for the gods cut short
With sudden scathe the foolishness of men.
CREON: Hardly indeed, but yet with forced consent
I'll do it, stooping to necessity.
CHORUS: Do it, and go; leave not this task to others.

CREON: Even as I am, I'll go; and, servants, haste,
That hear and hear me not: axes in hand,
All to yon spot, far-seen, make good your speed.
But I, since this way now my mind is bent,
Whom I myself have bound, myself will loose.
For now my heart misgives me, he lives best,
Whose feet depart not from the ancient ways.

(*Exit* CREON.)

Strophe 1

CHORUS: Worshipped by many names—
Glory of Theban Semele,
Child of loud-thundering Zeus—
Haunting the famed Italian fields,
Whom as a prince the hospitable vale
Of the Eleusinian Dame reveres—
Bacchus, that hast thy home
In Thebes, the home of Bacchanals,
Beside Ismenus' fertile stream,
Where the fell dragon's teeth of old were sown:

Antistrophe 1

O'er the two-crested peak,
With nymphs Corycian in thy train,
By springs of Castaly,
The streaming levin lights thy path:
And from steep Nysa's hills, with ivy clad,
And that green slope, with clustering grapes
Empurpled to the sea,
When thou wouldst visit Theban streets,
A jocund company divine
With acclamation loud conducts thee forth.

Strophe 2

Thebes of all cities most thou honourest,
Thou with thy mother, whom the lightning slew:
And now, when Thebes is sick,
And all her people the sore plague hath stricken,

Hear us and come with healing feet
O'er the Parnassian hill,
Or the resounding strait:

Antistrophe 2

Come, whom fire-breathing stars in dance obey,
The master of the voices of the night,
Of Zeus the puissant son—
Come at our call, girt with thy Thyiad troop,
That follow, with thy frenzy filled,
Dancing the livelong night,
Iacchus, thee their lord.

(*Enter a* MESSENGER.)

MESSENGER: Neighbours of Cadmus, and the royal house
Of old Amphion, no man's life would I,
How high or low soever, praise or blame,
Since, who to-day has fortune, good or ill,
To-morrow's fortune lifts or lays him low;
No seer a constant lot foresees for men.
For Creon before was happy, as I deemed,
Who saved this land of Cadmus from its foes,
And the sole sovereignty of Thebes receiving
Prospered therein, with noble children blest.
Now all is lost. For, when the joys of life
Men have relinquished, no more life indeed
I count their living, but a living death.
For in thy house heap riches, if thou wilt;
Keep kingly state; yet, if no joy withal
Thou hast, for all things else, compared with pleasure,
I would not change the shadow of a smoke.
CHORUS: Of what grief now of princes wilt thou tell?
MESSENGER: That one lies dead, whom those who live have
slain.
CHORUS: Say, who is slain? And what man is the slayer?
MESSENGER: Haemon is dead: his death no stranger's act.
CHORUS: Slain by himself, or by his father's hand?
MESSENGER: Wroth with his pitiless sire, he slew himself.
CHORUS: O prophet, how thy prophecy comes true!

MESSENGER: These things being so, consider of the rest.
CHORUS: Lo, hard at hand the miserable queen,
Eurydice: who from the house comes forth
Either by chance, or hearing of her son.

(*Enter* EURYDICE.)

EURYDICE: Good townsmen all, your conference I heard,
As to the doors I came, intending now
Of Pallas to entreat her heavenly aid.
Even as I loosed the fastenings of the gate,
That opened wide, there smote my ears a word
Of sorrow all my own: backward I swooned,
Surprised by terror, in my maidens' arms:
But tell me now your tidings once again—
For, not unlearned in sorrow, I shall hear.
MESSENGER: Dear mistress, I will tell thee what I saw,
And not leave out one word of all the truth.
Why should I flatter thee with glozing words,
Too soon found false? Plain truth is ever best.
Thy husband hence I followed at the heels
To that high plain, where torn by dogs the body
Of Polyneices lay, unpitied still.
A prayer we said to Hecate in the way
And Pluto, their displeasure to refrain,
Then, sprinkling with pure water, in new-stript boughs
Wrapped round and burned the fragments that remained.
A lofty funeral-mound of native earth
We heaped for him; then sought the maiden's bed,
Her bridal bed with Hades in the rock.
And from afar a voice of shrill lament
About the unhallowed chamber some one heard,
And came to Creon, and told it to his lord.
And in his ears, approaching, the wild cry
Rang doubtfully, till now there brake from him
A word of sharp despair, "O wretched man,
What fear is at my heart? and am I going
The wofullest road that ever I have gone?
It is my son's voice greets me. Good servants, go,
Go nearer quickly; and standing by the tomb,

Even to the throat of the vault peer through and look,
Where the wrenched stonework gapes, if Haemon's voice
I recognise indeed, or by the gods
Am cheated!" Crazed with his fear, he spake; and we
Looked, as he bade; and in the last of the tomb
We saw the maiden—hanged: about her neck
Some shred of linen had served her for a noose:
And fallen upon her, clasping her, he lay,
Wailing his wasted passion in the grave,
His fatal father, and his luckless bride.
His father saw, and crying a bitter cry
Went in, and with a lamentable voice
Called him, "O rash, what is it that thou hast done?
What wouldst thou? On what madness hast thou rushed?
My son, come forth: I pray thee—I implore."
But with fierce eyes the boy glared at his sire
And looks of loathing, and for answer plucked
Forth a two-hilted sword, and would have struck,
But missed him, as he fled: and in that minute,
Wroth with himself, in his own side amain
Thrust deep the steel, unhappy; and conscious still
Folded the maiden in his fainting arms;
Then, gasping out his life in one sharp breath,
Pelted her pale cheek with the crimson shower.
Dead with the dead he lies, such nuptial rites
In halls of Hades, luckless, having won;
Teaching the world, that of all human ills
With human folly is none that may compare.

(*Exit* EURYDICE.)

CHORUS: How should one deem of this? The queen, without
A word, of good or evil, has gone hence.
      MESSENGER: Indeed, 'tis strange: but yet I feed on hope
That to lament in public for her son
She will not deign; but, as for private sorrow,
Will charge her women in the house to weep.
She is well tried in prudence, not to fail.
      CHORUS: I know not; but to me the too-much silence,
No less than clamorous grief, seems perilous.

MESSENGER: I will go hence to the house, and know, if aught
Of secret purpose in her raging heart
She hath kept locked from us. Thou sayest well:
The too-much silence may bode mischief too.

(*Exit the* MESSENGER.)

CHORUS: Lo, the king comes hither himself, in his hands
The record, not doubtful its purport, bearing;
No grief (I dare to say) wrought by another,
But the weight of his own misdoing.

(*Enter* CREON *with the body of* HAEMON.)

Strophe

CREON: Alas, my purblind wisdom's fatal fault,
Stubborn, and fraught with death!
Ye see us, sire and son,
The slayer and the slain.
O counsels all unblest!
Alas for thee, my son,
So young a life and so untimely quenched—
Gone from me, past recall—
Not by thy folly, but my own!
    CHORUS: Ah, how too late thou dost discern the truth!
    CREON: Yea, to my cost I know: but then, methinks,
Oh then, some god with crushing weight
Leapt on me, drave me into frantic ways,
Trampling, alas for me,
In the base dust my ruined joy.
O toil and trouble of mortals—trouble and toil!

(*Enter a* SECOND MESSENGER.)

SECOND MESSENGER: Trouble, O king, thine own and none but
       thine,
Thou comest, methinks, part bearing in thy hands;
Part—in the house thou hast, and soon shalt see.
    CREON: What more, what worse than evil, yet remains?

SECOND MESSENGER: Thy wife is dead, with desperate hand ev'n
    now
Self-slain, for this dead son for whom she lived.

Antistrophe

CREON: O harbour of Hades, never to be appeased,
Why art thou merciless?
What heavy news is this?
Harsh news to me of grief,
That slays me, slain before!
A woful word indeed,
Telling of slaughter upon slaughter heaped,
To me, the twice-bereaved,
At one fell swoop, of son and wife!
    CHORUS: Behold and see: for now the doors stand wide.
    CREON: This second grief, ah me, my eyes behold.
What fate, ah what, remains behind?
My son I hold already in my arms:
And now, ah woe is me,
This other in my sight lies dead:
Mother and child—most piteous both to see!
    SECOND MESSENGER: Heartstricken at the altar as she fell,
Her swooning eyes she opened, and made moan
For Megareus, her son, who nobly died
Before, and for this other, and with her last
Breath cursed, the slayer of her children, thee.
    CREON: Ah me, will no one aim
Against my heart, made wild with fear,
With two-edged sword a deadly thrust?
O wretched that I am,
Fulfilled with sorrow, and made one with grief!
    SECOND MESSENGER: She did reproach thee, truly, ere she died,
And laid on thee the blame of both their deaths.
    CREON: What was the manner of her violent end?
    SECOND MESSENGER: Pierced to the heart, by her own hand, she
    died,
Hearing her son's most lamentable fate.
    CREON: All, all on me this guilt must ever rest,
And on no head but mine.

O my poor son, I slew thee, even I:
Let no one doubt, but that the deed was mine.
O servants, lead me quickly, lead me hence;
And let me be as one who is no more.
    CHORUS: 'Tis counselled well, if well with ill can be:
For bad is best, when soonest out of sight.
    CREON: I care not, let it come:
Let come the best of all my fate,
The best, the last, that ends my days:
What care I? come what will—
That I no more may see another day.
    CHORUS: Let be the future: mind the present need,
And leave the rest to whom the rest concerns.
    CREON: No other wish have I; that prayer is all.
    CHORUS: Pray not at all: all is as fate appoints:
'Tis not in mortals to avert their doom.
    CREON: Oh lead me hence, unprofitable; who thee
Unwittingly have slain,
Child, and my wife, unhappy; and know not now
Which way to look to either: for all things
Are crooked that I handle, and a fate
Intolerable upon my life hath leapt.

    (CREON *is led away.*)

    CHORUS: First of all happiness far is wisdom,
And to the gods that one fail not of piety.
But great words of the overweening
Lay great stripes to the backs of the boasters:
Taught by adversity,
Old age learns, too late, to be wise.

E U R I P I D E S

MEDEA

TRANSLATED BY R. C. TREVELYAN

CHARACTERS IN THE PLAY

MEDEA
JASON
CREON, *King of Corinth*
AEGEUS, *King of Athens*
NURSE *of Medea*
TWO BOYS, *children of Jason and Medea*
ATTENDANT *of the children*
A MESSENGER
CHORUS *of Corinthian Women*

MEDEA

NURSE: Ah would that Argo ne'er had flown between
The blue Symplegades to the Colchian land,
Nay, that in Pelion's glens ne'er had been felled
The pinetree, nor with oars had armed the hands
Of those chieftains who sailed to win the Fleece
Of Gold for Pelias: for then had my mistress,
Medea, ne'er embarked for towered Iolkos,
Smitten with love for Jason to the heart;
Nor yet had she beguiled Pelias' daughters
To slay their sire, nor with her lord and children
Dwelt here in Corinth, still by Jason loved,
And eager in all things to comply with him.
For then is the home's welfare most assured,
When the wife is not at variance with her lord.
But now all's enmity, cankered what was most dear.
For his own children and my mistress Jason
Would now betray, wedding a royal spouse,
The child of Creon, monarch of this land.
But miserable Medea, thus dishonoured,
Invokes their oaths, recalls their joined right hands,
That mightiest pledge, summons the Gods to witness
What recompense she receives from Jason now.
Fasting she lies, yielding to grief her body,
Wasting in tears continually since first
She had knowledge how her lord was wronging her;
Neither lifting her eyes, nor from the ground
Raising her face; but deaf as any rock
Or ocean wave, she heeds not chiding friends;
Save when she turns her beauteous neck aside,
And to herself bemoans her father dear,
Her country, and her house, which she betrayed

Following the man who now dishonours her.
Thus bitterly by misfortune has she learnt
The wisdom of cleaving to one's fatherland.
Her sons she hates, nor joys to see them more.
I am fearful lest some mischief she devise;
Since dangerous is her mood, nor to such wrong
Will she submit. I know her, and dread her wrath.
For terrible is she: if any rouse her hate,
Easy by no means will his triumph prove.
But here are the boys returning from their sports.
Naught of their mother's sorrows do they reck,
For in the young mind misery has no home.

(*Enter the two* BOYS *and their* ATTENDANT.)

ATTENDANT: Tell me, thou ancient house-serf of my lady,
Why dost thou stand here at the gate, alone,
Wailing aloud these sorrows to thyself?
How could Medea consent that thou shouldst leave her?
NURSE: Nay, old man, thou who guardest Jason's children,
The ill-fortunes of their masters must needs grieve
And touch the very souls of faithful slaves.
And I now to such anguish have been wrought
That a yearning took me to come forth and here
Proclaim to Earth and Heaven my lady's woes.
ATTENDANT: Has she not then yet ceased wailing her miseries?
NURSE: Would it were so! Her trouble is scarce begun.
ATTENDANT: Ah blind fool!—if we may speak so of our masters—
For of her latest troubles she knows naught.
NURSE: What mean you, old man? Grudge not to tell me all.
ATTENDANT: 'Tis nothing. I recall the words I spoke.
NURSE: I entreat you, hide naught from your fellow-slave.
I will keep silence, if need be, thereon.
ATTENDANT: As I approached the benches where the elders
Sit at draughts near Peirene's hallowed spring,
Pretending not to listen, I heard one say
That Creon, this land's ruler, has resolved

To expel these boys together with their mother
From Corinth. Yet if this report be true
I know not, but could wish it were not so.
  NURSE: Will Jason suffer his sons to be thus wronged,
Even though he be at discord with their mother?
  ATTENDANT: The old ties are grown weaker than the new;
And no more to this house is he a friend.
  NURSE: Then are we undone, if a new wave of woe
Must whelm us, ere of the old we are yet rid.
  ATTENDANT: But thou—since 'tis no moment for our mistress
To know of this—be calm and speak no word.
  NURSE: Children, hear you what love your father bears you?
Curse him I will not, for he is my master.
Yet to his dearest false has he been found.
  ATTENDANT: Who that lives is not? Now first dost thou learn
That all men love themselves more than their neighbour
(Some justly, some through greed), seeing that a father
For a new bride's sake loves his sons no more?
  NURSE: Go, boys, within the house.—All will be well.
But thou, keep them, as far as may be, aloof:
Bring them not near their mother in this dark mood.
Already have I seen her glaring upon them
Savagely, threatening mischief. From her rage
She will not cease till she strike down some victim.
Not among friends, but foes, may her wrath fall!
  MEDEA, *from within:* Ah woe!
What misery is mine! Utter grief and despair!
Ah woe, woe is me! Might I but die now!
  NURSE: It is she, dear children, she, your mother,
Goading her heart with wrath's bitter goad.
Enter the house now quickly, I pray you;
Yet venture not near, lest she behold you.
Do not approach: be wary; provoke not
That savage mood which sullenly dominates
Her relentless heart.
Tarry not: haste, go quickly within now.
This gathering cloud of wailing and tears,
It is plain she soon with stormier flashing
Wrath will enkindle. Such a spirit as hers

In its headstrong pride, stung by affliction,
What reckless deed may it not dare?

(Exeunt CHILDREN *with* ATTENDANT, *within the palace.)*

MEDEA, *from within:* Ai, ai!
Bitter my wrongs, ah bitter, and worthy
Of loud lamentations! Oh ye accursèd
Sons of an unloved mother, may ruin
Whelm you and your sire and the whole house!
   NURSE: Ah woe, woe is me! Ah ruthless heart!
In the father's guilt, say, how should the sons
Have a share? Why thus hate them?—Ah children,
I tremble aghast—what will befall you!
Strange are the moods of princes; and haply
Being wont to command, ill-schooled to obey,
Never easily will they remit their wrath.
For a life inured to equality is best.
Nay, mine be a fate that from Greatness afar
And in safety assured shall attain old age.
For first by its mere name all men know
Moderation is best: great gain doth it bring
To all who ensue it. But to no mortal
E'er of avail was excess of Greatness:
More cruel the doom it inflicts, when against
Some house God's anger is kindled.

(The CHORUS OF CORINTHIAN WOMEN *has now entered.)*

   LEADER OF CHORUS: Was it hers, that moan as of anguish—
         the woe-struck
Colchian queen?
Still unappeased is her wrath. I entreat thee, good mother,
Speak: for within from the court's double gate did I hear lamenta-
         tion:
And how in the anguish afflicting a house that is dear to me,
Alas, how should I rejoice, friend?
   NURSE: There is *no* house more. Gone is it utterly.
Lured by a royal bride is the lord's heart;
While she in her bower lies pining away,

Poor lady. No word spoken in kindness
May dissolve from her soul misery's frost.
      MEDEA, *from within:* Ai ai!
Would that a flash from heaven might cleave through
My brain! What profit is life to me henceforth?
Woe, woe! Would now that in death I could end
This abhorred living hell and be rid of it!

   Strophe

      CHORUS: Heardest thou?—Oh Zeus! Oh Earth! Oh Light!—
What a fierce wild dirge of woe broke forth
From the hapless wife!
Poor wretch, for the couch, that all men
Must dread to approach, why yearn you?
Death's end ever hasteneth nearer.
Cease then to invoke him.
Though thy lord by a new
Bride be bewitched, to all comes
Such misery: let that not wound thee.
By Zeus shall thy wrong be righted. Overmuch
Moan not wasting away for thy lost lord.
      MEDEA, *from within:* O thou divine Themis! O sovereign Zeus!
Look what I suffer, who with oaths of power
Once bound him fast, him my accursèd
Husband!—With his bride ere long may I see him
In one ruin crushed with the house of her sire—
They who unwronged find heart so to wrong me!
O father! O city! whom I abandoned
To my shame, having spilt my own brother's blood!
      NURSE: Did you hear her cries, loudly invoking
Themis who sanctions vows, and supreme Zeus,
Whom men call guardian of oath-pledge?
In no light blow surely our mistress
Will wreak her passionate anger.

   Antistrophe

      CHORUS: Ah, would she but come forth here in our midst!
To our kindly counselling words she then

Might give good heed;
If haply she might abate so
Her soul's bitter mood and passion.
Oh ne'er may I fail towards friends
In zeal and devotion!
Go then, bring her here
Forth from the house, we pray thee.
"Fear not, for they love thee," say thou.
Haste, ere upon those within her vengeance fall;
Since now mightily flows her grief's full tide.

NURSE: I go. But I doubt whether words will avail
To persuade her forth.
Yet gladly for your sakes this will I try:
Albeit she glares like to a cub-drawn
Lioness round her, if one of her handmaids
Should dare to approach her with soothing speech.
Ah truly I deem purblind was the skill,
And vainly employed the art of our fathers.
Songs would they fashion, whether for revelling
Holiday merriment, or for carousals,
Sweet tunes to delight luxurious ears.
But the art by magic of lyre and song
To heal or assuage man's torturing heart-ache
None yet has found: though thence cometh oft
Swift death, and the dire destruction of homes.
Yet such were the curses it most would beseem us
With song to essay. But if jovial and rich
Be the feast, why lift we an idle chant?
For the bounteous cheer spread for the revellers
Should alone for delight be sufficient.

(*Exit* NURSE *within palace.*)

CHORUS: Did I not hear a long lamenting cry of grief?
In bitter and clamorous misery she wails
The spouse untrue who is false to his troth-plight.
Maddened with rage, savagely she invoketh
Oath-sanctioning Themis, bride of Zeus,
Who from a far shore
Lured her to launch on the night,

And sped her to Hellas across the wave
Through those gates of the vast sea.

(*Enter* MEDEA *from the palace, followed by the* NURSE)

MEDEA: Women of Corinth, I have come forth thus
Lest you should blame me. For I know that many
Come to be thought proud; some who, seen in public
Are judged so by the eye; others, in quiet
Retirement, gain the ill name of indolence.
For there can be no justice in men's eyes
If, unprovoked, they hate at first sight one
Whose heart as yet they have not truly learnt.
So a stranger should conform to a city's ways;
Nay, even a citizen I blame, who offends
His fellows by self-willed discourtesy.
But upon me disaster unforeseen
Has fallen and crushed my soul. I am ruined, friends;
Life's joy is lost, and I desire to die.
For he who was all to me—too well I know—
My husband, is found now the worst of men.
Surely of all things that have life and feeling
We women are the unhappiest creatures born.
First we must waste a rich dower's price to purchase
A husband, and accept one to be tyrant
Over our body—an evil yet more bitter.
And here's the worst risk, whether the lord we choose
Be good or bad: for infamous is divorce
For women, nor may we disown our lords.
Next the wife, coming amid new ways and customs,
Must divine (since she learnt it not at home)
How she may best manage her bedfellow.
If in this task we fail not, and our lord
Dwells with us, nor rebels against the yoke,
Happy is our lot—else, it were best to die.
Should life within-doors vex him, a man goes forth
To solace a despondent heart elsewhere:
While we to him alone must look for comfort.
But we, say they, have a safe sheltered life
At home, while they are risking theirs at war.

Presumptuous error! Sooner would I three times
Stand in the shielded ranks, than bear one child.
Ah, but how different is your fate from mine!
You have a city and a father's house,
A blissful life and fellowship of friends.
But I, forlorn and citiless, by my lord
Despised, a prey robbed from a foreign land—
Mother, brother, nor kinsmen have I none
To give me harbour from this storm of troubles.
For this one favour therefore I entreat you:
If I should find some means, some stratagem
To requite my husband for these cruel wrongs,
Do not betray me. In all else full of fears
Is woman, a mere coward to face steel in battle;
But in the hour when she is wronged in wedlock
There is no spirit more murderous than hers.

LEADER: I will keep silence. Justly wilt thou requite him,
Medea; nor do I marvel at thy distress.
But yonder I see Creon, our city's ruler.
Doubtless he comes to announce some new purpose.

(*Enter* CREON *with* ATTENDANTS.)

CREON: Thou whose eyes scowl forth fury against thy lord,
Medea, I bid thee go hence from this land
Into exile, taking with thee thy two sons.
And tarry not: I am here to see this sentence
Fulfilled. Homeward I turn not, ere beyond
The boundaries of my realm I cast thee forth.

MEDEA: Ai ai! Now am I utterly destroyed.
My enemies with full sail bear down upon me:
Safe landing-place from ruin there is none.
Yet will I ask, downtrodden though I am,
For what cause, Creon, do you banish me?

CREON: I fear you—what need for veiled words?—I fear
Lest you wreak on my child some cureless mischief.
Much is there to confirm me in this dread.
You are subtle, and deep versed in evil lore:
Losing your husband's love, you are aggrieved.
Moreover 'tis reported that you threaten

Vengeance on sire, on bridegroom and on bride.
Ere it fall, I will guard me against that stroke.
'Twere wiser at once to earn thy hatred, woman,
Than relent now, but to repent hereafter.
    MEDEA: Alas!
Not the first time, Creon, but oft before
Has opinion wronged me and wrought grievous harm.
No prudent man should have his children taught
A subtler wisdom than the common wont.
For besides the reproach of idleness,
They earn the ill-will and envy of their neighbours.
For if to the ignorant you bring new learning,
Unserviceable, not learned, will they deem you;
While all dislike a citizen who excels
Those who to subtle knowledge make pretence.
In this unhappy fate I too must share:
For since I am wise, some find me odious,
Some hard to please, and indeed none too wise.
But you shrink from me, lest I disturb your peace.
Nay, Creon, fear not me: I am not such
That against princes I should seek to quarrel.
For wherein have you wronged me? You have but given
Your child to the man you chose. No, 'tis my husband
I hate. You doubtless have acted wisely here.
So now I grudge you not your happiness.
Go wed, and prosper: but within this land
Suffer me still to dwell. Wronged though I be,
I will keep silence, and yield, since I must.
    CREON: Mild words you speak: yet much I fear lest deep
Within your heart some wickedness you be plotting;
So less than ever do I trust you now.
For a cunning woman, aye, or a man, betrayed
To wrath, is easier watched than one who is silent.
Then straightway get you gone: speak no more speeches.
My sentence stands. Not all your craft shall help you
To stay here more, since you are known my foe.
    MEDEA: Now by thy knees! by thy new-wedded child! . . .
    CREON: You are wasting words. Never will you persuade me.
    MEDEA: So thou wilt drive me forth, spurning my prayers?

CREON: Why should I love you more than my own house?
MEDEA: O Fatherland! how I yearn for thee now!
CREON: Aye, there's naught else so dear, save haply a child.
MEDEA: O, what a fell curse for mankind is love!
CREON: Nay, rather curse or blessing as fortune falls.
MEDEA: Zeus, let not him escape thee, who caused these woes.
CREON: Go, fool—or must I drive you? Spare me that trouble.
MEDEA: I need none of *your* troubles. I have my own.
CREON: Haste, or I bid my menials thrust you forth.
MEDEA: Ah no, not that!—But I entreat thee, Creon . . .
CREON: So you compel me to use violence, woman.
MEDEA: I will go—Not for *that* boon do I implore you . . .
CREON: Why then do you struggle, and not depart forthwith?
MEDEA: Yet this one day suffer me to remain
And take thought for the manner of our exile,
And for my children's livelihood, since their father
Cares naught to make provision for his sons.
Ah pity them: thou art a father too.
Of myself and my banishment I reck not,
But weep for them, who now must learn adversity.
CREON: Mine is no tyrant's nature. Many a plan
Have I marred by relenting tenderness.
And now, though I see 'tis folly, yet this grace
I grant thee, woman. But heed well my warning:
If here within the borders of my realm,
Tomorrow's sunlight find thy sons or thee,
Thou diest. What I have spoken will I perform.

(*Exit* CREON *with* ATTENDANTS.)

CHORUS: Woe, woe! Sorrows past enduring are thine.
Nay, to what home, to what land will you turn
For welcome and shelter against these miseries?
For pathless and wild are the waves of despair,
Medea, wherein Heaven whelms thee.
MEDEA: From all sides defeat threatens; why gainsay it?
But think not the last word is said, not yet.
Perils are still in store for the new spouses,
And no slight miseries for the match-maker.
Think you I would have fawned upon that man,

Unless to gain some end or plot some guile?
Never had I addressed him or touched his hands.
But he to such a pitch of folly had come
That, though by banishing me he might have balked
My plottings, he now suffers me to abide
One day, wherein three foes will I destroy,
The father, and the daughter, and my husband.
So many are the roads of death I know,
That I doubt, friends, which it were best to choose.
Shall I set fire to their bridal chamber?
Or entering silently, to the nuptial bed
Steal near, and thrust a sharp sword through their hearts?
But there's one risk forbids me: if I be caught
Crossing the threshold, busy about my plot,
I shall die, mid the laughter of those that hate me.
No; best follow the forthright way, wherein
I have most skill. By poison must I slay them.
So then:
Suppose them slain: what city will receive me?
What friend will offer me a land of refuge,
A secure home, and so protect my life?
None.—Yet a little while then will I wait;
And if some tower of safety should appear,
By guile will I do this murder, secretly.
But if I am banished ere my plot be ripe,
Myself I'll seize the sword, and though I die for it,
Will slay them, and tread the path of utmost daring.
No, by that Mistress, whom beyond all others
I revere and have chosen for my helper,
Hecate, who dwells beside my secret hearth,
Not one of them shall wound my soul unpunished.
Bitter will I make their nuptials, bitter and doleful
Their wedlock, and their banishing of me.
Up then! neglect naught of thine art and skill,
Medea: some scheme now must thou devise.
On to dread deeds! Now is the hour for courage.
Thy wrongs thou seest. Become not a derision
To Jason and his Sisyphean bride.
Thou born of a noble sire, the Sun-god's race!

And skill thou hast: moreover—I am a woman;
And are not we for good most impotent,
But for all evil deeds subtlest artificers?

Strophe 1

CHORUS: Back now to their source will the sacred streams be
        mounting;
Changed is Nature's order, her laws are reversed.
Men it is now who are false, men now who break
Oaths that are sworn in the Gods' name.
So shall our estate be ennobled with fame and praised in story;
So to woman's race shall honour due be paid.
Scandal and slanderous tongues henceforth shall cease to assail us.

Antistrophe 1

Our falsity of old was your theme; but now, ye Muses,
Stint for shame those hoary traditional lays.
Phoebus, the leader of song, hath ne'er endowed
With lyric ardour and heaven-sent
Poetry's art my weak woman's mind; or against Man's race an
        answering
Hymn would I too uplift: for doth not Time record
Many a tale in reproach of men no less than women?

Strophe 2

With frenzied heart thou from thy father's home
Didst flee, setting sail in the bark that hath borne thee between
        the ocean's
Twin rocks to an alien land;
Whence now thou art chased, abandoned
Thus cruelly by thy husband,
Bereft of the joys of wedlock,
An unpitied exile.

Antistrophe 2

'Tis gone, the oath's spell; nor in mighty Hellas
Is piety to be found. To the skies has it fled from man's earth.
No home with thy sire awaits thee,
Poor wretch; from the storm of misery

No haven. A conquering rival
Now reigns in the halls, wherein once
He throned thee his heart's queen.

(*Enter* JASON.)

JASON: How often by experience have I learnt
That a stubborn humour is a pest incurable!
A home within this land might still be yours,
Could you but meekly endure the sovereign's will.
Now for your wild words banishment is the cost.
For myself I care naught: cease not to rail
At Jason as the basest among men.
But for those words you have spoken against our rulers,
Be thankful that exile is your only penance.
Oft as the royal anger rose, I strove
To check the fit, and would have had you stay;
But you in your stubborn folly would still revile
The princely house: so now you will be banished.
For all that, faithful ever to friends, I come,
Having so far prevailed that you should lack not
Gold, nor aught else besides, when with your sons
You are banished, lady. And many are the hardships
Exile brings in its train.—Aye, though you hate me,
Against you never will I make hard my heart.
  MEDEA: O thou all-basest!—well may I call you that
Do you come, you my worst foe—to me do you come?
No mere assurance, no mere hardihood
Is this, but that worst of all human plagues,
Shamelessness.—Ah, yet thou hast done well to come;
For the burden of my heart I now shall ease
Reviling thee, and thou be galled to hear.
Of that which first befell, first will I speak.
Thy life I saved—this every Hellene knows
Who upon Argo's benches sailed with thee—
When thou wast sent to tame fire-breathing bulls
To the yoke-collar, and sow a deadly tilth.
And the dragon, who kept guard with sleepless eye
Wreathed coil on coil around the Fleece of Gold,
I slew, and raised a light for thy deliverance.

Father and home willingly I forsook,
And to Iolkos beneath Pelion's crags
Fled with' thee—ah more passionate than wise!
A cruel death I wrought for Pelias, slain
By his own children, beguiling all their fears.
Such deeds, basest of men, for you have I done;
Yet to my bed you are false for a new bride's sake,
Though I bore you children. Had you still been childless,
Your wish for a second wife I might have pardoned.
Gone is all trust in oaths; nay how know I
Whether you deem the old Gods reign no more,
Or that new laws prevail now among men?
For your soul knows, towards me false were your oaths.
    Ah, this right hand—how often did you clasp it!
These knees—how have I felt them falsely embraced
By a traitor, but to be cheated of my hopes!
    Come, let me commune with you as with a friend!—
Though from you what fair dealing should I hope?
No matter: the viler shall my questioning show you.
Whither now should I turn? To my father's house?
To my country? I forsook them and fled with thee.
To those poor Peliad sisters? A kindly welcome
To me, their father's murderer, would they accord.
For thus it is: by those who loved me at home
I am hated now; while those who least deserved
My wrath, to please you I have turned to foes.
Blest therefore, in return for this, you have made me
In the eyes of all Greek wives; and I, poor wretch,
In you have a peerless and a loyal spouse,
If I must now be banished hence, cast forth
Forlorn of friends, alone with my lone children—
Verily a fine reproach for the new bridegroom:
Thy sons, and she who saved thee, wandering beggars!
O Zeus, why hast thou given to men clear signs
To reveal fraudulent alloy in gold,
While on man's outward form is set no stamp
Whereby to know if he be base or true?
    LEADER: Terrible and past healing is the wrath
When discord rises between friend and friend.

JASON: I have need, methinks, to be not mean in eloquence,
And, like the cunning helmsman of a ship,
With close-reefed sail must run before the fierce
Tempestuous violence of your woman's tongue.
I say then—since you would over-magnify
Your services—that the Cyprian, alone
Of Gods and men, was saviour of my voyage.
Though a subtle wit be yours . . . nay, but it were
Scarce generous to tell how Love compelled you
By his resistless shafts to save my life.
Howbeit I will not reckon this too strictly;
For with the way you helped me I find no fault.
Yet in delivering me you have received
More than you gave me, as I will show. For first
No more in a barbarian land you dwell,
But in Hellas, where you have learnt what justice means,
And how to live by rule of law, not might.
Then for your wisdom you are known and praised
By all the Greeks: but if still at the ends
Of the earth you dwelt, your fame none would have heard.
Not for me store of gold within my halls,
Nor skill in song that Orpheus might have envied,
Unless therewith my name be great in story.
Thus much, answering your challenge to debate,
Of my owns deeds I speak. But for your railings
Against my royal marriage, I will prove
That herein I act wisely, and moreover
With calm dispassion, last, as a potent friend
Both to you and my sons—nay hear me out.
When from Iolkos to this land I came,
Harassed by many a desperate mischance,
What happier fortune could I have lighted on
Than to wed a king's daughter, I, an exile?—
Not out of loathing for thy bed (the thought
That galls thee), nor through lust for a new bride,
Nor yet ambitious for a numerous offspring
(With those you have borne me I am well content),
But for this end chiefly, that we might live
In comfort, lacking naught; for well I know

How to be poor is to be shunned by friends.
Thus had I reared our children as beseems
My house, and raised up brethren for thy sons;
And thus, united in one princely family,
We had lived happily. What need now of children
For thee? But I by those yet to be born
Must help the living. Was my plan so unwise?
Even thou, wert thou not jealous, wouldst approve.
    Ah women, thus are you ever! While naught mars
Love's union, then you deem the whole world yours;
But if some shadow cloud your wedded bliss,
To you the best and fairest lot seems hateful.
Some other way to beget sons should mortals
Have found, and the race of women ne'er have been.
No woes then had there been to afflict mankind.
    LEADER: Jason, with subtle rhetoric have you argued.
Yet—for with boldness will I speak my thought—
You have done great wrong thus to betray your wife.
    MEDEA: How oft with the world's judgement mine conflicts!
For, to my mind, he who defends iniquity
With clever speech incurs more loss than gain.
With bold tongue making wrong seem right, he grows
Reckless in villainy, and so fails in wisdom.
Then be not thou specious and deft of tongue
Towards me; for one word shall lay thee low.
Wert thou not base, from me thou shouldst have sought
Consent to wed thus, not deceived my love.
    JASON: Nobly, I doubt not, wouldst thou have helped my purpose
Had I declared my marriage; since even now
Thou canst not calm thy spirit's violent rage.
    MEDEA: 'Twas not *that* stayed you; but your foreign wife
Ceased, as she lost her youth, to serve your pride.
    JASON: Be well assured, not for the woman's sake
Have I espoused this daughter of a king;
But, as I told thee, I wished to insure thy safety,
Begetting royal children of one blood
With our own sons, a bulwark to my house.
    MEDEA: May such bitter prosperity ne'er be mine;
Nor such well-being as would gall my heart!

JASON: Come, change that prayer, and thou wilt show more
  wisdom.
Bitter to thee may happiness ne'er seem.
When fate befriends thee, think it not unkind.
 MEDEA: Aye, mock me! You have a home wherein to dwell;
But I must flee this land, a friendless exile.
 JASON: Thine own free choice was that. Blame no one else.
 MEDEA: How so? Did I first wed you and then forsake you?
 JASON: No; thank thy wicked curses against the king.
 MEDEA: On thy house too a curse maybe I'll prove.
 JASON: Nay, hereon I dispute with you no more.
But if out of my wealth you will accept
Help for your children and yourself in exile,
Speak. With unstinting hand it shall be given,
And tokens sent to friends, bidding them aid you.
Folly it were should you reject these offers.
But cease from wrath, and great shall be your gain.
 MEDEA: No friend of yours will I allow to serve me,
Nor accept aught from you. Talk not of giving.
There is no blessing in a base man's gifts.
 JASON: At least I call the Gods to witness: gladly
You and your sons in all things would I serve.
But kindness offends you: stubbornly you spurn
Your friends. The bitterer then will be your woe.
 MEDEA: Go, go! Enthralled by love for your new bride
Too long far from her chamber you are lingering.
Go, wed.—But haply, if God so will, your bridal
Shall be such that you soon would fain renounce it.

(*Exit* JASON.)

 Strophe 1

 CHORUS: When Love with inordinate might
Invades the heart, he bringeth not
Virtue nor goodly renown:
Yet if with a temperate ardour
Cypris comes, no God hath a charm that excels hers.
Aim not, O great Queen, an invincible shaft in deadly passion
Steeped, nor draw thy golden bow against me.

Antistrophe 1

May chastity still be my shield!
What fairer gift may Heaven bestow?
Ne'er may the dread Cyprian
With lust for unlawful embraces
Smite my soul and drive me to moods of contention,
Restless hate and anger; but honouring rather peaceful unions,
Shrewdly may she adjudge the bonds of wedlock.

Strophe 2

Land of my home, ne'er may I flee
Forth from thy soil an exile,
To endure such a life of hardship,
Helpless and without hope!
Of miseries that were the worst.
Better death; better far were death than such fate.
Gladly of this brief day would I make an end.
Nay what woe may compare with theirs
Who from their home are banished?

Antistrophe 2

Yea, I have seen: 'tis not a tale
Told by the lips of others.
Fellow-countrymen hast thou none, nor
Friend to feel compassion,
Cruelly though thou art wronged.
By an unpitied death may he die, who thankless
Honours not his friends with an open heart
Where no secret is locked. Of such
Ne'er will I seek the friendship.

(*Enter* AEGEUS.)

AEGEUS: All hail to thee, Medea! With what greeting
Fairer than this may friend encounter friend?
MEDEA: All hail to thee too, wise Pandion's son,
Aegeus! Whence hast thou journeyed to this land?
AEGEUS: From Phoebus' ancient oracle am I come.
MEDEA: Why didst thou visit the earth's prophetic navel?

AEGEUS: How children might be born to me, I would ask.
MEDEA: Ah! Childless hast thou lived thy whole life long?
AEGEUS: Childless I am: some God would have it so.
MEDEA: Hast thou a wife; or art thou still unwed?
AEGEUS: Long have I lived in wedlock with a wife.
MEDEA: What answer to your hope did Phoebus utter?
AEGEUS: Riddles, too subtle for man's wit to read.
MEDEA: What was the God's response—if I may hear it?
AEGEUS: Surely; since here there needs a subtle wit.
MEDEA: What said he then? If naught forbids you, speak.
AEGEUS: "Thou shalt not spill the wineskin's jutting foot. . . ."
MEDEA: Till thou hast done what deed, or reached what land?
AEGEUS: Till to my native hearth-stone I return.
MEDEA: But say, what purpose brings you to this shore?
AEGEUS: There is one Pittheus, king of Troezen's town.
MEDEA: Aye, Pelops' son, renowned for piety.
AEGEUS: The God's response to him would I impart.
MEDEA: Yes, he is wise, and skilful in such lore.
AEGEUS: The dearest too of all my warrior friends.
MEDEA: All that thy heart desires mayst thou obtain.
AEGEUS: But why that downcast eye, that sunken cheek?
MEDEA: Aegeus, of all men basest is my husband.
AEGEUS: What mean you? Tell me your trouble in plain words.
MEDEA: Jason is false to me, who never wronged him.
AEGEUS: What has he done? Speak yet more clearly, I pray.
MEDEA: Another wife he is taking in my stead.
AEGEUS: He hath not dared to do a thing so shameful?
MEDEA: He hath. Those he once loved are now dishonoured.
AEGEUS: For some new love?—Or grows he weary of thee?
MEDEA: For love, a high love, he has betrayed his dearest.
AEGEUS: Fie on him, if indeed he is so base.
MEDEA: 'Tis with a princely wedlock he is in love.
AEGEUS: But who is the bride's father? Tell me more.
MEDEA: Creon it is, who reigns in Corinth here.
AEGEUS: Lady, thou hast but too much cause for grief.
MEDEA: 'Tis utter ruin.—Moreover I am banished.
AEGEUS: By whom? That were a crowning woe indeed.
MEDEA: 'Tis Creon who drives me an exile forth from Corinth.
AEGEUS: And Jason suffers it? Then he is doubly base.

MEDEA: His voice protests; yet he thinks best to endure it.
But now I implore thee by thy beard, and by
Thy knees, and as thy suppliant I entreat thee,
Pity, oh pity me in this evil plight;
Suffer me not to be cast out forlorn,
But to thy land and to thy hearth receive me:
So may thy wish for children by Heaven's grace
Be accomplished, and in death mayst thou be blest.
Thou know'st not what good fortune I shall bring thee.
I'll make thee a childless man no more; for sons
Shalt thou beget: such potent spells do I know.
AEGEUS: Lady, for many reasons I would fain
Grant you this boon: first for religion's sake;
Then for the sons whose birth you promise me,
Since other hope of offspring have I none.
Thus will I do. Once you have reached my land,
Then will I strive to befriend you, as justice bids.
But from this land you must escape unaided;
For towards all friends I would act blamelessly.
MEDEA: So be it. Yet by an oath were I assured . . .
AEGEUS: Do you mistrust me?—Or what fear troubleth you?
MEDEA: I trust you. But the house of Pelias hates me,
And Creon. Bound by oaths, you could not yield me
To them, when they would drag me from your land.
But, bound by mere words, not by solemn oath,
You will have no defence, and to their summons
Will yield perforce. For without strength am I,
While on their side is wealth and kingly power.
AEGEUS: What need for such far-sighted prudence here?
Yet may I not refuse, since so you wish.
Nay, thus the more secure shall be my ground,
If with this plea I am armed against your foes;
And you will stand the firmer.—Name your Gods.
MEDEA: Swear by the Earth below, and by the Sun,
My grandsire, and by the whole race of the Gods . . .
AEGEUS: To do what thing, or not to do? Say on.
MEDEA: Never thyself to expel me from thy land,
Nor to any foe of mine, who thence would force me,
Willingly yield me up while life is thine.

AEGEUS: By the firm Earth, by the Sun's light, by all
The Gods I swear by these terms to abide.
    MEDEA: 'Tis well. And if thou abide not by this oath? . . .
    AEGEUS: The doom reserved for sacrilege may I suffer.
    MEDEA: Go thy ways with my blessing. I am content.
Soon to thy city I too will follow thee,
When the deed I have purposed is achieved.

(*Exit* AEGEUS.)

    CHORUS: Now to thy home may the child of Maia
In safety escort thee; and may'st thou attain soon
That wish to thy heart so dear; for a nobler
Soul than is thine,
Aegeus, I know not among men.
    MEDEA: O Zeus, and thy child, Justice! O bright Sun!—
Now, women, a goodly triumph o'er my foes
Soon shall I win. My feet are on the path.
Where she was labouring most, my ship of counsel
Hath sighted a safe haven in yonder prince.
To him my stern-cable will I make fast,
When to the city of Pallas I am come.
Now to you my whole purpose will I tell.
Little shall you rejoice to hear my words.
To Jason will I send one of my household,
And beg that to my presence he return.
And when he comes, soft words I'll speak to him:
That this is my will too; that all is well—
A scheme most fortunately and wisely planned.
Then I'll entreat him that my sons may stay:
Not that I'ld leave them in a hostile land;
But this king's daughter by craft would I kill.
For to her will I send them bearing gifts,
A delicate robe and wreath of beaten gold.
These fineries if she accept and put them on,
Horribly shall she die, and all who touch her;
With such fell poisons will I anoint my gifts.
But on that theme let me be silent now.
I must bewail the deed that yet remains
To do. For my own children I will slay.

None shall deliver them. Then, having wrecked
The house of Jason utterly, hence will I flee
From my dear children's blood, that I must spill,
Daring a deed most impious. For, oh friends,
The laughter of foes is not to be endured.
    Be it so!—What then do I live for? No home now,
No country is mine, from misery no refuge.
Then did I err, when from my father's halls
I fled, beguiled by the phrases of a Greek,
Who (grant it Heaven!) shall pay just penance now.
Never again shall he behold alive
The sons I bore him, nor from this new bride
A child shall he beget; since she, my bane,
By a baneful death must die, slain by my drugs.
Feeble and poor of spirit let none deem me,
No, nor indolent, but of quite other mood—
Grievous to foes, and serviceable to friends;
For such the lives that win the fairest fame.
    LEADER: Since thou hast opened to us thy resolve,
Wishing to help thee, and yet reverencing
The laws of men, I adjure thee, do not this.
    MEDEA: It must be so; naught else. Yet I excuse
Thy censuring words. Thou art not wronged as I.
    LEADER: Wilt thou find heart to slay thine offspring, woman?
    MEDEA: My husband's soul thus shall I wound most deeply.
    LEADER: And thus shalt thou become of wives most wretched.
    MEDEA: So be it. Wasted are all words henceforth.
(*to the* NURSE) But thou go, go hence, and bring me Jason
      hither.
Your prudence on such service I may trust.
Speak no word of my purpose, would you serve
Your mistress loyally. You are a woman too.

   (*The* NURSE *goes out.*)

   Strophe 1

   CHORUS: Fortunate in ancient days was the house of Erechtheus,
Those children of blessed Deities,
Sprung from a sacred land by foes never ravaged,

On glorious wisdom nurtured,
Through that most limpid air evermore luxuriously moving,
There where once to the nine
Holy Pierian Muses, so 'tis told,
Golden-haired Harmonia gave birth.

Antistrophe 1

Also they sing how the Cyprian Goddess drew
From the streams of the fair-flowing river
Kephisus, and watered the land, breathing thereon
Winds of sweet-scented breath.
With a fragrant wreath of rose-buds were her tresses
Ever garlanded, and the Loves
Escorted her, those colleagues of fair wisdom,
Her fellow-workers in all gentlest deeds.

Strophe 2

How then may that city
Of sacred rivers, that land
That welcomes those it loves,
Receive thee among her citizens,
The child-murderess, the accurst?
Wilt thou smite them?—Ah, bethink thee!—
Of the clinging guilt bethink thee!
Nay, by thy knees, with our whole strength,
Our whole soul, we beseech thee,
Slay not thy children.

Antistrophe 2

How shall thy soul find courage?
Whence shalt thou arm thy hand
And heart with savage fury
To wreak such a deed of horror?
How, gazing upon thy children,
Wilt thou with a tearless eye
Still murder them? Ah thou canst not,
While kneeling they supplicate thee,

With merciless soul pollute
Thy hands with their bloodshed.

(*Re-enter* JASON.)

JASON: I come, since you have bidden me. Though my foe,
I must not grudge you, lady, this small boon.
Speak then: what now do you desire from me?
  MEDEA: Jason, I entreat you, pardon what was spoken.
You must bear with me in my passionate moods;
For was there not much love between us once?
I have been reasoning with myself, and chiding
My spirit thus: What is this madness, fool?
Why at enmity with the rulers of the land,
And with my lord who acts but for my good
Wedding a princess, that so for my sons
He may get brethren? Should I not put by
My wrath? What ails me? Doth not Heaven grow kind?
And have I not my children? Do I not know
That we are exiles and bereft of friends?
Thus pondering, I was aware how far astray
Had been my judgement, how senseless my wrath.
So now I approve, and deem thee wise to seek
This new alliance for our good. 'Twas I
Was foolish, who in these counsels should have shared
And lent my aid, countenancing the match
And ministering joyfully to your bride.
But we are what we are—evil I say not—
But women. Why then vie with us at our worst,
Or contend with us—folly matched with folly?
I yield, and do confess that I was then
Unwise; but better counsel now is mine.
  Come, children, children—hither from the house!

(*Enter the* CHILDREN *with their* ATTENDANT.)

Come forth! Welcome your father; speak to him;
Be reconciled, you and your mother too,
That so this enmity with friends may cease.
Our peace is made: the old anger is no more.
There, clasp his hand.—Oh misery! How by thoughts

Of hidden woes to come I am haunted still!
Can it be, children, you will live long years
And still reach forth your dear arms thus?—Alas!
How swift am I to tears, how full of dread!
Ended is now the long strife with your father;
And lo, with tears my softened eyes are filled.

LEADER: From mine eyes too there wells forth a pale tear.
May no new misery worse than this befall!

JASON: Lady, I praise thee now, nor what is past
Do I blame. Small wonder a wife's wrath should be kindled
When her lord turns elsewhere to treat for a bride.
But now your heart is changed to a saner mood,
And you perceive, though late, what policy
Is best. Herein you act like a wise woman.
And you, my sons, with forethought has your father
Assured your welfare, if but Heaven so will.
For I dare hope that in this realm of Corinth
You with your brethren will be foremost yet.
Wax then; grow strong: leave all else to the care
Of me, your father, and the Gods that love us.
May I live to see you reach the goodly prime
Of youthful vigour, the envy of my foes.—
But thou, why thus with tears dost thou bedew
Thine eyelids, turning thy pale cheek away,
As though my friendly words gave thee no joy?

MEDEA: 'Tis naught. My heart was brooding o'er these children.

JASON: But why for them so sorely do you weep?

MEDEA: I bare them. And when you prayed that they might live,
A sad doubt came to me whether that shall be.

JASON: Take heart. My guarding care they shall not lack.

MEDEA: I will take heart then, nor mistrust your words.
Yet a weak thing is woman, born for tears.
But that whereon I sought to speak with you
In part is said: the rest will I now declare
Since 'tis the ruler's will that I be banished
And well I know 'twere best for me that here
I dwell not, a vexation both to thee
And to the king, to whose house I am deemed a foe,
I then go forth an exile from this land;

But our sons—that by thee they may be reared,
Entreat Creon that them he banish not.
    JASON: I doubt my power to move him: yet will I try.
    MEDEA: Bid then your bride entreat him in your stead . . .
    JASON: That will I—and with good hope to persuade her.
    MEDEA: Aye, if she be as other women are.
In this kind task I too will share with you.
Our children will I send bearing her gifts
In beauty far surpassing aught now seen,
Sure am I, among men.—One of my maidens,
Go, fetch me the robings hither with all speed.—

(A handmaiden goes into the house.)

Blest will she be, not once, but thousandfold,
Winning thee, best of heroes, for her spouse,
And dowered with treasures that once Helios,
My father's father, to his own offspring gave.

(The handmaiden has returned with the gifts.)

Children, take in your hands these nuptial gifts,
And to the royal maid, the blissful bride,
Bear them. Gifts are they that she may not scorn.
    JASON: Oh folly! Why would you cast away these treasures?
Think you the royal palace lacks fine robes,
Or gold perchance? Nay keep them: make no gift.
For if my lady esteem me of any worth,
More than all wealth she'll prize my wish, I know.
    MEDEA: Chide me not. Gifts, they say, tempt even the Gods:
And gold sways mortals more than a myriad words.
Hers now is fortune; her fate Heaven exalts.
She is young, a princess. Life, not gold alone,
To save my sons from exile would I barter.
    Now, children, when you enter yon rich halls,
Entreat, beseech this new bride of your sire,
My mistress now, from banishment to save you,
Offering her these treasures. And forget not:
With her own hands she must receive my gifts.

Haste now: speed well; and to your mother soon
Return with the glad news she longs to hear.

(*Exeunt* JASON *with the* CHILDREN.)

Strophe 1

CHORUS: Now hope have I none that the children yet may live.
Hope is none: yea now to their death they are going.
Soon the hapless bride will receive it, the gold-wrought
Crown—receive her own destruction.
Those fair locks with her own hands will she garland
With the bright wreath of death.

Antistrophe 1

Their splendour and beauty divine shall tempt her soul
Thus with robe and chaplet of gold to adorn her.
Midst the dead new-decked as a bride she will pass now.
Such the snare wherein the hapless
Death-doomed maiden, alas, shall fall, a dread fate,
Whence to escape, hope is none.

Strophe 2

And thou, wretched wooer accurst, a princely spouse pursuing,
Blindly upon thy children
Thou art bringing destruction, and dooming thy bride
To torturing anguish of death.
Ill-fated wretch, thus from glory fallen!

Antistrophe 2

Thy misery last do I wail, O mother, woeful mother,
Thou who wilt slay thy children
To avenge thee on him who abandoning thee,
And scorning the troth he hath sworn,
With lawless heart fain would wed a new bride.

(*Re-enter the* CHILDREN *with their* ATTENDANT.)

ATTENDANT: Mistress, thy sons from banishment are spared.
With gracious hands the royal bride received

Their gifts. Henceforth between them there is peace.
Ah!
Why stand you as though distraught at such good hap?
    MEDEA: Ah woe!
    ATTENDANT: Such moans accord but ill with my glad news.
    MEDEA: Ah woe, indeed!
    ATTENDANT: Lurks there within my tidings
Some mishap that to grief can change their joy?
    MEDEA: You have told what you have told. I blame not thee.
    ATTENDANT: Why then this downcast eye, these tears that flow?
    MEDEA: Needs must I weep, old man. This thing the Gods.
Nay I myself in folly of heart, have schemed.
    ATTENDANT: Take heart. Thy sons shall some day bring thee
        home.
    MEDEA: Others ere that shall I send home, woe's me!
    ATTENDANT: Has no one else save thee been reft of her children?
Patiently must we mortals bear mischance.
    MEDEA: That will I do.—Now go within the house,
And prepare what is needful for the boys.

(*Exit* ATTENDANT.)

O children, children, a city shall be yours,
A home, where severed from my wretchedness
Evermore you shall dwell, reft of your mother.
And I to another land must flee, banished,
Ere I have joyed in you, or seen you prosperous,
Ere I have graced your nuptials, decked the bride
And bridal bed, and lifted high the torches.
Ah woe is me! Woe to my stubborn pride!
Vain was it then, my children, that I reared you;
Vain were the toils, the wasting agonies,
The cruel pangs of childbirth I endured.
Verily once, poor wretch, fond hopes were mine
That in my old age you would cherish me,
And with your own hands tend my corpse, a boon
All mortals covet. But now that sweet thought
Has perished; for, bereft of you, a life
Of bitterness and grief must I drag on.

And you—no more shall your loved eyes behold
Your mother: to a changed life must you depart.
   Nay, nay; why thus do you gaze on me, my children?
Why do you smile on me with that last smile?
Ay me! What can I do? Women, my heart
Fails me, at sight of their gay laughing eyes.
I cannot; no. Farewell my late resolves!
Far from this land my sons will I take with me.
Why must I, wronging them to grieve their sire,
Myself reap twice the woe I inflict on him?
No, no, not I! Then farewell my resolves!
   And yet what thoughts are these? Do I wish to leave
My foes unpunished, and so earn their mockery?
This must be dared. Shame on my craven mood,
That I should admit soft pleadings to my mind!—
Go, boys, within.—Whoever deems it impious
To attend my sacrifice, what seems to him fit
May do: but I will not make weak my hand.
Ah, Ah!
No, my heart, do not—no, not such a thing!
Let them live, wretched mother: spare thy children,
Living, though far away, joy shall they give me.
   Nay, by the avenging fiends of Hades, never
Shall this thing be, that to the spiteful outrage
Of foes I should abandon my own sons.
Too late! The deed is done! she shall not scape.
Crowned by the wreath, swathed in the robe, already
The royal bride is perishing, I know well.
Yet since this woeful journey I now must go,
And must send these on one more woeful still,
Fain would I bid my sons farewell.—Come, children;
Give your right hand to mother, for one last kiss.—
O darling hand! lips dear, how dear, to me!
Features and form of childish gentleness!
May you be bless'd—but elsewhere! Of all here
Your father is robbing you.—O sweet embrace!
O tender cheeks, and fragrant breath of childhood!—
Go from me; go. No more can I endure
To see you. I am broken by this misery.

Well do I know the fell deed I must do:
But vanquished are all sober counsels now
By passionate anger, cause of man's worst woes.

(*She goes into the house with the* CHILDREN.)

CHORUS: Ofttimes ere now have I ventured on themes
Far more subtle, and boldly debated
Problems more deep and grave than behoves
Our feminine sex.
Yet have we also, we women, our Muse.
Wisdom in converse with her may we learn.
She consorts not with all: but a few such surely
Among so many perchance may be found
Not wholly unblest by the Muses.
Now I say that of mortals they who have known
Neither a father's cares nor a mother's,
In fortunate destiny far surpass
Those who have offspring.
They who are childless, who have avoided
A parent's task, knowing not whether children
Are most a delight or a misery to men,
Such doubtless escape many troubles;
While those whose homes are gay with the flowering
Beauty of children, too oft have I seen
Worn out evermore with labour and care:
First how they may rear them wisely and well,
Then leave them enough to sustain their lives:
Yet again, whether good children or evil
Will prove the reward
Of such toil, *that* can they ne'er know.
One last crowning woe there remaineth,
Which every mortal needs must dread:
Albeit the wealth they have gotten suffice,
And their sons be to manhood and virtue grown,
Even then, if fortune so should befall,
Lo at the door stands Death who shall bear
Their children away to the darkness of Hades.
How then may it profit a man that the Gods
Should lay on his soul, as the price to be paid

For children, the burden
Of this most grievous affliction?

(*Re-enter* MEDEA.)

MEDEA: Friends, I have long been waiting eagerly
To learn how yonder the event shall issue.
And lo, is it not one of Jason's servants
Hastening hither? His wild gasping breath
Proclaims him bearer of some strange ill news.

(*Enter* MESSENGER.)

MESSENGER: O thou who hast wrought this horror, this foul
          crime,
Flee, flee, Medea; pause not in thy flight
Whether in swift chariot or on sea-borne bark.
MEDEA: Say, what has chanced that calls for flight so wild?
MESSENGER: Dead is the maiden princess, Creon too,
Her father, dead but now, slain by thy poisons.
MEDEA: Most glorious are thy tidings; nay, henceforth
My friend and benefactor will I deem thee.
MESSENGER: What! Are you sane? Are you not raving, woman,
Since you can hear with joy this outrage done
To the hearth of a king, and shudderest not?
MEDEA: I too might find some words to give fit answer
To your reproaches. But, friend, take your ease;
Tell how they perished. Double were my delight,
Could you but say: by a most foul death they died.
MESSENGER: When we saw thy two children with their father
Passing within the chambers of the bride,
Glad were we thralls who had sorrowed for thy woes;
And straightway rumour filled our ears of truce
To former feuds betwixt thy lord and thee.
One kissed the hand, another the golden head
Of the boys; and I myself for very joy
Within the women's chambers followed them.
Our mistress, whom now in thy stead we honoured,
Ere yet she was aware of thy two sons,
With eager welcoming glance gazed upon Jason;
But then, drawing her veil before her eyes,

Turned her white cheek away, as though she loathed
That the boys should come near her. But your husband
Strove to dispel the maiden's angry mood,
Chiding her thus: "Be not hostile to friends.
Cease from thy wrath; turn hither again thy face.
Deem to be friends all whom thy spouse holds dear.
Accept their gifts, and then plead with thy father
That he remit their exile, for my sake."
She, seeing those fineries, could resist no more,
But yielded wholly to his will: and scarce
Had Jason left her chamber with your sons,
She took the broidered robe and put it on,
Then with the golden crown circled her hair,
And in the shining mirror ranged her locks,
Smiling back at her lifeless image there.
Then, rising from her seat, around the room
She paced with white feet treading delicately,
Exulting in the gifts, and many a time
Casting her eyes down at her pointed foot.
   But now a fearful change was visible.
Suddenly she turns pale, and reeling back
With limbs atremble, sinks down into a seat
Scarce in time ere she tottered to the ground.
Then an old handmaid, deeming it perchance
A frenzy sent by Pan or some God else,
Cried out in prayer; when lo, through the bride's lips
She sees white foam-flakes issue, sees her eyeballs
Rolled upwards, and no blood left in her face.
Then she sent forth a shrill wail, different far
From her first cry. Forthwith one maiden flew
To the King's chamber, another to tell the bridegroom
Of his young bride's sad plight; and the whole house
Echoed with footsteps hurrying to and fro.
And now might a swift walker with long strides
Have paced a furlong's course and reached the goal,
When from her speechless trance she opened wide
Her eyes in agony with a fearful groan.
For twofold was the torment that assailed her:
From the gold chaplet wreathed around her head

There gushed a marvellous stream of ravening fire;
While those fine robes, the gift thy children brought,
Were eating away the poor maid's fair white flesh;
Till all aflame leaping up from her seat
She fled, tossing her hair this way and that,
Seeking to cast the wreath off: but the gold
Clung firmly fixed; and as she tossed her locks,
The fire did but the faster lap them up.
Then spent with anguish to the ground she sinks,
A mere shape, even her father scarce might know.
For hard to trace were what had been her eyes;
Marred were her lovely features; from her head
Ran down blood mingled in one stream with fire:
From her bones, like the pinetree's tears, the flesh
Dript, by the poison's unseen jaws devoured,
A ghastly sight! And we all feared to touch
The body, warned by the horror we had seen.
But, ignorant of his woe, the wretched father,
Suddenly entering, falls upon the corpse,
Then with a wail folding her in his arms
Kisses her, crying: "O my hapless daughter,
What God by a death so shameful hath destroyed thee
Bereaving thus my old age, for the tomb
Long ripe? Ah, child, would I might die with thee!"
And when he had made an end of moans and tears,
And fain would have raised up his ancient limbs,
He clave to the fine-spun robes, as ivy clings
To laurel boughs; and a grim wrestling followed:
For while *he* strove to rise to his feet, *she* held him
Fast-gripped; and when he pulled with his whole strength,
His aged flesh from off his bones he tore.
At last the poor wretch yielded and breathed forth
His soul, vanquished at length by that fell bane.
So there, the old man dead beside his child,
They are lying, a woeful sight that craves for tears.
Of what concerns thee I say naught. Thyself
Wilt know how best to escape punishmen'.
This mortal life ever do I deem a shadow;
For among mortals there is no man happy.

In the flood-tide of fortune one may seem
More prosperous than his fellows; but happy—none.

(*Exit* MESSENGER.)

LEADER: Verily hath just-judging Fate this day
Whelmed Jason beneath misery heaped on misery.
MEDEA: Friends, on this deed I am resolved, forthwith
To slay my children, and then flee this land,
Lest, lingering, I be forced to yield them up
For some more merciless hand to slaughter them.
They must die; there's no help: and since they must,
I alone will slay them, I who gave them birth.
Come then, my heart, steel thyself! Why delay
To perform those dread deeds that must be done?
Haste, wretched hand of mine, grasp the sword, grasp it!
On to the line whence life must run to woe!
And turn not craven: remember not thy children,
How dear they are, how thou didst bear them. No,
For this short day forget they are thy sons;
Thereafter mourn them: for though thou shalt slay them,
Dear are they still, and I—but a mother accurst.

(*She goes into the house.*)

Strophe

CHORUS: O hear, Earth, and thou, Sun, by whose
Bright beams all is revealed! hither, look hither, behold
This parricidal mother, ere yet she spill
With self-scathing hand her own children's blood.
Thine was it, that golden race wherefrom
She sprang. O beware! Man with a fell stroke
Threatens the seed of Gods.
Nay then, O Light divine, hear us, arrest her hand,
Suffer her not to strike, but chase forth from the house
This fell witch, by fiends driven to crime and blood.

Antistrophe

Alas, pangs of birth vainly endured!
Alas, motherly love tenderly lavished in vain!

Thou who of old between the blue Clashing Rocks,
That dread bane of ships, on swift keel didst flee!
Poor wretch, why doth fiercely brooding wrath
Assail thus thy soul, while fatal thoughts
Gather, till murder looms?
For a polluting curse heavy for men to bear
Verily is kindred blood; and fresh storms of woe
Ever, I wot, shall Heaven fling at the guilty house.

> A CHILD'S VOICE: Oh what shall I do? Oh whither flee from
> mother's hands?
>
> THE OTHER CHILD: I know not, darling brother. She will kill
> us both.

Strophe

CHORUS: A cry! heard you not? The children—'twas they!
Alas, wretch accurst! mother of evil fate!
Should I bring help within? There's hope yet from death
To save them . . . Oh but haste!

> A CHILD: Yes, haste, for God's sake; help, oh help! Our need is
> sore.
>
> THE OTHER CHILD: We cannot escape—the sword comes nearer—
> we are trapped.

CHORUS: Ah wretch, hard of heart, harder than rock or iron!
Who thus wouldst destroy with savage and pitiless hand
The sons thine own womb hath borne.

Antistrophe

But one, one alone among wives of yore
Of her sons, so 'tis told, ever was murderess.
To the waves down she leapt, the poor wretch who shed
Her own children's blood.
Shall aught e're befall terrible as such a deed?
O bride-bed accurst! Of myriad miseries oft
To men 'tis thou art found the cause.

(*Enter* JASON.)

JASON: Tell me, ye women gathered near my house,
Is she still here within, she who has wrought

This horrible crime, Medea—or is she fled?
For either deep in the earth she must now hide,
Or wings must lift her to the heights of heaven,
Would she escape the vengeance of her lords.
Thinks she to slay the rulers of the land,
Then from this house herself to flee unscathed?
But not for her—for my sons would I take thought.
Let those she has wronged requite her: it is the life
Of my dear children I come here to save,
Lest upon them the kinsmen of the slain
Should venge their mother's impious deed of blood.

LEADER: Poor wretch, you know not in what woes you are sunk;
Else, Jason, such words never had you uttered.

JASON: What mean you? Has she a mind to kill me too?

LEADER: Your sons are dead, slain by their mother's hand.

JASON: Ah woman, take back your words. Would you destroy
    me?

LEADER: Your children are no more: of that be sure.

JASON: Where did she slay them? Yonder, within those doors?

LEADER: Open, and you shall see your slaughtered children.

JASON: Haste, slaves! thrust back the bolts, undo the fastenings.
Haste, that this twofold woe I may behold,
The murdered and their murderess—and requite her.

(*Enter* MEDEA *above, on a chariot of winged Dragons, in which
are the dead bodies of the* CHILDREN.)

MEDEA: Why strive thus to unbar the doors, in quest
Of the dead children and of me who slew them?
Cease from such vain toil. Wouldst thou aught of me,
Speak what thou wilt: but touch me shalt thou never.
So dread a team my father's sire, the Sun,
Has given me, a safe refuge from my foes.

JASON: O monster! O you woman most abhorred
By the Gods, and by me, and all mankind!
You who could find the heart to stab the sons
You had borne, and leave me a childless broken man!
This impious deed you have dared and done, yet still
Can look upon the sunlight and the earth.
I curse you! Now I see—what then I saw not,

When hither from your barbarian halls I brought you
To a Greek home, you my life's bane, traitress
To your father, and the land that nurtured you—
The Gods have laid on me the curse of your house.
For at the altar you had slain your brother,
When first you embarked on fair-prowed Argo's deck.
Such was your prelude. Then did you wed with me
And bear me children, whom, enraged by a rival
To your embraces, you have thus destroyed.
Not one of all the women of Greece had dared
This wickedness; yet before them all I chose
To wed thee, a bride to be my foe, my bale,
No woman, but a lioness, a fell fiend
More savage-natured than Tyrrhenian Scylla.
Nay, but with myriad reproaches never
Could I wound thee, so obdurate is thy heart.
Avaunt, foul miscreant, thou child-murderess!
Go, leave me to bemoan my evil fate,
Who in my new-wed bride shall ne'er find joy,
Ne'er to the sons whom I begat and reared
Shall I speak word more: them thou hast destroyed.
   MEDEA: To all these words of yours a lengthy answer
Might I retort; but father Zeus knows well
How I have dealt with you, and you with me.
Hoped you then that my bed you could dishonour,
And live in bliss, making a mock of me?
Or that your princess, or your match-maker,
Creon, could banish me and rue it not?
Nay then, a lioness call me, if so thou wilt,
Or a Scylla lairing in Tyrrhenian caves;
I have wrung thy heart in turn; thou art justly paid.
   JASON: Thou too art grieved: my misery thou sharest.
   MEDEA: Aye, but such grief is gain, so it foil thy laughter.
   JASON: Alas my children, born of a wicked mother!
   MEDEA: Alas, my sons, destroyed by a father's lewdness!
   JASON: How so? It was not *my* hand that destroyed them.
   MEDEA: No, but thy wantonness and thy new nuptials.
   JASON: Could you think jealousy justified this murder?
   MEDEA: Such outrage deem you a slight thing to a wife?

JASON: If she be wise. To thee, vile wretch, 'tis all.

MEDEA: Your sons are dead. Let that knowledge torment you.

JASON: Ah no, they live, avenging spirits to haunt thee.

MEDEA: The Gods know who began these miseries.

JASON: Verily they know that abhorred heart of thine.

MEDEA: Yes, hate me! but I am weary of thy harsh snarl.

JASON: And I of thine. But let us part forthwith.

MEDEA: How? On what terms? I too would fain begone.

JASON: Yield me the dead to bury and bewail.

MEDEA: Not so. Myself will I bear them to the shrine
Of Mountain Hera, and there bury them,
Lest those that hate me insult them, casting down
Their tomb-stones. But for this land of Sisyphus
I will ordain a solemn feast, with rites
To atone for blood thus impiously shed.
Then to the land of Erechtheus will I go,
And dwell with Aegeus there, Pandion's son.
But thou, vile wretch, by a vile death shalt thou die,
Thy head crushed by a beam from thine own Argo.
So shall our nuptials reach their bitter end.

JASON: But thee may the just fiend, venging the blood
Of our sons, destroy!

MEDEA: What God, what demon will hear thy prayer,
O thou false friend, thou breaker of oaths?

JASON: Oh fie on thee, foul child-murdering wretch!

MEDEA: Go to your bride's home, go now and bury her.

JASON: I go home—childless, of both sons reft.

MEDEA: Wait; weep not yet. Soon cometh old age.

JASON: O my belov'd sons!

MEDEA: Mine were they, not thine.

JASON: Yet you could slay them . . .

MEDEA: To wound your soul.

JASON: Woe's me, for my children's darling lips
Heart-broken I yearn—one last sad kiss.

MEDEA: Now you would greet them, now kiss fondly,
Whom then you repulsed.

JASON: O grant me, I pray,
Yet again to embrace those tender limbs.

MEDEA: In vain! To the winds are your words flung forth.

JASON: Zeus, thou hast heard her? Thus am I cruelly
Spurned and derided by this ravening
Lioness, this foul murderess of children!
Yet, fiend, in thy spite, for the dead will I raise
A lamenting dirge, loudly invoking
Heaven to be witness, how thou hast slaughtered
These children, and wilt not suffer their sire
To embrace them, or give them burial due.
Ah, would I had ne'er been doomed to beget,
Then live to behold thee destroy them!
    CHORUS: Many fates doth Olympian Zeus dispense,
Many chances unhoped do the Gods ordain,
And events men looked for are not fulfilled,
But to things undreamed Heaven findeth a way.
Of these deeds such was the issue.

EURIPIDES

HIPPOLYTUS

TRANSLATED BY ARTHUR S. WAY

CHARACTERS IN THE PLAY

APHRODITE (*or Kypris*), *Goddess of Love*
HIPPOLYTUS, *son of Theseus and Hippolyta, Queen of the Amazons*
PHAEDRA, *daughter of Minos, King of Crete, and wife of Theseus*
NURSE *of Phaedra*
THESEUS, *King of Athens and Troezen*
ARTEMIS, *Goddess of Hunting*
MESSENGER, *henchman of Hippolytus*
CHORUS *of women of Troezen*
ATTENDANTS, *huntsmen, and handmaids*

HIPPOLYTUS

(SCENE: *Before the palace of* THESEUS *at Troezen, where* THESEUS *dwelt, being self-exiled for a year from Athens, to expiate the shedding of the blood of kinsmen who had sought to dethrone him. To left and right, statues and altars of* APHRODITE *and* ARTEMIS. APHRODITE *is alone.*)

APHRODITE: Mighty on earth, and named by many a name
Am I, the Goddess Kypris, as in heaven.
And of all dwellers 'twixt the Pontic Sea
And Atlas' bourn, which look on the sun's light,
I honour them which reverence my power,
But bring the proud hearts that defy me low.
For even to the Gods this appertains,
That in the homage of mankind they joy.
And I will give swift proof of these my words.
For Theseus' son, born of the Amazon,
Hippolytus, pure-hearted Pittheus' ward,
Sole mid the folk of this Troezenian land
Sayeth that vilest of the Gods am I;
Rejects the couch; of marriage will he none;
But Phoebus' sister Artemis, Zeus' child,
Honours, of all Gods chiefest holding her:
And through the greenwood in the Maid's train still
With swift hounds sweeps the wild beasts from the earth,
Linked with companionship for men too high.
Yet this I grudge not: what is this to me?
But that his wrong to me will I avenge
Upon Hippolytus this day: the path
Well-nigh is cleared; scant pains it needeth yet.
For, as from halls of Pittheus once he sought
Pandion's land, to see and to be sealed
In the Great Mysteries, Phaedra, high-born wife
Of his own father, saw him; and her heart
Of fierce love was enthralled by my device.

And, ere she came to this Troezenian land,
Hard by the Rock of Pallas, which looks down
On this land, built she unto me a shrine
For love of one afar; and his memorial
That fane divine she named for days to be.
But since from Kekrops' land forth Theseus passed
Fleeing the blood-guilt of the sons of Pallas,
And unto this shore with his wife hath sailed,
From his land brooking one year's banishment,
Thenceforward, sighing and by stings of love
Distraught, the hapless one wastes down to death
Silent: her malady no handmaid knows.
Ah, but not so shall this love's issue fall.
Theseus shall know this thing; all bared shall be:
And him that is my foe his sire shall slay
By curses, whose fulfilment the Sea-king
Poseidon in this boon to Theseus gave,
That, to three prayers, he should ask nought in vain.
She, how high-born soe'er, yet perisheth,
Phaedra:—I will not so regard her pain
That I should not exact such penalty
Of them which hate me as shall do me right.
But,—forasmuch as Theseus' son I see
Yonder draw near, forsaking hunting's toil,
Hippolytus,—forth will I from this place.
And a great press of henchmen following shout,
Honouring with songs the Goddess Artemis.
He knows not Hades' gates wide flung for him,
And this day's light the last his eyes shall see.

(*Exit* APHRODITE.)

(*Enter* HIPPOLYTUS *and attendant* HUNTSMEN *with their*
LEADER.)

HIPPOLYTUS: Follow on, follow on, ring out the lay
Unto Artemis high enthroned in the sky
Zeus' child, in her keeping who hath us aye.
HUNTSMEN: O Majesty, Daughter of Zeus, dread Queen,
I hail thee, Artemis, now,

O Leto's Daughter, O Zeus's child,
Loveliest far of the Undefiled!
In the Hall, "of the Mighty Father" styled,
The palace of Zeus, mid the glory-sheen
        Of gold—there dwellest thou.
O Fairest, to theeward in greeting I call,
O fairest Artemis thou of all
The Maidens Divine in Olympus' hall!
   HIPPOLYTUS: For thee this woven garland from a mead
Unsullied have I twined, O Queen, and bring.
There never shepherd dares to feed his flock,
Nor steel of sickle came: only the bee
Roveth the springtide mead undesecrate:
And Reverence watereth it with river-dews.
They which have heritage of self-control
In all things,—not taught, but the pure in heart,—
These there may gather flowers, but none impure.
Now Queen, dear Queen, receive this anadem
From reverent hand to deck thy golden hair;
For to me sole of men this grace is given,
That I be with thee, converse hold with thee,
Hearing thy voice, yet seeing not thy face.
And may I end life's race as I began.
   LEADER: Prince,—for the Gods we needs must call our Lords,—
Wouldst thou receive of me good counselling?
   HIPPOLYTUS: Yea surely: else were I fool manifest.
   LEADER: Knowest thou then the stablished wont of men?
   HIPPOLYTUS: Not I: whereof is this thou questionest me?
   LEADER: To hate the proud reserve that owns few friends.
   HIPPOLYTUS: Rightly: what proud man is not odious?
   LEADER: And in the gracious is there nought of charm?
   HIPPOLYTUS: Yea, much, and profit won with little pains.
   LEADER: And deem'st thou not this same may hold with Gods?
   HIPPOLYTUS: Yea, if men live by laws derived from Gods.
   LEADER: Why not then greet a Goddess worshipful?
   HIPPOLYTUS: Whom?—have a care thy lips in no wise err.
   LEADER: Even Kypris, there above thy portals set.
   HIPPOLYTUS: From far I greet her, who am undefiled.
   LEADER: Worshipful is she, glorious among men.

HIPPOLYTUS: Of Gods, of men, each maketh still his choice.
LEADER: Now prosper thou;—be needful wisdom thine!
HIPPOLYTUS: No God who hath night-homage pleaseth me.
LEADER: Guerdons of Gods, my son, ought men to use.
HIPPOLYTUS: Depart, mine henchmen, enter ye the halls,
And set on bread. The full board welcome is
When hunting's done. And one must groom my steeds,
That I may yoke them to the chariot-pole,
Being full of meat, and breathe them in the race.
But to thy Kypris wave I long farewell.

(*Exeunt* HIPPOLYTUS *and* HUNTSMEN *except the* LEADER.)

LEADER: But we, who must not tread in steps of youth,
Who are wise—so far as thralls dare claim to be,—
Make supplication to thine images,
Queen Kypris. It beseems thee to forgive,
If one that bears through youth a vehement heart
Speak folly. Be as though thou heardest not;
For wiser Gods should be than mortal men.

(*Exit* LEADER.)

(*Enter* CHORUS OF TROEZENIAN WOMEN.)

Strophe 1

CHORUS: A rock there is, wherefrom, as they tell, the springs of
        the heart of the Ocean well,
    Whence the rifts of the crags overbeetling send
For the plunging urns their founts outstreaming:
    Even there did I light on a maiden my friend,
As she drenched the mantles purple-gleaming
        In the riverward-glittering spray,
And spread the dye of the Tyrian shell on the rocks where glowing
        the sunbeams fell.
    Hers were the lips that I first heard say
        How wasteth our lady away:

Antistrophe 1

For a tale they told of a fevered bed, of the feet that forth of her
    bower ne'er tread,

Of the dainty-woven veil that is cast
For a darkness over the tresses golden.
    Yea, and by this hath the third day past
That the queen from her fainting lips hath withholden
            The gift of the Lady of Corn,
Keeping her body thereof unfed, as though 'twere pollution to
        taste of bread,
With anguish unuttered longing forlorn
            One haven to win—death's bourn.

Strophe 2

O queen, what if this be possession
    Of Pan or of Hekate?—
        Of the Mother of Dindymus' Hill?—
        Or the awful Corybant thrill?—
Or Dictynna hath found transgression
    Of offerings unrendered in thee—
        If the hand of the Huntress be here?—
        For she flasheth o'er mountain and mere,
And rideth her triumph-procession
    Over surges and swirls of the sea.

Antistrophe 2

Or thy princely lord, in whose leading
    Be the hosts of Erechtheus' race,
        Hath one in his halls beguiled,
        That thy couch is in secret defiled?
Or hath some sea-trafficker, speeding
    From Crete over watery ways
        To the haven where shipmen would be,
        Brought dolorous tidings to thee
        That hath bowed thee with anguish exceeding
            On thy bed through thy soul's prison-days?

Epode

Or shall this be the discord mournful, weirdly haunting,
    That ofttimes jarreth and jangleth the strings of woman's
        being?
'Tis the shadow of travail-throes nigh, a delirium spirit-daunting:

Yea, I have known it, through mine own bosom have felt it
    shiver:
But I cried to the Queen of the Bow, to the Helper in travail-throe
    for refuge fleeing;
And by grace of the Gods she hearkeneth ever my fervent
    request, she is there to deliver.

But lo, through the doors where cometh the grey-haired nurse
    Leading the stricken one forth of her bowers:
    On her brows aye darker the care-cloud lowers.
My spirit is yearning to know what is this strange curse,
      Wherefore the queen's cheek is paling,
      And her strength is failing.

(*Enter* PHAEDRA, NURSE, *and* HANDMAIDS.)

NURSE: O afflictions of mortals, O bitter pain!
What shall I do unto thee, or refrain?
    Lo here is the light of the sun, the sky:
    Brought forth of the halls is thy bed; hereby
      Thy cushions lie.

Hitherward wouldst thou come; it was all thy moan:
Yet aback to thy bowers wilt thou fret to be gone.
    Thou art soon disappointed, hast pleasure in nought,
    Nor the present contents thee; a thing far-sought
      Thy fancy hath caught.

Better be sick than tend the sick:
    Here is but one pain; grief of mind
    And toil of hands be there combined.
O'er all man's life woes gather thick;

Ne'er from its travail respite is.
    If better life beyond be found,
    The darkness veils, clouds wrap it round;
Therefore infatuate-fond to this

We cling—this earth's poor sunshine-gleam:
    Nought know we of the life to come,
    There speak no voices from the tomb:
We drift on fable's shadowy stream.

PHAEDRA: Uplift ye my body, mine head upraise.
Friends, faint be my limbs, and unknit be their bands.
Hold, maidens, my rounded arms and mine hands.
Ah, the coif on mine head all heavily weighs:
Take it thence till mine hair o'er my shoulders strays!
　NURSE: Take heart, my child, nor in such wild wise
　Toss thou thy body so feveredly.
　Lighter thy sickness to bear shall be,
If thine high-born courage in calm strength rise:
For the doom of sorrow on all men lies.
　PHAEDRA: Oh but to quaff, where the spray-veil drifteth
　O'er taintless fountains, the dear cool stream!
Oh to lie in the mead where the soft wind lifteth
　Its tresses—'neath poplars to lie and dream!
　NURSE: My child, my child, what is this thou hast cried?
Ah, speak not thus, with a throng at thy side,
Wild words that on wings of madness ride!
　PHAEDRA: Let me hence to the mountain afar—I will hie me
　To the forest, the pines where the stag-hounds follow
Hard after the fleet dappled hinds as they fly me!
　Oh, I long to cheer them with hunter's hollo,—
　　　Ah God, were I there!—
And to grasp the Thessalian shaft steel-gleaming,
And to swing it on high by my hair outstreaming—
　　　My golden hair!
　NURSE: What wouldst thou, my darling, of suchlike things?
　Will nought save the hunt and the hounds content?
And why art thou yearning for fountain-springs?
　Lo, nigh to thy towers is a soft-sloped bent
　With streams for thy drinking dew-besprent.
　PHAEDRA: Lady of Limne, the burg looking seaward,
　Of the thunder of hoofs on the wide race-courses,
Oh for the plains where the altars to theeward
　Flame, there to be curbing the Henetan horses!
　NURSE: What speech in thy frenzy outflingest thou?
　The mountain-ward path then fain hadst thou taken
On the track of the beasts; and thou yearnest now
　For the steeds on the sea-sands wave-forsaken!
Of a surety the lore of a seer we lack

To tell what God, child, reineth thee back,
And scourgeth thy spirit from reason's track.
    PHAEDRA: O hapless I—what is this I have done?
    Whitherward have I wandered from wisdom's way?
I was mad, by a God's curse overthrown.
           Oh ill-starred—welladay!
Dear Nurse, veil over mine head once more;
   For I blush for the words from my lips that came.
Veil me: the tears from mine eyes down pour,
        And mine eyelids sink for shame.
For anguish wakes when re-dawneth the mind.
Though a curse be madness, herein is it kind,
That the soul that it ruins it striketh blind.
    NURSE: I veil thee:—ah that death would veil
    Me too!—with many a lesson stern
    The years have brought, this too I learn—
Be links of mortal friendship frail:

Let heart-strings ne'er together cling,
   Nor be indissolubly twined
    The cords of love, but lightly joined
For knitting close or severing.

Ah weary burden, where one soul
   Travails for twain, as mine for thee!
   Ruin, not bliss, say they, shall be
Care's life-absorbing heart-control.

Yea, that way sickness, madness, lies.
   Therefore "the overmuch" shall be
   Less than "the nought-too-much" for me:
So say I; so shall say the wise.

    CHORUS: Thou grey-haired dame, queen Phaedra's loyal nurse,
In sooth I mark her lamentable plight,
Yet what her malady, to us is dark.
Fain would we question thee and hear thereof.
    NURSE: I know not, though I ask: she will not tell.
    CHORUS: Nor what was the beginning of these woes?

NURSE: The same thy goal: nought sayeth she of all.
CHORUS: How strengthless and how wasted is her frame!
NURSE: No marvel, being three days foodless now.
CHORUS: Madness is this, or set resolve to die?
NURSE: To die: she fasteth to make end of life.
CHORUS: Strange is thy tale, if this content her lord.
NURSE: Nay, but she hides her pain, nor owns she ails.
CHORUS: Should he not guess?—one glance upon her face?
NURSE: Nay, absent is he from this land of late.
CHORUS: But thou—dost not constrain her, strive to learn
Her malady and wandering of her wit?
NURSE: All have I tried, and nought the more availed.
Yet will I not even now abate my zeal:
So stand thou by and witness unto me
How true am I to mine afflicted lords.
Come, darling child, the words said heretofore
Forget we both; more gracious-souled be thou:
Thy lowering brow, thy wayward mood, put by.
And I, wherein I erred in following thee,
Refrain, and unto wiser counsels seek.
If thy disease be that thou mayst not name,
Lo women here to allay thy malady.
But if to men thy trouble may be told,
Speak, that to leeches this may be declared.
Ha, silent?—silence, child, beseems thee not.
Or thou shouldst chide me if I speak not well,
Or unto pleadings wisely uttered yield.
One word!—look hitherward!—ah, woe is me!
Women, we toil and spend our strength for nought,
And still are far as ever: of my words
Unmelted was she then, nor hearkeneth now.
Howbeit know thou—then be waywarder
Than is the sea,—thy death shall but betray
Thy sons, who shall not share their father's halls.
Yea, by that chariot-queen, the Amazon,
Who bare unto thy sons a bastard lord,—
Not bastard-thoughted,—well thou knowest him,
Hippolytus—
PHAEDRA: Woe's me!

NURSE: It stings thee, this?

PHAEDRA: Thou hast undone me, nurse: by heaven, I pray,
Speak thou the name of this man nevermore.

NURSE: Lo there!—thy wit is sound: yet of thy wit
Thou wilt not help thy sons nor save thy life!

PHAEDRA: I love them: in that storm of fate I toss not.

NURSE: Sure, thine are hands, my child, unstained with blood?

PHAEDRA: Pure be mine hands: the stain is on my soul.

NURSE: Not, not of sorcery-spells by some foe cast?

PHAEDRA: A friend—unwitting he, nor wilful I.

NURSE: Hath Theseus wrought against thee any sin?

PHAEDRA: May I be found as clear of wrong to him.

NURSE: What then is this strange thing that deathward drives
        thee?

PHAEDRA: Let be my sin!—Not against thee I sin.

NURSE: Of my will, never!—On mine head my failure!

(*Clings to* PHAEDRA's *hands.*)

PHAEDRA: Violence to me!—on mine hand hangest thou?

NURSE: Yea, and thy knees I never will let go.

PHAEDRA: Thy bane, unhappy, shouldst thou hear in mine.

NURSE: What greater bane for me than thee to lose?

PHAEDRA: Thy death:—the selfsame thing shall save mine
        honour.

NURSE: Still dost thou hide it, when I pray thy good?

PHAEDRA: Yea, for I fashion honour out of shame.

NURSE: If then thou tell me, more shall be thine honour.

PHAEDRA: For God's sake hence away: let go mine hand.

NURSE: No!—while thou grantest not the boon my due.

PHAEDRA: I will, in reverence of thy suppliant hand.

NURSE: I am dumb: henceforth thy part it is to speak.

PHAEDRA: O hapless mother!—what strange love was thine!

NURSE: Love for the bull, my child?—or what wouldst name?

PHAEDRA: And thou, sad sister, Dionysus' bride!

NURSE: What ails thee, child?—dost thou revile thy kin?

PHAEDRA: And I the third—how am I misery-wrecked!

NURSE: I am 'wildered all—whereunto tend thy words?

PHAEDRA: To the rock that wrecks us all, yea, from of old.

NURSE: None the more know I that I fain would know.

PHAEDRA: Ah, couldst thou say for me what I must say!
NURSE: No seer am I to interpret hidden things.
PHAEDRA: What mean they when they speak of this—to love?
NURSE: The sweetest thing, my child—the bitterest too.
PHAEDRA: For me, the second only have I proved.
NURSE: What say'st thou?—child, dost thou love any man?
PHAEDRA: Whate'er his name—'tis he—the Amazon's—
NURSE: Hippolytus!
PHAEDRA: Thou sayest it, not I.
NURSE: Woe, child! What wilt thou say? Thou hast dealt me
     death!
Friends, 'tis past bearing. I will not endure
To live. O hateful life, loathed light to see!
I'll cast away, yield up, my frame, be rid
Of life by death! Farewell, I am no more.
The virtuous love—not willingly, yet love
The evil. Sure no Goddess Kypris is,
But, if it may be, something more than God,
Who hath ruined her, and me, and all this house.
    CHORUS: Hast thou heard?—the unspeakable tale hast thou
         hearkened,
         The wail of my lady's anguish-throe?
         O may I die, ah me! ere I know,
Dear lady, a spirit as thine so darkened.
         O misery burdened, O whelmed in woe!
         O troubles that cradle the children of men!
         Undone!—all's bared to the daylight's ken.
Ah, weariful season for thee remaining!
   · Dark looms o'er the household the shadow of doom.
Plain now where the star of thy love is waning,
    O hapless daughter of Crete's proud home!
    PHAEDRA: Troezenian women, ye which here abide
Upon the utmost march of Pelops' land,
Oft sleepless in the weary-wearing night
Have I mused how the life of men is wrecked.
And not, meseems, through evil thoughts inborn
So ill they fare,—discretion dwells at least
With many,—but we thus must look hereon:—
That which is good we learn and recognise,

Yet practise not the lesson, some from sloth,
And some preferring pleasure in the stead
Of duty. Pleasures many of life there be—
Long gossip, idlesse,—pleasant evils sooth,—
And sense of shame—twofold: no ill the one,
But one drags houses down. Were men's choice clear,
These twain had never borne the self-same names.
Forasmuch then as I knew this before,
No philtre-spell was like to change mine heart
To make me fall away from this my faith.
Thee will I tell the path my reason trod;—
When love's wound smote me, straight I cast about
How best to bear it: wherefore I began
Thenceforth to hush my moan, to veil my pang.
For the tongue none may trust, which knoweth well
To lesson rebel thoughts of other men,
Yet harboureth countless evils of its own.
Then did I take thought nobly to endure
My folly, triumphing by self-control.
Lastly, when even so I nought availed
To o'ermaster Love's Queen, then I deemed it best
To die: no man shall gainsay my resolve.
For be it mine to do not good unseen,
Nor ill before a cloud of witnesses.
I knew the deed, the very pang, was shame.
Yea, well I knew withal myself a woman,
The all-abhorred. Foul curses upon her
Who showed the way the first, with alien men
To shame the couch! Ah, 'twas from princely homes
That first this curse on womankind had birth.
For, when the noble count their shame their good,
The lowly sure will hold it honourable.
And O, I hate the continent-professed
Which treasure secret recklessness of shame.
How can they, O Queen Kypris, Sea-born One,
Look ever in the faces of their lords,
Nor shudder lest their dark accomplice, night,
And their own bowers may utter forth a voice?
Me—friends, 'tis even this dooms me to die,

That never I be found to shame my lord,
Nor the sons whom I bare; but free, with tongues
Unfettered, flourish they, their home yon burg
Of glorious Athens, blushing ne'er for me.
For this cows man, how stout of heart soe'er,
To know a father's or a mother's sin.
And this alone can breast the shocks of life,
An honest heart and good, in whomso found.
But vile ones Time unmasketh in his hour,
Holding his mirror up, as to a maid.
With such consorting ne'er may I be seen.
    CHORUS: Lo now, how fair is virtue everywhere,
Which yieldeth fruit of good repute mid men!
    NURSE: Mistress, thy mischance, suddenly revealed
But now, wrought in me terrible dismay.
Yet I discern my folly now. 'Tis strange
How second thoughts for men are wisest still.
Thine is the common lot, not past cool weighing:
The Goddess's passion-bolts have smitten thee.
Thou lov'st—what marvel this?—thou art as many—
And lo, for love's sake wouldst fling life away!
Sooth, 'twere small gain for them which love their fellows,
Or yet shall love, if help be none save death.
For Kypris crusheth, swooping in her might;
Yet gently stealeth she on whoso yield.
But whom she findeth wayward, arrogant-souled,
She graspeth, mocketh, past imagining.
Through air she roveth, in the ocean-surge
Is Kypris; all things have their birth of her.
'Tis she that sows love, gives increase thereof,
Whereof all we that dwell on earth are sprung.
Whoso have scrolls writ in the ancient days,
And wander still themselves by paths of song,
They know how Zeus of yore desired the embrace
Of Semele; they know how radiant Dawn
Up to the Gods snatched Kephalus of yore,
And all for love; yet these in Heaven their home
Dwell, neither do they flee the face of Gods,
Content, I trow, in their mischance's triumph.

Thou—wilt not yield? Thy sire by several treaty
Thee should have gotten, or with other Gods
For lords, if thou wilt bow not to these laws.
How many men, think'st thou, and wise men they,
Knowing their beds dishonoured, shut their eyes?
How many a father in his son's transgression
Playeth love's go-between?—the maxim this
Of wise men, that dishonour be not seen.
Why should men toil to over-perfect life?
Lo, even the house-roof's pitch the craftsman's rule
Can make not utter-true. How thinkest thou,
Plunged in fate's deep abyss, to swim thereout?
Tush—if more good than evil is in thee,
Who art but human, thou shalt do full well.
Nay, darling, from thy deadly thoughts refrain
And from presumption—sheer presumption this,
That one should wish to be more strong than Gods.
In love, flinch not; a God hath willed this thing.
In pain, victorious wrestle with thy pain.
Lo, charms there be, and words of soothing spell.
Some cure for this affliction shall appear.
Sooth, it were long ere *men* would light thereon,
Except we women find devices forth.

    CHORUS: Phaedra, she speaketh words that more avail
For this thine imminent plight: yet thee I praise.
But haply this my praise shall gall thee more
Than those her words, and harsher sound to thee.

    PHAEDRA: This is it which doth ruin goodly towns
And homes of men, these speeches over-fair.
It needeth not to speak words sweet to ears,
But those whereby a good name shall be saved.

    NURSE: Out on thine high-flown talk! No speech tricked fair
Thou needest! Haste we must and learn the mind
Of this man, telling all thy tale straight out.
For, were thy life not in such desperate case,
Or thou a woman strong in self-control,
Never for thy lust's sake and pleasure I
To this would bring thee: but we must fight hard
Now for thy life, and void of blame is this.

PHAEDRA: Speaker of horrors!—wilt not seal thy lips?
Wilt not refrain from utter-shameful words?
  NURSE: Shameful—yet better than the good for thee.
Better this deed, so it but save thy life,
Than that name, whose proud vaunt shall be thy death.
  PHAEDRA: No, by the Gods!—fair words, but words of shame!—
No farther go: I have schooled mine heart to endure
This love: but if thou plead shame's cause so fair,
I shall be trapped in that sin which I flee.
  NURSE: If such thy mind, thine heart should not have sinned:
But now—obey me: thank me or thank me not:—
I have within some certain charms to assuage
Love: 'twas but now they came into my thought.
These, not with shame, nor hurt unto thy mind,
Shall lull thy pang, so thou be not faint-hearted.
Howbeit there needs of him thou yearnest for
Some token, or a word, or fragment caught
From vesture, so to knit two loves in one.
  PHAEDRA: A salve, or potion, is this charm of thine?
  NURSE: I know not: be content with help, not knowledge.
  PHAEDRA: I fear lest over-cunning thou shalt prove.
  NURSE: Then know thyself all fears. What dreadest thou?
  PHAEDRA: Lest thou show aught of this to Theseus' son.
  NURSE: Let be, my child: this will I order well.
Only do thou, Queen Kypris, Sea-born One,
Work with me. Whatso else I have in mind
Shall it suffice to speak to friends within.

(*Exit* NURSE.)

  Strophe 1

CHORUS: O Eros, O Eros, how melts love's yearning
From thine eyes, when thy sweet spell witcheth the heart
    Of them against whom thou hast marched in thy might!
    Not me, not me for mine hurt do thou smite,
My life's heart-music to discord turning.
    For never so hotly the flame-spears dart,
      Nor so fleet are the star-shot arrows of light,
      As the shaft from thy fingers that speedeth its flight,

As the flame of the Love-queen's bolts fierce-burning,
  O Eros, the child of Zeus who art!

Antistrophe 1

O vainly, O vainly by Alpheus' river
  And in Phoebus's Pythian shrine hath the land
    Of Hellas the blood of her oxen outpoured.
  But Eros, but Love, who is all men's lord,
Unto whom Aphrodite is wont to deliver
  Her keys, that the doors be unsealed by his hand
    Of her holy of holies, we have not adored.
    Though he marcheth through ruin victory-ward,
Though he raineth calamity forth of his quiver
  On mortals against his on-coming that stand.

Strophe 2

For I call to remembrance Oechalia's daughter,
Who, ere Love 'neath his tyrannous car-yoke had brought her,
  Had been spouseless and free—overseas how she hasted,
When Kypris the dear yoke of home had disparted,
Like a bacchanal fiend out of hell that hath darted,
  And with blood, and with smoke of a palace flame-wasted,
And with death-shrieks for hymns at her bridal-feast chanted,
By Love's Queen to the son of Alkmena was granted—
  Woe, woe for the joys of espousal she tasted!

Antistrophe 2

And ye, O ye ramparts of hallowèd Thebe,
And ye lips wave-welling of Dirke, might ye be
  Witness how dire was the Love-queen's coming,
When a slumber that knoweth not waking was given
Of her spells by the flame-enfolded levin
  To the mother of Zeus' seed Bacchus: for dooming
Of death had she blent with the bride-chant's singing.
For the Dread One breatheth on all life, winging
  Softly her flight as a bee low-humming.

(*Voices within.*)

PHAEDRA: Hush ye, O hush ye, women! . . . . Lost am I!

CHORUS: What is this dread thing, Phaedra, in thine halls?
PHAEDRA: Peace—let me hear the voice of them within.
CHORUS: I am dumb: an ominous prelude sure is this.
PHAEDRA: Ah me! ah me! alas!
O wretched, wretched!—ah, mine agonies!
CHORUS: What cry dost thou utter? What word dost thou
    shriek?
What boding of terror hath rushed on thy soul?—O lady, speak!
PHAEDRA: I am undone! O stand ye by these doors,
And hear what clamour clasheth in the house.
CHORUS: Nay, thou art thereby, and the cry from the palace
    sped forth is for thee.
O tell me what evil came forth—tell it me!
PHAEDRA: The son of the Amazon, Hippolytus,
Shouts, hurling fearful curses at mine handmaid.
CHORUS: A noise do I hear; yet it passeth me clearly to tell
    whereby
It came—through the doors to thee came that cry.
PHAEDRA: Ah clear—ah clear!—yea, pandar of foul sin,
Traitress to her lord's bed, he calleth her.
CHORUS: Woe! Thou art betrayed, belovèd one!
What shall I counsel? Thy secret is bared: thou art wholly undone.
PHAEDRA: Woe's me! ah woe!
CHORUS: From the hand that loved came the traitor's blow.
PHAEDRA: She hath undone me, telling my mischance:
In love, in shame, she sought these pangs to heal.
CHORUS: What wilt thou do, O thou in desperate plight?
PHAEDRA: No way save one I know—straightway to die—
The one cure for the ills that compass me.

(*Enter* HIPPOLYTUS, *followed by the* NURSE.)

HIPPOLYTUS: O mother Earth, unveilings of the sun,
What words unutterable have I heard!
NURSE: Hush, O my son, ere one have heard thy cry.
HIPPOLYTUS: I have heard horrors—should I hold my peace?
NURSE: Yea, I beseech thee by thy fair right hand.
HIPPOLYTUS: Hence with thine hand!—touch not my vesture
    thou.
NURSE: Oh, by thy knees, do not—ah, slay me not!

HIPPOLYTUS: How, if thou hast said no wrong, as thou dost say?
NURSE: No tale is this, my son, for all men's ears.
HIPPOLYTUS: Tush, a fair tale is fairer told to the world.
NURSE: My son, thine oath!—dishonour not thine oath.
HIPPOLYTUS: My tongue hath sworn: no oath is on my soul.
NURSE: O son, what wilt thou do?—wilt slay thy friends?
HIPPOLYTUS: Avaunt the word!—no villain is my friend.
NURSE: Forgive, son: men are men, they needs must err.
HIPPOLYTUS: Why hast thou given a home beneath the sun,
Zeus, unto woman, specious curse to man?
For, were thy will to raise a mortal seed,
This ought they not of women to have gotten,
But in thy temples should they lay its price,
Or gold, or iron, or a weight of bronze,
And so buy seed of children, every man
After the worth of that his gift, and dwell
Free in free homes unvexed of womankind.
But now—soon as we go about to bring
This bane to the home, we hurl to earth its weal.
Hereby is woman proved a grievous bane—
He, who begat and reared her, banishes,
Yea, adds a dower, to rid him of his bane;
While he which taketh home the noisome weed
Rejoices, decks with goodly bravery
The loathly image, and tricks out with robes,—
Filching away, poor wretch! his household's wealth.
He may not choose: who getteth noble kin
With her, content must stomach his sour feast:
Who getteth a good wife, but worthless kin,
Must muffle up the evil 'neath the good.
Happiest who wins a cipher, in whose halls
A brainless fadge is throned in uselessness.
But the keen-witted hate I: in mine house
Ne'er dwell one wiser than is woman's due;
For Kypris better brings to birth her mischief
In clever women: the resourceless 'scapes
That folly by the short-weight of her wit.
Handmaids should ne'er have had access to wives,
But brutes, with teeth, no tongue, should dwell with them,

That so they might not speak to any one,
Nor win an answering word from such as these.
But now the vile ones weave vile plots within,
And out of doors their handmaids bear the web:
As thou hast come, foul quean, to tender me
Commerce in mine own father's sacred couch!—
Words that with fountain-streams I'll wash away,
Sluicing mine ears. How should I be so vile,
Who even with hearing count myself defiled?
Woman, I fear God: know, that saveth thee.
For, had I not by oaths been trapped unwares,
I had ne'er forborne to tell this to my sire.
Now from mine home, while Theseus yet is far,
I go, and I will keep my lips from speech.
But—with my father I return, to see
How thou wilt meet his eye, thou and thy mistress,
And so have taste of thy full shamelessness.
Curse ye! My woman-hate shall ne'er be sated,
Not though one say that this is all my theme:
For they be ever strangely steeped in sin.
Let some one now stand forth and prove them chaste,
Or leave me free to trample on them ever.

    (*Exit* HIPPOLYTUS.)

    CHORUS: O drear dark doom that on women hath lighted!
    By what cunning of pleading, when feet once trip,
    Shall we loose the accuser's iron grip?
    PHAEDRA: O earth, O sun, I am justly requited!
    Through the snares of calamity how shall I slip?
How, friends, shall I cloke my woe, how hide?
What God or what man shall stand forth on my side,
Shall consent in my sin to be made partaker?
    For all life's anguish, and all life's shame,
Are upon me, and whelm like a shipwrecking breaker!
    Most accurst of my fate among women I am.
    CHORUS: Woe, woe! 'Tis done. Queen, it hath nought availed,
Thy bower-maid's device: 'tis ruin all.
    PHAEDRA: Vilest of vile! destroyer of thy friends!
How hast thou ruined me! May Zeus my sire

Smite thee with flame, and wholly abolish thee!
Did I not tell thee—not divine thy purpose?—
To speak not that whereby I am now dishonoured?
But thou wouldst not forbear. I shall not now
Even die unshamed!   (*A pause.*)
                              Some new plea must I find.
For yonder boy with soul keen-edged with wrath
Shall to his sire accuse me of thy sin,
Shall tell to agèd Pittheus my mischance,
Shall blaze the shameful tale through every land.
Curses on thee, and whoso thrusteth in
To do base service to unwilling friends!

NURSE: Mistress, thou may'st revile mine evil work,
For rankling pain bears thy discernment down:
Yet somewhat might I answer, wouldst thou hear.
I nursed thee, loved thee, sought for thy disease
A healing balm,—and found not that I would.
Had I sped well, right wise had I been held;
For, as we speed, so is our wisdom's fame.

PHAEDRA: Ha! is this just?—should this suffice me now,
To have stabbed me, and then close in strife of words?

NURSE: We waste the time in speech. I was not wise.
Yet even from this there is escape, my child.

PHAEDRA: Peace to thy talk. Thy counsel heretofore
Was shame, and mischief thine endeavour was.
Hence from my sight: for thine own self take thought.
I with my needs will deal—and honourably.

(*Exit* NURSE.)

But ye, O Troezen's daughters nobly born,
Grant to my supplication this, but this—
With silence veil what things ye here have heard.

CHORUS: I swear by reverend Artemis, Zeus' child,
Never to bare to light of thine ills aught.

PHAEDRA: Thou hast well said. Now, as I muse, I find
One refuge, one, from this calamity,
So to bequeath my sons a life of honour,
And what I may from this day's ruin save.
For never will I shame the halls of Crete,

Nor will I meet the face of Theseus ever,
For one poor life's sake, after all this shame.
   CHORUS: Ah, wilt thou do a deed of ill past cure?
   PHAEDRA: Die will I. How—for this will I take thought.
   CHORUS: Ah hush!
   PHAEDRA: O yea, advise me wisely thou.
But I shall gladden Kypris my destroyer
By fleeting out of life on this same day,
And vanquished so by bitter love shall be.
Yet in my death will I become the bane
Of one beside, that he may triumph not
Over my woes, and taking of my pain
His share, may learn sound wisdom's temperance.

   (*Exit* PHAEDRA.)

   Strophe 1

   CHORUS: Under the arched cliffs O were I lying,
   That there to a bird might a God change me,
And afar mid the flocks of the winged things flying
   Over the swell of the Adrian sea
     I might soar—and soar,—upon poised wings dreaming,
   O'er the strand where Eridanus' waters be,
     Where down to the sea-swell purple-gleaming
     The tears of the Sun-god's daughters are streaming,
Of the thrice-sad sisters for Phaethon sighing,
     Star-flashes of strange tears amber-beaming!

   Antistrophe 1

O to win to the strand where the apples are growing
   Of the Hesperid chanters kept in ward,
Where the path over Ocean purple-glowing
   By the Sea's Lord is to the seafarer barred!
     O to light where Atlas hath aye in his keeping
   The bourn twixt earth and the heavens bestarred,
     Where the fountains ambrosial sunward are leaping
     By the couches where Zeus in his hall lieth sleeping,
Where the bounty of Earth the life-bestowing
     The bliss of the Gods ever higher is heaping!

Strophe 2

O white-winged galley from Crete's far shore,
  Whose keel over deep-sea surges speeding,
Through their flying brine and their battle-roar,
Onward and onward my lady bore,
  From a bliss-fraught palace a princess leading
  To the joy of a bridal of woe exceeding!—
For, a bird ill-boding, thy sail flitted o'er,
For a curse to the Cretan land and to Athens' glorious strand,
When the seafarers lashed to the beach Munychian the hawser-
      band,
          And sprang unto earth's firm floor.

Antistrophe 2

Wherefore, with love-pangs all unblest
  For her gift, entered in Aphrodite, wringing
Her heart-strings asunder, a fearful guest.
Like a wrecked ship sinking, disaster-oppressed
  Over her bride-bower's rafters flinging
  The noose, shall she cast the coil close-clinging
Round the neck that was whitest and loveliest,
Because that with shuddering shame she shrank from a loathèd
      name,
And she chose, for its foulness, the stainless renown of a wife's
      fair fame,
          And, for anguish of love, heart-rest.

(*A cry within.*)

Run to the rescue, all ye nigh the house!
In the strangling noose is Theseus' wife, our mistress!

CHORUS: Woe! Woe! 'Tis done! No more—no more is she,
The queen—in yon noose rafter-hung upcaught!

(*Cry within.*)

O haste!—will no one bring the steel two-edged,
Wherewith to loose this cincture of her neck?

SEMI-CHORUS 1: What shall we do, friends? Deem ye we should
    pass
The doors, and from the noose-grip loose the queen?
  SEMI-CHORUS 2: Wherefore?—Are no young handmaids at her
    side?
The busy meddler treadeth perilous paths.

(*Cry within.*)

Uncramp the limbs, streak out the hapless corpse.
ʻBitter house-warding this is for my lords!

CHORUS: Dead is the woeful lady, by that cry:
Even now they streak her as a corpse is streaked.

(*Enter* THESEUS.)

THESEUS: Women, know ye what means this cry within?
A dolorous shriek of handmaids reached mine ears.
Nor deigns the house to open doors and greet me
Blithely, as from the oracle come home.
Hath aught untoward happed to Pittheus' eld?
Well-stricken in years is he, yet dole were ours
If haply fare his feet from these halls forth.
  CHORUS: Not to the old pertains this thy mischance,
Theseus: the young have died, for grief to thee.
  THESEUS: Woe!—is a child's life by the spoiler reft?
  CHORUS: They live, their mother dead—alas for thee!
  THESEUS: What say'st thou?—dead—my wife?—by what mishap?
  CHORUS: The strangling noose she coiled about her neck.
  THESEUS: By grief's touch frozen, or of what mischance?
  CHORUS: No more I know, for to thine halls but now,
Theseus, I came, o'er these thine ills to mourn.
  THESEUS: Woe! with these wreathèd leaves why is mine head
Crowned—ill-starred harbinger of oracles?
Shoot back the bolts, my servants, of the doors:
Loose bars, that I may see this bitter sight,
My wife, who hath destroyed me by her death.

(*The palace is thrown open, and the corpse of* PHAEDRA *dis-
closed, with her handmaids grouped round it.*)

CHORUS: Woe for thy misery! Woe for thine ills, who hast
　　　suffered and wrought
Such a thing as in ruin shall whelm thine home!
Ah for thy desperate deed, who by violence unhallowed hast
　　　sought
Death, who with hand despairing the all-quelling wrestler hast
　　　caught!
Who shroudeth thy life, O hapless, in gloom?

Strophe

THESEUS: Ah me for my woes!—I have suffered calamity, great
Beyond all ills overpast!—O foot of fate,
　　　How hast thou heavily trampled me and mine,
　　　Unlooked-for blight from some avenging fiend—
Nay, but destruction that blasteth my life evermore!
On a sea of disaster I look, on a sea without shore,
　　　So vast, that never can I swim thereout,
　　　Nor ride the surge of this calamity.
What word can I speak unto thee?—how name, dear wife,
The doom that on thee hath descended and crushed thy life?
　　　Like a bird hast thou fleeted from mine hands,
　　　And with swift leap hast rushed to Hades' halls.
Never sorrow of sorrows was like unto mine.
　　　On mine head have I gathered the load
Of the far-off sins of an ancient line;
　　　And this is the vengeance of God.
　　CHORUS: Not to thee only, king, this grief hath come;
With many more a dear wife's loss thou sharest.

Antistrophe

THESEUS: In the darkness under the earth—ah me, to have died,
That in blackness of darkness under the earth I might hide,
　　　Who am reft of thy most dear companionship!
　　　For thou hast dealt worse death than thou hast suffered.
Of whom shall I hear whence came it, the deadly stroke
Of doom, that the heart of thee, my belovèd, broke?
　　　Will none speak what befell?—or all for nought
　　　Doth this my palace roof a menial throng?

Woe's me, my belovèd, stricken because of thee!
Ah for the grief of mine house, for the travail I see,
   Past utterance, past endurance!—lost am I:
   Mine house is desolate, motherless my babes.
O my darling, my wife, thou art gone, thou art gone,
     O best upon whom the light
Looketh down of the all-beholding sun,
     Or the splendour of star-eyed night!
   CHORUS: Woe's me for thine house! woe's me for its burden of
     ill!
With ruth for thy fate running o'er do mine eyelids the tear-drops
     pour:
   (*Aside.*) But for woe which must follow I shudder and shudder
     still.
   THESEUS: Ha!
What is this tablet, what, to her dear hand
Fastened? What new thing meaneth it to tell?
Now hath she writ, unhappy one, to pray
Touching my marriage or my children aught?
Fear not, lost love: the woman is not born
Shall lie in Theseus' couch, or tread his halls.
Lo, how the impress of the carven gold
Of her that is no more smiles up at me!
Come, let me uncoil the seal's envelopings,
And see what would this tablet say to me.
   CHORUS: Woe, woe! How God bringeth evil following hard on
     the track
    Of evil! I count for living unmeet
The lot of a life such as this, as on deeds that are wrought I
    look back:
For the house of my lords standeth not any more, but in ruin and
    wrack
    I behold it hurled from its ancient seat.
    Ah God, if this may be, wreck not the house,
    But hearken my beseeching, for I trace,
    Seer-like, an evil omen from his face.
   THESEUS: Ah me!—a new curse added to the old,
Past utterance, past endurance! Woe is me!
   CHORUS: What is it? Speak, if I may share the tale.

THESEUS: It shrieketh,—ah, horrors the tablet outshrieketh! O
    how can I flee
    My burden of woes? I am utterly ruin-sped!
They sing—what curses they sing, the words I have read
    Graved on the wax—woe's me!
    CHORUS: Alas! thou utterest speech that heralds ill.
    THESEUS: No more within my lips' gates will I pen
The horror that chokes utterance—ah wretch!
Hippolytus hath dared assail my bed
With violence, flouting Zeus's awful eye!
Father Poseidon, thou didst promise me
Three curses once. Do thou with one of these
Destroy my son: may he not 'scape this day,
If soothfast curses thou hast granted me.
    CHORUS: O King, recall thou from the Gods this prayer!
Thou yet shalt know thine error: yield to me.
    THESEUS: Never! Yea, I will drive him from the land,
And, of two dooms, with one shall he be scourged:—
Either Poseidon, reverencing my prayers,
Shall slay and speed him unto Hades' halls,
Or, banished from this land, a vagabond
On strange shores, shall he drain life's bitter dregs.
    CHORUS: Lo, where thy son's self comes in season meet,
Hippolytus: refrain thy wrath, O king
Theseus, and for thine house the best devise.

    (*Enter* HIPPOLYTUS.)

    HIPPOLYTUS: Father, I heard thy crying, and I came
In haste: yet for what cause thou makest moan
I know not, but of thee I fain would hear.
Ha! what is this?—Father, thy wife I see—
Dead!—matter this for marvel passing great.
But now I left her, who upon this light
Looked, it is not yet a long season since.
What hath befallen her? How perished she?
Father, I fain would learn it from thy mouth.
Silent!—In trouble silence nought avails.
The heart that yearns to know all cares of thine
Fain shall be found to prove thy troubles too.

Sure from thy friends—yea, and thy more than friends,
Father, it is not right to hide thy griefs.
 THESEUS: O men that ofttimes err, and err in vain,
Why are ye teaching ever arts untold,
And search out manifold inventions still,
But one thing know not, no, nor hunt for it,
To teach them wit, in whom no wisdom dwells?
 HIPPOLYTUS: A cunning sophist hast thou named, of power
Them to constrain to sense who sense have none:
But—so ill-timed thy speculations are—
Father, I fear thy tongue for grief runs wild.
 THESEUS: Out! There should dwell in men some certain test
Of friendship, a discerner of the heart,
To show who is true friend and who is false.
Yea, all men should have had two several voices,
One honest, one—how it might chance soe'er;
That so the traitor voice might be convict
Before the honest, nor we be deceived.
 HIPPOLYTUS: How?—to thine ear hath some friend slandered
  me,
That I the innocent am in evil case?
Astonied am I, for thy words amaze me,
Thus wandering wide astray from reason's throne.
 THESEUS: Out on man's heart!—to what depths will it sink?
Where shall assurance end and hardihood?
For if it swell with every generation,
And the new age reach heights of villainy
Above the old, the Gods must needs create
A new earth unto this, that room be found
For the unrighteous and unjust in grain.
Look on this man, who, though he be my son,
Hath shamed my couch, and shall be manifest proved
Most vile, by testimony of the dead.
Hither,—since to this foulness thou hast come,—
And set thy face against thy father's face.
Dost thou with Gods—O thou no common man!—
Consort? Art thou the chaste, the stainless one?
I will not trust thy boasts, for so should I
Impute to Gods unwisdom's ignorance.

Now vaunt, ay now!—set out thy paltry wares
Of lifeless food: take Orpheus for thy king:
Rave, worship vapourings of many a scroll:
For ah, thou'rt caught! I warn all men to shun
Such hypocrites as this; for they hunt souls
With canting words, the while they plot foul sin.
Dead is she: thinkest thou this saveth thee?
Hereby thou art most convicted, basest thou!
What oaths, what protestations shall bear down

(Shows tablet.)

This, for thine absolution of the charge?
And wilt thou say, "She hated me: the bastard
Is foe by blood of those in wedlock born?"
Fools' traffic this in life—to fling away
For hate of thee the dearest thing she owed!
Or—say'st thou?—"Frailty is not in men,
But in the blood of women." Youths, I have proved,
Are no whit more than women continent
When Kypris stirs a heart in flush of youth:
Yet all the strength of manhood helpeth them.
But wherefore thus contend against thy pleas,
When there the corpse lies, witness faithful and true?
Hence from this land, an exile, with all speed.
Never come thou to god-built Athens more,
Nor any marches where my spear hath sway:
For if 'neath thy mishandling I sit still,
Never shall Isthmian Sinis testify
That I slew him, but name it idle vaunt;
Nor those Skironian Rocks that skirt the sea
Shall call me terrible to evil-doers.
    CHORUS: I dare not name of mortals any man
Happy, for lo, the first is made the last.
    HIPPOLYTUS: Father, thy rage and strong-strained fury of
        soul
Are fearful: yet, fair-seeming though the charge,
If one unfold it, all unfair it is.
I have no skill to speak before a throng:
My tongue is loosed with equals, and those few.

And reason: they that are among the wise
Of none account, to mobs are eloquent.
Yet needs I must, now this mischance hath lighted,
Unrein my tongue. And first will I begin
Where thou didst first assail, as thou wouldst crush me,
And I find no reply. See'st thou yon sun
And earth?—within their compass is no man—
Though thou deny it—chaster-souled than I.
For I have learnt, first, to revere the Gods,
Then, to have friends which seek to do no wrong,
Friends who think shame to proffer aught of base,
Yea, or to render others shameful service.
No mocker am I, father, at my friends,
But to the absent even as to the present:
In one thing flawless,—where thou think'st me trapped,—
For to this day my body is clean of lust.
I know this commerce not, save by the ear
And sight of pictures,—little will have I
To look thereon, who keep a virgin soul.
Yet, grant my virtue wins not thy belief,
Sure 'tis for thee to show whereby I fell.
Wilt say this woman's form in grace outshone
All women?—that I hoped thy state to inherit
By winning for mine own thine heiress-queen?
Vain fool were I—nay rather, wholly mad!
"Nay," (say'st thou) "sweet is power, though one be chaste."
Nay verily!—save the lust of sovereignty
Poison the wit of all who covet it.
Fain would I foremost victor be in games
Hellenic, and be second in the realm,
And with pure-hearted friends be happy still.
For there is true well-being, peril far,
Which giveth sweeter joys than sovereignty.
So hast thou all my counterpleas, save one:—
Had I a witness,—one who knows mine heart,—
And made defence while she stood living there,
By deeds shouldst thou search out and know the wicked:
But now—by Zeus Oath-warden, by Earth's plain,
Swear I, I ne'er attempted couch of thine,

No, nor had wished it, nor had dreamed thereof.
God grant I perish nameless, fameless all,
Cityless, homeless, exile, vagabond
On earth,—may sea nor land receive my corpse
When I am dead, if I be this vile thing!
Now if through fear she flung away her life
I know not:—more I cannot sinless say.
Honest she was, yet honest could not be:
I, caught at disadvantage, bore with wrong.

CHORUS: Thou hast said enough to turn this charge from thee
In tendering the Gods' oath, that dread pledge.

THESEUS: Lo, is not this a mountebank, a juggler,
Who thinks by his unruffled calm to outface
My mood, when his own father he hath shamed?

HIPPOLYTUS: Nay, but I marvel, father, at this in thee:—
For, if my son thou wert, and I thy sire,
I had slain thee: exile should not be thy mulct,
If on my wife thou hadst dared to lay a hand.

THESEUS: Good sooth, well said: yet not so shalt thou die
After the doom thou speakest for thyself;
For easiest for the wretched is swift death.
But from the home-land exiled, wandering
To strange soil, shalt thou drain life's bitter dregs.
For this is meet wage for the impious man.

HIPPOLYTUS: Woe's me!—what wilt thou do? Wilt not receive
Time's witness in my cause, but banish now?

THESEUS: Beyond the sea, beyond the Atlantic bourn,
If this I could; so much I hate thy face.

HIPPOLYTUS: Nor oath, nor pledge, nor prophet's utterance
Wilt test, but cast me forth the land untried?

THESEUS: This tablet, though it bear no prophet's sign,
Accuseth thee, nor lieth:—but the birds
That roam o'erhead, I wave them long farewell.

HIPPOLYTUS (aside): O Gods, why can I not unlock my lips,
Who am destroyed by you whom I revere?
No—whom I need persuade, I should not so,
And all for nought should break the oaths I swore.

THESEUS: Faugh!—how it chokes me, this thy saintly mien!
Out from thy fatherland! Straightway begone!

HIPPOLYTUS: Unhappy! whither shall I flee?—What home
Of what friend enter, banished on such charge?
    THESEUS: Of whoso joys in welcoming for guests
Defilers of men's wives, which dwell with sin.
    HIPPOLYTUS: Alas! this stabs mine heart well-nigh to weep-
        ing,
If I be published villain, thou believe it!
    THESEUS: Then shouldest thou have moaned and taken thought,
Then, when thou dar'dst insult thy father's wife.
    HIPPOLYTUS: O halls, could ye but find a voice for me,
And witness if I be a wicked man!
    THESEUS: To speechless witnesses thou fleest?—Clearly
This deed, though it speak not, declares thee vile.
    HIPPOLYTUS: Ah, to stand face to face and see myself,
That for the wrongs I suffer I might weep!
    THESEUS: Yea, 'tis thy wont to gaze on thy perfections
More than to render parents righteous honour.
    HIPPOLYTUS: Ah, hapless mother!—ah, my bitter birth!
Base-born be never any that I love!
    THESEUS: Will ye not hale him hence, thralls?—heard ye not
Long since his banishment pronounced of me?
    HIPPOLYTUS: Who layeth hand on me of them shall rue!
Thou thrust me from the land if such thy mood.
    THESEUS: That will I, an thou wilt not heed mine hest.
No pity for thine exile visits me.

    (*Exit* THESEUS.)

    HIPPOLYTUS: So then my fate is sealed. Ah, woe is me!
I know the truth, yet know not how to tell it.
Dearest of Gods to me, O Leto's Child,
Companion, fellow-huntress, I shall flee
Athens the glorious. Farewell ye, O burg,
Land of Erechtheus! O Troezenian plain,
How many pleasant paths of youth hast thou!
Farewell: I see thee, hail thee, the last time.
Come, O ye youths, mine age-mates in this land,
Speak parting word: escort me from this soil:
For never shall ye see a chaster man,
Albeit this my sire believeth not.

(*Exit* HIPPOLYTUS.)

Strophe 1

CHORUS: When faith overfloweth my mind, God's providence
    all-embracing
Banisheth griefs: but when doubt whispereth "Ah but to
    know!"
No clue through the tangle I find of fate and of life for my
    tracing:
      There is ever a change and many a change,
And the mutable fortune of men evermore sways to and fro
      Over limitless range.

Antistrophe 1

Ah, would the Gods hear prayer!—would they grant to me these
    supplications—
A lot with prosperity sweet, and a soul unshadowed of pain,
And a faith neither fixed foursquare on the flint, nor on sandy
    foundations!
      Quick-shifting my sail to the coming breeze
Of the morrow, so may I fleet, ever voyaging life's wide main
      Over stormless seas.

Strophe 2

For my mind is a fountain stirred, and I see things all undreamed:
      For the Star of Athens, that beamed
      The brightest withal in Hellas-land,
      We have seen him driven to an alien strand,
      By the wrath of a father have seen him banned.
      Ah, cityward sands, ye shall wait him in vain,
      And ye mountain woods, where streamed
'Twixt the oaks the pack on the wild boar's track
    In dread Dictynna's hunter-train,
      Till the quarry was slain.

Antistrophe 2

Nevermore shall he harness the Henetan horses and leap on his
    car,
      O'er the race-course of Limne afar

To speed the coursers' feet of fire:
And the songs, that once 'neath the strings of the lyre
Slept never, shall cease in the halls of his sire.
Ungarlanded Artemis' bowers shall be
    In the greenwood depths that are.
By thine exile have perished the sweet hopes cherished
    Of our maids, and their gentle rivalry
            In love for thee.

Epode

For thy woeful fate shall I pass amid tears fast-flowing
A fortuneless fortune. O mother evil-starred,
        This day thy birth-joy effaces!
        I am wroth with the Gods:—O Graces
        Aye linkèd in loving embraces,
Why do ye suffer that he from his land should be going,
From his home, who hath nowise earned a doom so bitter-hard?

But lo, I see Hippolytus' henchman nigh
Hasting unto the halls with clouded brows.

(*Enter* MESSENGER.)

MESSENGER: Where should I go and find this country's king,
Theseus, ye women? If ye know, declare
Straightway to me. Within these halls is he?
CHORUS: Lo yonder where he cometh forth the halls.

(*Enter* THESEUS.)

MESSENGER: Theseus, I bring a sorrow-kindling tale
To thee and all the citizens which dwell
In Athens and the bounds of Troezen-land.
THESEUS: What now?—Hath some disaster unforeseen
Fallen on these two neighbour-citied states?
MESSENGER: Hippolytus is no more, one may say,
Though yet a little space he seeth light.
THESEUS: Of whom slain?—Hath one met him in his wrath,
Whose wife he had outraged, even as his sire's?

MESSENGER: His proper chariot-team hath dealt him death,
And thy mouth's curses, which thou didst call down
From the Sea's Lord, thy father, on thy son.
THESEUS: O Gods! Poseidon! how thou wast indeed
My father, who hast heard my malison!
How perished he? In what way did the gin
Of justice snap on him who wrought me shame?
MESSENGER: We, hard beside the beach that greets the surf,
With combs were smoothing out his horses' manes
Weeping: for word had come to us to say
That no more in this land Hippolytus
Might walk, of thee to wretched exile doomed.
Then came he, bringing the same tale of tears
To us upon the strand: a countless throng
Of friends his age-mates following with him came.
But, ceasing at the last from moan, he cried:
"Why rave I thus? I must obey my sire.
Harness the horses to the chariot-yoke,
My thralls: this city is no more for me."
Then, then did every man bestir himself.
Swifter than one could say it were the steeds
Harnessed, and by our lord's side set we them.
Then the reins caught he from the chariot-rail,
Settling his feet, all buskined as he was;
And to the Gods first stretched his hands and cried:
"Zeus, may I die if I a villain am!
May my sire know that he is wronging me,
When I am dead, if not while I see light!"
Then in his hands he took the scourge and smote
At once the steeds. We henchmen by the car
Fast by the reins attended on our lord
Towards Argos straight and Epidauria.
And, as we entered on a desert tract,
Beyond this Troezen's border lies a beach
Sloping full down to yon Saronic Sea.
There from earth's womb a noise like Zeus's thunder
Made muffled roaring, a blood-curdling sound.
Then the steeds lifted head and pricked the ear;
And thrilled through us most vehement dismay

Whence might the sound be. To the sea-lashed shores
Then glanced we, and a surge unearthly saw
Up-columned to the sky, that from my sight
Shrouded was all the beach Skironian;
Veiled was the Isthmus and Asklepius' Crag.
Then swelling higher, higher, and spurting forth
All round a cloud of foam and sea-blown spray,
Shoreward it rusheth toward the four-horse car.
Then from the breaker's midst and hugest surge
The wave belched forth a bull, a monster fierce,
With whose throat-thunder all the land was filled
And echoed awfully, as on our gaze
He burst, a sight more dread than eyes could bear.
Straightway wild panic falleth on the steeds:
Yet their lord, wholly conversant with wont
Of horses, caught the reins in both his hands,
And tugs, as shipman tugs against the oar,
Throwing his body's weight against the reins.
But on the fire-forged bits they clenched their teeth,
And whirl him on o'ermastered, recking not
Of steering hand, or curb, or strong car's weight.
And if, yet holding to the chariot-helm,
Toward the smooth ground he strove to guide their course,
Aye showed that bull in front, to turn them back,
Maddening with fright the fourfold chariot-team.
If toward the rocks they rushed with frenzied heart,
Fast by the rail in silence followed he
On, till he fouled and overset the car,
Dashing against a rock the chariot felly.
Then all was turmoil: upward leapt in air
Naves of the wheels and linchpins of the axles.
And he, unhappy, tangled in the reins,
Bound in indissoluble bonds, is haled
Dashing his head against the cruel rocks,
Rending his flesh, outshrieking piteous cries—
"O stay, ye horses nurtured at my cribs,
Destroy me not!—ah, father's curse ill-starred!
Who wills to save an utter-innocent man?"
Ah, many willed, but far behind were left

With feet outstripped. Loosed from the toils at last
Of clean-cut reins,—I know not in what wise,—
He falls, yet breathing for short space of life.
Vanished the steeds and that accursèd monster,
The bull, mid rock-strewn ground, I know not where.
Thrall am I verily of thine house, O king;
Howbeit so foul a charge—I never can
Believe it of thy son, that he is vile,
Not though all womankind should hang themselves,
Though one should fill with writing all the pine
In Ida:—he is righteous, this I know.

CHORUS: Woe for accomplishment of new disaster!
No refuge is there from the doom of fate.

THESEUS: For hatred of the man who thus hath fared,
Glad for this tale was I: but now, for awe
Of heaven, and for that he is yet my son,
Nor glad am I nor sorry for these ills.

MESSENGER: How then?—must we bear yonder broken man
Hither?—or in what wise perform thy pleasure?
Bethink thee: if my counsel thou wilt heed,
Harsh to thy stricken son thou wilt not be.

THESEUS: Bear him, that I may see before mine eyes
Him who denied that he had stained my bed,
By words and heaven's judgment to convict him.

(*Exit* MESSENGER.)

CHORUS: Love, under thy dominion
    Unbending hearts bow low
  Of Gods, and hearts of mortals,
  When, flashing through thy portals
On glory-gleaming pinion,
    Flits Eros to and fro;
      Love, under thy dominion
      Unbending hearts bow low.

Gold-glittering wings wide-soaring,
  They rain down witchery,
O'er maddened hearts prevailing,
O'er earth triumphant sailing,

O'er music of the roaring
　Of spray-bemantled sea,
　　　Gold-glittering wings wide-soaring,
　　　They rain down witchery.

He kindleth with his yearning
　All things of earth-born race;
The mountain's whelps he thrilleth,
The ocean's brood he filleth,
Where'er the sun's eye burning
　Down-looketh on earth's face,
　　　He kindleth with his yearning
　　　All things of earth-born race.

They bend—all, all are bending,
　Love-queen, beneath thy hand!
O crownèd brows, whom loyal
Vassals acclaim sole-royal
By spells all-comprehending
　In sky and sea and land;
　　　They bend—all, all are bending,
　　　Love-queen, beneath thy hand!

(*Enter* ARTEMIS.)

ARTEMIS: Thou high-born scion of Aigeus, I call upon thee:
　　Theseus, give ear unto me.
It is Artemis, Leto's Daughter, that nameth thy name:
　　Why dost thou joy in thy shame?
Thou hast murdered thy son unrighteously, thereto moved
　　Of the lies of thy wife unproved.
By infatuate folly all-manifest, lo, thou wast bound.
　　How wilt thou hide underground
Thy dishonour, or soar to the heaven, by changing thy life
　　To escape from this anguish-strife?
For the part that was erstwhile thine in the good man's lot,
　　Behold, it is not.
Theseus, hear thou the posture of thy woes;—
Yet have I no help for thee, only pain;

But I have come to show the righteousness
Of thy son, that in fair fame he may die,
And thy wife's fever-flame,—yet in some sort
Her nobleness,—who, stung by goads of her
Whom most we loathe, who joy in purity,
Of all the Gods, was lovesick for thy son,
Yet strove by reason to o'ermaster passion,
And died through wiles unsanctioned of her nurse,
Who under oath-seal told thy son her pangs;
And he, even as was righteous, would not heed
The tempting; no, nor when sore-wronged of thee
Broke he the oath's pledge, for he feared the Gods.
But she, adread to be of sin convict,
Wrote that false writing, and by treachery so
Destroyed thy son:—and thou believedst her!

   THESEUS: Ah me!

   ARTEMIS: Is it torture, Theseus?—Nay, but hear me out,
That hearing all thou mayst the more lament.
Three soothfast curses hadst thou of thy sire:
One hast thou thus misused, O villain thou,
Against thy son, which might have quelled a foe!
Thy sire the Sea-king, in his love's despite,
Gave as he needs must, seeing he had pledged him:
Yet wicked in his eyes and mine art thou,
Who wouldst not wait for proof, nor prophet's voice,
Nor yet make inquisition, nor wouldst trace
Time's slow step, but with haste that did thee wrong
Didst hurl the curse upon thy son, and slay.

   THESEUS: Queen, ruin seize me!

   ARTEMIS: Deep thy sin; but yet
Even thou for this mayst win forgiveness still:
For Kypris willed that all this should befall
To glut her spite. And this the Gods' wont is:—
None doth presume to thwart the fixed design
Willed by his fellow: still aloof we stand.
Else be thou sure that, but for dread of Zeus,
I never would have known this depth of shame,
To suffer one, of all men best beloved
Of me, to die. But thy transgression, first,

Thine ignorance from utter sin redeems;
Then, by her death thy wife made void all test
Of these her words, and won thy credence so.
Now, most on thee this storm of woe hath burst;
Yet grief is mine: for when the righteous die
The Gods joy not. The wicked, and withal
Their children and their homes, do we destroy.
   CHORUS: Lo, lo, the stricken one borne
   Hitherward, with his young flesh torn
And his golden head of its glory shorn!
   Ah, griefs of the house!—what doom
   Twofold on thine halls hath come
By the Gods' will shrouded in sorrow's gloom!

   (*Enter bearers with* HIPPOLYTUS.)

HIPPOLYTUS:
   Woe, woe for a son
     By the doom of his sire
   All marred and undone!
     Through mine head leapeth fire
Of the agony-flashes, and throbbeth my brain like a hard-stricken
   lyre.

   Let me rest—ah forbear!
     For my strength is sped.
   Cursèd horses, ye were
     Of mine own hands fed,
Yet me have ye wholly destroyed, yet me have ye stricken dead!

   For the Gods' sake, bear
     Me full gently, each thrall!
   Thou to right—have a care!—
     Soft let your hands fall;
Tenderly bear the sore-mangled, on-stepping in time, one and
   all,

   The unhappy on-bearing,
     And cursèd, I ween,

    Of his father's own erring:—
      Ah Zeus, hast thou seen?
Innocent I, ever fearing the Gods, who was wholly heart-clean

    Above all men beside,—
      Lo, how am I thrust
    Unto Hades, to hide
      My life in the dust!
All vainly I reverenced God, and in vain unto man was I just.

    Let the stricken one be!—
      Ah, mine anguish again!—
    Give ye sleep unto me,
      Death-salve for my pain,
The sleep of the sword for the wretched—I long, oh I long to be
    slain.

    Dire curse of my father!—
      Sins, long ago wrought
    Of mine ancestors, gather:
      Their doom tarries not,
But the scourge overfloweth the innocent—wherefore on me is it
    brought?

    Ah for words of a spell,
      That my soul might take flight
    From the tortures, with fell
      Unrelentings that smite!
Oh for the blackness of Hades, the sleep of Necessity's night!

ARTEMIS: Unhappy, bowed 'neath what disaster's yoke!
Thine own heart's nobleness hath ruined thee.
  HIPPOLYTUS: Ah, perfume-breath celestial!—mid my pains
I feel thee, and mine anguish is assuaged.
Lo in this place the Goddess Artemis!
  ARTEMIS: Yea, hapless one, of Gods best friend to thee.
  HIPPOLYTUS: O Queen, seest thou my plight—the stricken one?
  ARTEMIS: I see—but tears are to mine eyes forbid.
  HIPPOLYTUS: None now shall hark thine hounds, nor do thee
    service—

ARTEMIS: Ah no!—Yet dear to me thou perishest.

HIPPOLYTUS: Nor tend thy steeds, nor guard thine images.

ARTEMIS: This all-pernicious Kypris hath contrived—

HIPPOLYTUS: Ah me! what Goddess blasts me now I know—

ARTEMIS: Jealous for honour, wroth with chastity.

HIPPOLYTUS: Three hath one hand destroyed; I see it now.

ARTEMIS: Thy father—thee—thy father's wife the third.

HIPPOLYTUS: Yea, and I wail my father's misery.

ARTEMIS: By plots of deity was he beguiled.

HIPPOLYTUS: Ah father, woe is thee for this mischance!

THESEUS: I am slain, my son: no joy have I in life!

HIPPOLYTUS: More than myself I mourn thee for thine error.

THESEUS: Would God I could but die for thee, my son!

HIPPOLYTUS: Ah, bitter gifts of that Sea-god, thy sire!

THESEUS: Ah that the word had never passed my lips!

HIPPOLYTUS: Wherefore?—thou wouldst for wrath have slain
        me still.

THESEUS: Yea, for the Gods had caused my wit to stumble.

HIPPOLYTUS: Oh that men's curses could but strike the Gods!

ARTEMIS: Let be: for even in the nether gloom
Not unavenged shall be the stroke that fell
Upon thy frame through rage of Kypris' spite,
For thy pure soul's and for thy reverence' sake.
For upon one, her minion, with mine hand—
One who is dearest of all men to her—
With these unerring shafts will I avenge me.
And to thee, hapless one, for these thy woes
High honours will I give in Troezen-town.
Ere their espousals shall all maids unwed
For thee cut off their hair: through age on age
Full harvests shalt thou reap of grief in tears.
Ever of thee song-waking memory
Shall live in virgins; nor shall Phaedra's love
Forgotten in thy story be unhymned.
But thou, O son of ancient Aigeus, take
Thy child into thine arms, and fold him close.
Not of thy will thou slewest him, and well
May men transgress when Gods are thrusting on.
Thee too I charge, Hippolytus—hate not

Thy father: 'tis by fate thou perishest.
Farewell: I may not gaze upon the dead,
Nor may with dying gasps pollute my sight:
And now I see that thou art near the end.

(*Exit Artemis.*)

HIPPOLYTUS: Farewell to thy departing, maiden blest.
Light falls on thee long fellowship's severance!
Lo, I forgive my father at thy suit,
As heretofore have I obeyed thy word.
Ah, o'er mine eyes even now the darkness draws!
Take, father, take my body, and upraise.
THESEUS: Ah me! what dost thou, child, to hapless me?
HIPPOLYTUS: I am gone—yea, I behold the gates of death!
THESEUS: Wilt leave me—and my conscience murder-stained?
HIPPOLYTUS: No, no! I do absolve thee of my death.
THESEUS: How say'st thou?—dost assoil me of thy blood?
HIPPOLYTUS: I call to witness Bow-queen Artemis.
THESEUS: Dearest, how noble show'st thou to thy sire!
HIPPOLYTUS: Father, farewell thou too—untold farewells!
THESEUS: Woe for thy reverent soul, thy righteous heart!
HIPPOLYTUS: Pray to have such sons—sons in wedlock born.
THESEUS: Forsake me not, my son!—be strong to bear!
HIPPOLYTUS: My strength is overborne—I am gone, my father.
Cover my face with mantles with all speed.

(*Dies.*)

THESEUS: O bounds of Athens, Pallas' glorious realm,
What hero have ye lost! Ah, woe is me!
Kypris, how oft shall I recall thy wrong!
CHORUS: On the city hath lighted a stroke without warning,
        On all hearts desolation.
Rain down, O ye fast-falling tears of our mourning!
When the mighty are fallen, their burial-oblation
        Is the wail of a nation.

ARISTOPHANES

LYSISTRATA

TRANSLATED BY CHARLES T. MURPHY

CHARACTERS IN THE PLAY

LYSISTRATA ⎫
CALONICE ⎬ *Athenian women*
MYRRHINE ⎭
LAMPITO, *a Spartan woman*
LEADER *of the Chorus of Old Men*
CHORUS *of Old Men*
LEADER *of the Chorus of Old Women*
CHORUS *of Old Women*
ATHENIAN MAGISTRATE
THREE ATHENIAN WOMEN
CINESIAS, *an Athenian, husband of Myrrhine*
SPARTAN HERALD
SPARTAN AMBASSADORS
ATHENIAN AMBASSADORS
TWO ATHENIAN CITIZENS
CHORUS *of Athenians*
CHORUS *of Spartans*

(As is usual in ancient comedy, the leading characters have significant names. LYSISTRATA is "She who disbands the armies"; MYRRHINE's name is chosen to suggest *myrton,* a Greek word meaning *pudenda muliebria;* LAMPITO is a celebrated Spartan name; CINESIAS, although a real name in Athens, is chosen to suggest a Greek verb *kinein, to move,* then *to make love, to have intercourse,* and the name of his deme, Paionidai, suggests the verb *paiein,* which has about the same significance.)

LYSISTRATA

(SCENE: *In Athens, beneath the Acropolis. In the center of the stage is the Propylaea, or gate-way to the Acropolis; to one side is a small grotto, sacred to Pan. The Orchestra represents a slope leading up to the gate-way.*

It is early in the morning. LYSISTRATA *is pacing impatiently up and down.*)

LYSISTRATA: If they'd been summoned to worship the God of Wine, or Pan, or to visit the Queen of Love, why, you couldn't have pushed your way through the streets for all the timbrels. But now there's not a single woman here—except my neighbour; here she comes.

(*Enter* CALONICE.)

Good day to you, Calonice.

CALONICE: And to you, Lysistrata. (*noticing* LYSISTRATA'S *impatient air*) But what ails you? Don't scowl, my dear; it's not becoming to you to knit your brows like that.

LYSISTRATA (*sadly*): Ah, Calonice, my heart aches; I'm so annoyed at us women. For among men we have a reputation for sly trickery—

CALONICE: And rightly too, on my word!

LYSISTRATA: —but when they were told to meet here to consider a matter of no small importance, they lie abed and don't come.

CALONICE: Oh, they'll come all right, my dear. It's not easy for a woman to get out, you know. One is working on her husband, another is getting up the maid, another has to put the baby to bed, or wash and feed it.

LYSISTRATA: But after all, there are other matters more important than all that.

CALONICE: My dear Lysistrata, just what is this matter you've summoned us women to consider? What's up? Something big?

LYSISTRATA: Very big.

CALONICE (*interested*): Is it stout, too?

LYSISTRATA (*smiling*): Yes indeed—both big and stout.

CALONICE: What? And the women still haven't come?

LYSISTRATA: It's not what you suppose; they'd have come soon enough for *that*. But I've worked up something, and for many a sleepless night I've turned it this way and that.

CALONICE (*in mock disappointment*): Oh, I guess it's pretty fine and slender, if you've turned it this way and that.

LYSISTRATA: So fine that the safety of the whole of Greece lies in us women.

CALONICE: In us women? It depends on a very slender reed then.

LYSISTRATA: Our country's fortunes are in our hands; and whether the Spartans shall perish—

CALONICE: Good! Let them perish, by all means.

LYSISTRATA: —and the Boeotians shall be completely annihilated.

CALONICE: Not completely! Please spare the eels.

LYSISTRATA: As for Athens, I won't use any such unpleasant words. But you understand what I mean. But if the women will meet here—the Spartans, the Boeotians, and we Athenians—then all together we will save Greece.

CALONICE: But what could women do that's clever or distinguished? We just sit around all dolled up in silk robes, looking pretty in our sheer gowns and evening slippers.

LYSISTRATA: These are just the things I hope will save us: these silk robes, perfumes, evening slippers, rouge, and our chiffon blouses.

CALONICE: How so?

LYSISTRATA: So never a man alive will lift a spear against the foe—

CALONICE: I'll get a silk gown at once.

LYSISTRATA: —or take up his shield—

CALONICE: I'll put on my sheerest gown!

LYSISTRATA: —or sword.

CALONICE: I'll buy a pair of evening slippers.

LYSISTRATA: Well then, shouldn't the women have come?

CALONICE: Come? Why, they should have *flown* here.

LYSISTRATA: Well, my dear, just watch: they'll act in true Athenian fashion—everything too late! And now there's not a woman here from the shore or from Salamis.

CALONICE: They're coming, I'm sure; at daybreak they were laying—to their oars to cross the straits.

LYSISTRATA: And those I expected would be the first to come—the women of Acharnae—they haven't arrived.

CALONICE: Yet the wife of Theagenes means to come: she consulted Hecate about it. (*seeing a group of women approaching*) But look! Here come a few. And there are some more over here. Hurrah! Where do they come from?

LYSISTRATA: From Anagyra.

CALONICE: Yes indeed! We've raised up quite a stink from Anagyra anyway.

(*Enter* MYRRHINE *in haste, followed by several other women.*)

MYRRHINE (*breathlessly*): Have we come in time, Lysistrata? What do you say? Why so quiet?

LYSISTRATA: I can't say much for you, Myrrhine, coming at this hour on such important business.

MYRRHINE: Why, I had trouble finding my girdle in the dark. But if it's so important, we're here now; tell us.

LYSISTRATA: No. Let's wait a little for the women from Boeotia and the Peloponnesus.

MYRRHINE: That's a much better suggestion. Look! Here comes Lampito now.

(*Enter* LAMPITO *with two other women.*)

LYSISTRATA: Greetings, my dear Spartan friend. How pretty you look, my dear. What a smooth complexion and well-developed figure! You could throttle an ox.

LAMPITO: Faith, yes, I think I could. I take exercises and kick my heels against my bum. (*She demonstrates with a few steps of the Spartan "bottom-kicking" dance.*)

LYSISTRATA: And what splendid breasts you have.

LAMPITO: La! You handle me like a prize steer.

LYSISTRATA: And who is this young lady with you?

LAMPITO: Faith, she's an Ambassadress from Boeotia.

LYSISTRATA: Oh yes, a Boeotian, and blooming like a garden too.

CALONICE (*lifting up her skirt*): My word! How neatly her garden's weeded!

LYSISTRATA: And who is the other girl?

LAMPITO: Oh, she's a Corinthian swell.

MYRRHINE (*after a rapid examination*): Yes indeed. She swells very nicely (*pointing*) here and here.

LAMPITO: Who has gathered together this company of women?

LYSISTRATA: I have.

LAMPITO: Speak up, then. What do you want?

MYRRHINE: Yes, my dear, tell us what this important matter is.

LYSISTRATA: Very well, I'll tell you. But before I speak, let me ask you a little question.

MYRRHINE: Anything you like.

LYSISTRATA (*earnestly*): Tell me: don't you yearn for the fathers of your children, who are away at the wars? I know you all have husbands abroad.

CALONICE: Why, yes; mercy me! my husband's been away for five months in Thrace keeping guard on—Eucrates.

MYRRHINE: And mine for seven whole months in Pylus.

LAMPITO: And mine, as soon as ever he returns from the fray, readjusts his shield and flies out of the house again.

LYSISTRATA: And as for lovers, there's not even a ghost of one left. Since the Milesians revolted from us, I've not even seen an eight-inch dingus to be a leather consolation for us widows. Are you willing, if I can find a way, to help me end the war?

MYRRHINE: Goodness, yes! I'd do it, even if I had to pawn my dress and—get drunk on the spot!

CALONICE: And I, even if I had to let myself be split in two like a flounder.

LAMPITO: I'd climb up Mt. Taygetus if I could catch a glimpse of peace.

LYSISTRATA: I'll tell you, then, in plain and simple words. My friends, if we are going to force our men to make peace, we must do without—

MYRRHINE: Without what? Tell us.

LYSISTRATA: Will you do it?

MYRRHINE: We'll do it, if it kills us.

LYSISTRATA: Well then, we must do without sex altogether. (*general consternation*) Why do you turn away? Where go you? Why turn so pale? Why those tears? Will you do it or not? What means this hesitation?

MYRRHINE: I won't do it! Let the war go on.

CALONICE: Nor I! Let the war go on.

LYSISTRATA: So, my little flounder? Didn't you say just now you'd split yourself in half?

CALONICE: Anything else you like. I'm willing, even if I have to walk through fire. Anything rather than sex. There's nothing like it, my dear.

LYSISTRATA (*to* MYRRHINE): What about you?

MYRRHINE (*sullenly*): I'm willing to walk through fire, too.

LYSISTRATA: Oh vile and cursed breed! No wonder they make tragedies about us: we're naught but "love-affairs and bassinets." But you, my dear Spartan friend, if you alone are with me, our enterprise might yet succeed. Will you vote with me?

LAMPITO: 'Tis cruel hard, by my faith, for a woman to sleep alone without her nooky; but for all that, we certainly do need peace.

LYSISTRATA: O my dearest friend! You're the only real woman here.

CALONICE (*wavering*): Well, if we do refrain from—(*shuddering*) what you say (God forbid!), would that bring peace?

LYSISTRATA: My goodness, yes! If we sit at home all rouged and powdered, dressed in our sheerest gowns, and neatly depilated, our men will get excited and want to take us; but if you don't come to them and keep away, they'll soon make a truce.

LAMPITO: Aye; Menelaus caught sight of Helen's naked breast and dropped his sword, they say.

CALONICE: What if the men give us up?

LYSISTRATA: "Flay a skinned dog," as Pherecrates says.

CALONICE: Rubbish! These make-shifts are no good. But suppose they grab us and drag us into the bedroom?

LYSISTRATA: Hold on to the door.

CALONICE: And if they beat us?

LYSISTRATA: Give in with a bad grace. There's no pleasure in it for them when they have to use violence. And you must torment them in every possible way. They'll give up soon enough; a man gets no joy if he doesn't get along with his wife.

MYRRHINE: If this is your opinion, we agree.

LAMPITO: As for our own men, we can persuade them to make a just and fair peace; but what about the Athenian rabble? Who will persuade them not to start any more monkey-shines?

LYSISTRATA: Don't worry. We guarantee to convince them.

LAMPITO: Not while their ships are rigged so well and they have that mighty treasure in the temple of Athene.

LYSISTRATA: We've taken good care for that too: we shall seize the Acropolis today. The older women have orders to do this, and while we are making our arrangements, they are to pretend to make a sacrifice and occupy the Acropolis.

LAMPITO: All will be well then. That's a very fine idea.

LYSISTRATA: Let's ratify this, Lampito, with the most solemn oath.

LAMPITO: Tell us what oath we shall swear.

LYSISTRATA: Well said. Where's our Policewoman? (*to a Scythian slave*) What are you gaping at? Set a shield upside-down here in front of me, and give me the sacred meats.

CALONICE: Lysistrata, what sort of an oath are we to take?

LYSISTRATA: What oath? I'm going to slaughter a sheep over the shield, as they do in Aeschylus.

CALONICE: Don't, Lysistrata! No oaths about peace over a shield.

LYSISTRATA: What shall the oath be, then?

CALONICE: How about getting a white horse somewhere and cutting out its entrails for the sacrifice?

LYSISTRATA: White horse indeed!

CALONICE: Well then, how shall we swear?

MYRRHINE: I'll tell you: let's place a large black bowl upside-down and then slaughter—a flask of Thasian wine. And then let's swear—not to pour in a single drop of water.

LAMPITO: Lord! How I like that oath!

LYSISTRATA: Someone bring out a bowl and a flask.

(*A slave brings the utensils for the sacrifice.*)

CALONICE: Look, my friends! What a big jar! Here's a cup that 'twould give me joy to handle. (*She picks up the bowl.*)

LYSISTRATA: Set it down and put your hands on our victim. (*as* CALONICE *places her hands on the flask*) O Lady of Persuasion and dear Loving Cup, graciously vouchsafe to receive this sacrifice from us women. (*She pours the wine into the bowl.*)

CALONICE: The blood has a good colour and spurts out nicely.

LAMPITO: Faith, it has a pleasant smell, too.

MYRRHINE: Oh, let me be the first to swear, ladies!

CALONICE: No, by our Lady! Not unless you're allotted the first turn.

LYSISTRATA: Place all your hands on the cup, and one of you repeat on behalf of all what I say. Then all will swear and ratify the.oath. *I will suffer no man, be he husband or lover,*

CALONICE: *I will suffer no man, be he husband or lover,*

LYSISTRATA: *To approach me all hot and horny.* (*as* CALONICE *hesitates*) Say it!

CALONICE (*slowly and painfully*): *To approach me all hot and horny.* O Lysistrata, I feel so weak in the knees!

LYSISTRATA: *I will remain at home unmated,*

CALONICE: *I will remain at home unmated,*

LYSISTRATA: *Wearing my sheerest gown and carefully adorned,*

CALONICE: *Wearing my sheerest gown and carefully adorned,*

LYSISTRATA: *That my husband may burn with desire for me.*

CALONICE: *That my husband may burn with desire for me.*

LYSISTRATA: *And if he takes me by force against my will,*

CALONICE: *And if he takes me by force against my will,*

LYSISTRATA: *I shall do it badly and keep from moving.*

CALONICE: *I shall do it badly and keep from moving.*

LYSISTRATA: *I will not stretch my slippers toward the ceiling,*

CALONICE: *I will not stretch my slippers toward the ceiling,*

LYSISTRATA: *Nor will I take the posture of the lioness on the knife-handle.*

CALONICE: *Nor will I take the posture of the lioness on the knife-handle.*

LYSISTRATA: *If I keep this oath, may I be permitted to drink from this cup,*

CALONICE: *If I keep this oath, may I be permitted to drink from this cup,*

LYSISTRATA: *But if I break it, may the cup be filled with water.*

CALONICE: *But if I break it, may the cup be filled with water.*

LYSISTRATA: Do you all swear to this?

ALL: I do, so help me!

LYSISTRATA: Come then, I'll just consummate this offering.

(*She takes a long drink from the cup.*)

CALONICE (*snatching the cup away*): Shares, my dear! Let's drink to our continued friendship.

(A shout is heard from off-stage.)

LAMPITO: What's that shouting?

LYSISTRATA: That's what I was telling you: the women have just seized the Acropolis. Now, Lampito, go home and arrange matters in Sparta; and leave these two ladies here as hostages. We'll enter the Acropolis to join our friends and help them lock the gates.

CALONICE: Don't you suppose the men will come to attack us?

LYSISTRATA: Don't worry about them. Neither threats nor fire will suffice to open the gates, except on the terms we've stated.

CALONICE: I should say not! Else we'd belie our reputation as unmanageable pests.

(LAMPITO leaves the stage. The other women retire and enter the Acropolis through the Propylaea.)

(Enter the CHORUS OF OLD MEN, carrying fire-pots and a load of heavy sticks.)

LEADER OF MEN: Onward, Draces, step by step, though your shoulder's aching.

Cursèd logs of olive-wood, what a load you're making!

FIRST SEMI-CHORUS OF OLD MEN *(singing)*:

Aye, many surprises await a man who lives to a ripe old age;

For who could suppose, Strymodorus my lad, that the women we've nourished (alas!),

    Who sat at home to vex our days,

    Would seize the holy image here,

    And occupy this sacred shrine,

    With bolts and bars, with fell design,

    To lock the Propylaea?

LEADER OF MEN: Come with speed, Philourgus, come! to the temple hast'ning.

There we'll heap these logs about in a circle round them,

And whoever has conspired, raising this rebellion,

Shall be roasted, scorched, and burnt, all without exception,

Doomed by one unanimous vote—but first the wife of Lycon.

SECOND SEMI-CHORUS *(singing)*:

No, no! by Demeter, while I'm alive, no woman shall mock at me.

Not even the Spartan Cleomenes, our citadel first to seize,
>   Got off unscathed; for all his pride
>   And haughty Spartan arrogance,
>   He left his arms and sneaked away,
>   Stripped to his shirt, unkempt, unshav'd,
>   With six years' filth still on him.
LEADER OF MEN: I besieged that hero bold, sleeping at my
>   station,
Marshalled at these holy gates sixteen deep against him.
Shall I not these cursèd pests punish for their daring,
Burning these Euripides-and-God-detested women?
Aye! or else may Marathon overturn my trophy.
>   FIRST SEMI-CHORUS (*singing*):
>   There remains of my road
>   Just this brow of the hill;
>   There I speed on my way.
Drag the logs up the hill, though we've got no ass to help.
>   (God! my shoulder's bruised and sore!)
>   Onward still must we go.
>   Blow the fire! Don't let it go out
>   Now we're near the end of our road.
>   ALL (*blowing on the fire-pots*):
Whew! Whew! Drat the smoke!
>   SECOND SEMI-CHORUS (*singing*):
>   Lord, what smoke rushing forth
>   From the pot, like a dog
>   Running mad, bites my eyes!
This must be Lemnos-fire. What a sharp and stinging smoke!
>   Rushing onward to the shrine
>   Aid the gods. Once for all
>   Show your mettle, Laches my boy!
>   To the rescue hastening all!
>   ALL (*blowing on the fire-pots*): Whew! Whew! Drat the smoke!

(*The chorus has now reached the edge of the Orchestra nearest the stage, in front of the Propylaea. They begin laying their logs and fire-pots on the ground.*)

LEADER OF MEN: Thank heaven, this fire is still alive. Now let's first put down these logs here and place our torches in the pots to catch; then let's make a rush for the gates with a battering-ram. If the women don't unbar the gate at our summons, we'll have to smoke them out.

Let me put down my load. Ouch! That hurts! (*to the audience*) Would any of the generals in Samos like to lend a hand with this log? (*throwing down a log*) Well, *that* won't break my back any more, at any rate. (*turning to his fire-pot*) Your job, my little pot, is to keep those coals alive and furnish me shortly with a red-hot torch.

O mistress Victory, be my ally and grant me to rout these audacious women in the Acropolis.

(*While the men are busy with their logs and fires, the* CHORUS OF OLD WOMEN *enters, carrying pitchers of water.*)

LEADER OF WOMEN: What's this I see? Smoke and flames? Is that a fire ablazing?
Let's rush upon them. Hurry up! They'll find us women ready.
FIRST SEMI-CHORUS OF OLD WOMEN (*singing*):
    With wingèd foot onward I fly,
    Ere the flames consume Neodice;
    Lest Critylla be overwhelmed
  By a lawless, accurst herd of old men.
  I shudder with fear. Am I too late to aid them?
  At break of the day filled we our jars with water
Fresh from the spring, pushing our way straight through the crowds. Oh, what a din!
    Mid crockery crashing, jostled by slave-girls,
    Sped we to save them, aiding our neighbours,
    Bearing this water to put out the flames.
SECOND SEMI-CHORUS OF OLD WOMEN (*singing*):
    Such news I've heard: doddering fools
    Come with logs, like furnace-attendants,
    Loaded down with three hundred pounds,
  Breathing many a vain, blustering threat,
  That all these abhorred sluts will be burnt to charcoal.
  O goddess, I pray never may they be kindled;
Grant them to save Greece and our men; madness and war help them to end.
    With this as our purpose, golden-plumed Maiden,

Guardian of Athens, seized we thy precinct.
Be my ally, Warrior-maiden,
'Gainst these old men, bearing water with me.

(*The women have now reached their position in the Orchestra,
and their* LEADER *advances toward the* LEADER OF THE MEN.)

LEADER OF WOMEN: Hold on there! What's this, you utter
scoundrels? No decent, God-fearing citizens would act like this.

LEADER OF MEN: Oho! Here's something unexpected: a swarm
of women have come out to attack us.

LEADER OF WOMEN: What, do we frighten you? Surely you don't
think we're too many for you. And yet there are ten thousand
times more of us whom you haven't even seen.

LEADER OF MEN: What say, Phaedria? Shall we let these women
wag their tongues? Shan't we take our sticks and break them over
their backs?

LEADER OF WOMEN: Let's set our pitchers on the ground; then if
anyone lays a hand on us, they won't get in our way.

LEADER OF MEN: By God! If someone gave them two or three
smacks on the jaw, like Bupalus, they wouldn't talk so much!

LEADER OF WOMEN: Go on, hit me, somebody! Here's my jaw!
But no other bitch will bite a piece out of you before me.

LEADER OF MEN: Silence! or I'll knock out your—senility!

LEADER OF WOMEN: Just lay one finger on Stratyllis, I dare you!

LEADER OF MEN: Suppose I dust you off with this fist? What
will you do?

LEADER OF WOMEN: I'll tear the living guts out of you with my
teeth.

LEADER OF MEN: No poet is more clever than Euripides: "There
is no beast so shameless as a woman."

LEADER OF WOMEN: Let's pick up our jars of water, Rhodippe.

LEADER OF MEN: Why have you come here with water, you
detestable slut?

LEADER OF WOMEN: And why have you come with fire, you
funeral vault? To cremate yourself?

LEADER OF MEN: To light a fire and singe your friends.

LEADER OF WOMEN: And I've brought water to put out your fire.

LEADER OF MEN: What? You'll put out my fire?

LEADER OF WOMEN: Just try and see!

LEADER OF MEN: I wonder: shall I scorch you with this torch of mine?

LEADER OF WOMEN: If you've got any soap, I'll give you a bath.

LEADER OF MEN: Give *me* a bath, you stinking hag?

LEADER OF WOMEN: Yes—a bridal bath!

LEADER OF MEN: Just listen to her! What crust!

LEADER OF WOMEN: Well, I'm a free citizen.

LEADER OF MEN: I'll put an end to your bawling. (*The men pick up their torches.*)

LEADER OF WOMEN: You'll never do jury-duty again. (*The women pick up their pitchers.*)

LEADER OF MEN: Singe her hair for her!

LEADER OF WOMEN: Do your duty, water! (*The women empty their pitchers on the men.*)

LEADER OF MEN: Ow! Ow! For heaven's sake!

LEADER OF WOMEN: Is it too hot?

LEADER OF MEN: What do you mean "hot"? Stop! What are you doing?

LEADER OF WOMEN: I'm watering you, so you'll be fresh and green.

LEADER OF MEN: But I'm all withered up with shaking.

LEADER OF WOMEN: Well, you've got a fire; why don't you dry yourself?

(*Enter an Athenian* MAGISTRATE, *accompanied by four Scythian policemen.*)

MAGISTRATE: Have these wanton women flared up again with their timbrels and their continual worship of Sabazius? Is this another Adonis-dirge upon the roof-tops—which we heard not long ago in the Assembly? That confounded Demostratus was urging us to sail to Sicily, and the whirling women shouted, "Woe for Adonis!" And then Demostratus said we'd best enroll the infantry from Zacynthus, and a tipsy woman on the roof shrieked, "Beat your breasts for Adonis!" And that vile and filthy lunatic forced his measure through. Such license do our women take.

LEADER OF MEN: What if you heard of the insolence of these women here? Besides their other violent acts, they threw water all over us, and we have to shake out our clothes just as if we'd leaked in them.

MAGISTRATE: And rightly, too, by God! For we ourselves lead the women astray and teach them to play the wanton; from these roots such notions blossom forth. A man goes into the jeweler's shop and says, "About that necklace you made for my wife, gold-smith: last night, while she was dancing, the fastening-bolt slipped out of the hole. I have to sail over to Salamis today; if you're free, do come around tonight and fit in a new bolt for her." Another goes to the shoe-maker, a strapping young fellow with manly parts, and says, "See here, cobbler, the sandal-strap chafes my wife's little—toe; it's so tender. Come around during the siesta and stretch it a little, so she'll be more comfortable." Now we see the results of such treatment: here I'm a special Councillor and need money to procure oars for the galleys; and I'm locked out of the Treasury by these women.

But this is no time to stand around. Bring up crow-bars there! I'll put an end to their insolence. (to one of the policemen) What are you gaping at, you wretch? What are you staring at? Got an eye out for a tavern, eh? Set your crow-bars here to the gates and force them open. (retiring to a safe distance) I'll help from over here.

(The gates are thrown open and LYSISTRATA comes out followed by several other women.)

LYSISTRATA: Don't force the gates; I'm coming out of my own accord. We don't need crow-bars here; what we need is good sound common-sense.

MAGISTRATE: Is that so, you strumpet? Where's my policeman? Officer, arrest her and tie her arms behind her back.

LYSISTRATA: By Artemis, if he lays a finger on me, he'll pay for it, even if he is a public servant.

(The policeman retires in terror.)

MAGISTRATE: You there, are you afraid? Seize her round the waist—and you, too. Tie her up, both of you!

FIRST WOMAN (as the second policeman approaches LYSIS-TRATA): By Pandrosus, if you but touch her with your hand, I'll kick the stuffings out of you.

(*The second policeman retires in terror.*)

MAGISTRATE: Just listen to that: "kick the stuffings out." Where's another policeman? Tie *her* up first, for her chatter.

SECOND WOMAN: By the Goddess of the Light, if you lay the tip of your finger on her, you'll soon need a doctor.

(*The third policeman retires in terror.*)

MAGISTRATE: What's this? Where's my policeman? Seize *her* too. I'll soon stop your sallies.

THIRD WOMAN: By the Goddess of Tauros, if you go near her, I'll tear out your hair until it shrieks with pain.

(*The fourth policeman retires in terror.*)

MAGISTRATE: Oh, damn it all! I've run out of policemen. But women must never defeat us. Officers, let's charge them all together. Close up your ranks!

(*The policemen rally for a mass attack.*)

LYSISTRATA: By heaven, you'll soon find out that we have four companies of warrior-women, all fully equipped within!

MAGISTRATE (*advancing*): Twist their arms off, men!

LYSISTRATA (*shouting*): To the rescue, my valiant women!
O sellers-of-barley-green-stuffs-and-eggs,
O sellers-of-garlic, ye keepers-of-taverns, and vendors-of-bread,
    Grapple! Smite! Smash!
Won't you heap filth on them? Give them a tongue-lashing!

(*The women beat off the policemen.*)

Halt! Withdraw! No looting on the field.

MAGISTRATE: Damn it! My police-force has put up a very poor show.

LYSISTRATA: What did you expect? Did you think you were attacking slaves? Didn't you know that women are filled with passion?

MAGISTRATE: Aye, passion enough—for a good strong drink!

LEADER OF MEN: O chief and leader of this land, why spend
    your words in vain?

Don't argue with these shameless beasts. You know not how we've
    fared:
A soapless bath they've given us; our clothes are soundly soaked.
   LEADER OF WOMEN: Poor fool! You never should attack or strike
    a peaceful girl.
But if you do, your eyes must swell. For I am quite content
To sit unmoved, like modest maids, in peace and cause no pain;
But let a man stir up my hive, he'll find me like a wasp.

   CHORUS OF MEN (*singing*):
O God, whatever shall we do with creatures like Womankind?
This can't be endured by any man alive. Question them!
    Let us try to find out what this means.
    To what end have they seized on this shrine,
      This steep and rugged, high and holy,
        Undefiled Acropolis?
   LEADER OF MEN: Come, put your questions; don't give in, and
    probe her every statement.
For base and shameful it would be to leave this plot untested.

   MAGISTRATE: Well then, first of all I wish to ask her this: for
what purpose have you barred us from the Acropolis?
   LYSISTRATA: To keep the treasure safe, so you won't make war
on account of it.
   MAGISTRATE: What? Do we make war on account of the
treasure?
   LYSISTRATA: Yes, and you cause all our other troubles for it, too.
Peisander and those greedy office-seekers keep things stirred up so
they can find occasions to steal. Now let them do what they like:
they'll never again make off with any of this money.
   MAGISTRATE: What will you do?
   LYSISTRATA: What a question! We'll administer it ourselves.
   MAGISTRATE: *You* will administer the treasure?
   LYSISTRATA: What's so strange in that? Don't we administer the
household money for you?
   MAGISTRATE: That's different.
   LYSISTRATA: How is it different?
   MAGISTRATE: We've got to make war with this money.
   LYSISTRATA: But that's the very first thing: you mustn't make
war.

MAGISTRATE: How else can we be saved?

LYSISTRATA: We'll save you.

MAGISTRATE: *You?*

LYSISTRATA: Yes, we!

MAGISTRATE: God forbid!

LYSISTRATA: We'll save you, whether you want it or not.

MAGISTRATE: Oh! This is terrible!

LYSISTRATA: You don't like it, but we're going to do it none the less.

MAGISTRATE: Good God! it's illegal!

LYSISTRATA: We *will* save you, my little man!

MAGISTRATE: Suppose I don't want you to?

LYSISTRATA: That's all the more reason.

MAGISTRATE: What business have you with war and peace?

LYSISTRATA: I'll explain.

MAGISTRATE: (*shaking his fist*): Speak up, or you'll smart for it.

LYSISTRATA: Just listen, and try to keep your hands still.

MAGISTRATE: I can't. I'm so mad I can't stop them.

FIRST WOMAN: Then you'll be the one to smart for it.

MAGISTRATE: Croak to yourself, old hag! (*to* LYSISTRATA) Now then, speak up.

LYSISTRATA: Very well. Formerly we endured the war for a good long time with our usual restraint, no matter what you men did. You wouldn't let us say "boo," although nothing you did suited us. But we watched you well, and though we stayed at home we'd often hear of some terribly stupid measure you'd proposed. Then, though grieving at heart, we'd smile sweetly and say, "What was passed in the Assembly today about writing on the treaty-stone?" "What's that to you?" my husband would say. "Hold your tongue!" And I held my tongue.

FIRST WOMAN: But I wouldn't have—not I!

MAGISTRATE: You'd have been soundly smacked, if you hadn't kept still.

LYSISTRATA: So I kept still at home. Then we'd hear of some plan still worse than the first; we'd say, "Husband, how could you pass such a stupid proposal?" He'd scowl at me and say, "If you don't mind your spinning, your head will be sore for weeks. *War shall be the concern of Men.*"

MAGISTRATE: And he was right, upon my word!

LYSISTRATA: Why right, you confounded fool, when your proposals were so stupid and we weren't allowed to make suggestions?

"There's not a *man* left in the country," says one. "No, not one," says another. Therefore all we women have decided in council to make a common effort to save Greece. How long should we have waited? Now, if you're willing to listen to our excellent proposals and keep silence for us in your turn, we still may save you.

MAGISTRATE: We men keep silence for you? That's terrible; I won't endure it!

LYSISTRATA: Silence!

MAGISTRATE: Silence for *you,* you wench, when you're wearing a snood? I'd rather die!

LYSISTRATA: Well, if that's all that bothers you—here! take my snood and tie it round your head. (*During the following words the women dress up the* MAGISTRATE *in women's garments.*) And *now* keep quiet! Here, take this spinning-basket, too, and card your wool with robes tucked up, munching on beans. *War shall be the concern of Women!*

LEADER OF WOMEN: Arise and leave your pitchers, girls; no time
          is this to falter.
We too must aid our loyal friends; our turn has come for action.
    CHORUS OF WOMEN (*singing*):
I'll never tire of aiding them with song and dance; never may
Faintness keep my legs from moving to and fro endlessly.
      For I yearn to do all for my friends;
      They have charm, they have wit, they have grace,
        With courage, brains, and best of virtues—
          Patriotic sapience.
    LEADER OF WOMEN: Come, child of manliest ancient dames,
          offspring of stinging nettles,
Advance with rage unsoftened; for fair breezes speed you onward

LYSISTRATA: If only sweet Eros and the Cyprian Queen of Love shed charm over our breasts and limbs and inspire our men with amorous longing and priapic spasms, I think we may soon be called Peacemakers among the Greeks.

MAGISTRATE: What will you do?

LYSISTRATA: First of all, we'll stop those fellows who run madly about the Marketplace in arms.

FIRST WOMAN: Indeed we shall, by the Queen of Paphos.

LYSISTRATA: For now they roam about the market, amid the pots and greenstuffs, armed to the teeth like Corybantes.

MAGISTRATE: That's what manly fellows ought to do!

LYSISTRATA: But it's so silly: a chap with a Gorgon-emblazoned shield buying pickled herring.

FIRST WOMAN: Why, just the other day I saw one of those long-haired dandies who command our cavalry ride up on horseback and pour into his bronze helmet the egg-broth he'd bought from an old dame. And there was a Thracian slinger too, shaking his lance like Tereus; he'd scared the life out of the poor fig-peddler and was gulping down all her ripest fruit.

MAGISTRATE: How can you stop all the confusion in the various states and bring them together?

LYSISTRATA: Very easily.

MAGISTRATE: Tell me how.

LYSISTRATA: Just like a ball of wool, when it's confused and snarled: we take it thus, and draw out a thread here and a thread there with our spindles; thus we'll unsnarl this war, if no one prevents us, and draw together the various states with embassies here and embassies there.

MAGISTRATE: Do you suppose you can stop this dreadful business with balls of wool and spindles, you nit-wits?

LYSISTRATA: Why, if *you* had any wits, you'd manage all affairs of state like our wool-working.

MAGISTRATE: How so?

LYSISTRATA: First you ought to treat the city as we do when we wash the dirt out of a fleece: stretch it out and pluck and thrash out of the city all those prickly scoundrels; aye, and card out those who conspire and stick together to gain office, pulling off their heads. Then card the wool, all of it, into one fair basket of good-will, mingling in the aliens residing here, any loyal foreigners, and anyone who's in debt to the Treasury; and consider that all our colonies lie scattered round about like remnants; from all of these collect the wool and gather it together here, wind up a great ball, and then weave a good stout cloak for the democracy.

MAGISTRATE: Dreadful! Talking about thrashing and winding balls of wool, when you haven't the slightest share in the war!

LYSISTRATA: Why, you dirty scoundrel, we bear more than twice as much as you. First, we bear children and send off our sons as soldiers.

MAGISTRATE: Hush! Let bygones be bygones!

LYSISTRATA: Then, when we ought to be happy and enjoy our youth, we sleep alone because of your expeditions abroad. But never mind us married women: I grieve most for the maids who grow old at home unwed.

MAGISTRATE: Don't men grow old, too?

LYSISTRATA: For heaven's sake! That's not the same thing. When a man comes home, no matter how grey he is, he soon finds a girl to marry. But woman's bloom is short and fleeting; if she doesn't grasp her chance, no man is willing to marry her and she sits at home a prey to every fortune-teller.

MAGISTRATE (coarsely): But if a man can still get it up—

LYSISTRATA: See here, you: what's the matter? Aren't you dead yet? There's plenty of room for you. Buy yourself a shroud and I'll bake you a honey-cake. (handing him a copper coin for his passage across the Styx) Here's your fare! Now get yourself a wreath.

(During the following dialogue the women dress up the MAGISTRATE as a corpse.)

FIRST WOMAN: Here, take these fillets.

SECOND WOMAN: Here, take this wreath.

LYSISTRATA: What do you want? What's lacking? Get moving; off to the ferry! Charon is calling you; don't keep him from sailing.

MAGISTRATE: Am I to endure these insults? By God! I'm going straight to the magistrates to show them how I've been treated.

LYSISTRATA: Are you grumbling that you haven't been properly laid out? Well, the day after tomorrow we'll send around all the usual offerings early in the morning.

(The MAGISTRATE goes out still wearing his funeral decorations. LYSISTRATA and the women retire into the Acropolis.)

LEADER OF MEN: Wake, ye sons of freedom, wake! 'Tis no time for sleeping. Up and at them, like a man! Let us strip for action.

(*The* CHORUS OF MEN *remove their outer cloaks.*)

CHORUS OF MEN (*singing*):
Surely there is something here greater than meets the eye;
For without a doubt I smell Hippias' tyranny.
Dreadful fear assails me lest certain bands of Spartan men,
Meeting here with Cleisthenes, have inspired through treachery
All these god-detested women secretly to seize
Athens' treasure in the temple, and to stop that pay
        Whence I live at my ease.

LEADER OF MEN: Now isn't it terrible for them to advise the state and chatter about shields, being mere women?

And they think to reconcile us with the Spartans—men who hold nothing sacred any more than hungry wolves. Surely this is a web of deceit, my friends, to conceal an attempt at tyranny. But they'll never lord it over me; I'll be on my guard and from now on,
        "The blade I bear   A myrtle spray shall wear."
I'll occupy the market under arms and stand next to Aristogeiton.

Thus I'll stand beside him. (*He strikes the pose of the famous statue of the tyrannicides, with one arm raised.*) And here's my chance to take this accurst old hag and—(*striking the* LEADER OF WOMEN) smack her on the jaw!

LEADER OF WOMEN: You'll go home in such a state your Ma
        won't recognize you!
Ladies all, upon the ground let us place these garments.

(*The* CHORUS OF WOMEN *remove their outer garments.*)

CHORUS OF WOMEN (*singing*):
Citizens of Athens, hear useful words for the state.
Rightly; for it nurtured me in my youth royally.
As a child of seven years carried I the sacred box;
Then I was a Miller-maid, grinding at Athene's shrine;
Next I wore the saffron robe and played Brauronia's Bear;
And I walked as Basket-bearer, wearing chains of figs,
        As a sweet maiden fair.

LEADER OF WOMEN: Therefore, am I not bound to give good advice to the city?
Don't take it ill that I was born a woman, if I contribute some-

thing better than our present troubles. I pay my share; for I contribute MEN. But you miserable old fools contribute nothing, and after squandering our ancestral treasure, the fruit of the Persian Wars, you make no contribution in return. And now, all on account of you, we're facing ruin.

What, muttering, are you? If you annoy me, I'll take this hard, rough slipper and— (*striking the* LEADER OF MEN) smack you on the jaw!

CHORUS OF MEN (*singing*):
This is outright insolence! Things go from bad to worse.
If you're men with any guts, prepare to meet the foe.
Let us strip our tunics off! We need the smell of male
Vigour. And we cannot fight all swaddled up in clothes.

(*They strip off their tunics.*)

Come then, my comrades, on to the battle, ye who once to
          Leipsydrion came;
Then ye were MEN. Now call back your youthful vigour.
          With light, wingèd footstep advance,
     Shaking old age from your frame.
LEADER OF MEN: If any of us give these wenches the slightest hold, they'll stop at nothing: such is their cunning.

They will even build ships and sail against us, like Artemisia. Or if they turn to mounting, I count our Knights as done for: a woman's such a tricky jockey when she gets astraddle, with a good firm seat for trotting. Just look at those Amazons that Micon painted, fighting on horseback against men!

But we must throw them all in the pillory— (*seizing and choking the* LEADER OF WOMEN) grabbing hold of yonder neck!

CHORUS OF WOMEN (*singing*):
'Ware my anger! Like a boar 'twill rush upon you men.
Soon you'll bawl aloud for help, you'll be so soundly trimmed!
Come, my friends, let's strip with speed, and lay aside these
          robes;
Catch the scent of women's rage. Attack with tooth and nail!

(*They strip off their tunics.*)

Now then, come near me, you miserable man! you'll never eat
    garlic or black beans again.
And if you utter a single hard word, in rage I will "nurse" you
    as once
      The beetle requited her foe.

LEADER OF WOMEN: For you don't worry me; no, not so long as
my Lampito lives and our Theban friend, the noble Ismenia.

You can't do anything, not even if you pass a dozen—decrees!
You miserable fool, all our neighbours hate you. Why, just the
other day when I was holding a festival for Hecate, I invited as
playmate from our neighbours the Boeotians a charming, well-
bred Copaic—eel. But they refused to send me one on account of
your decrees.

And you'll never stop passing decrees until I grab your foot
and— (tripping up the LEADER OF MEN) toss you down and break
your neck!

(Here an interval of five days is supposed to elapse. LYSISTRATA
comes out from the Acropolis.)

LEADER OF WOMEN (dramatically): Empress of this great
    emprise and undertaking,
Why come you forth, I pray, with frowning brow?

LYSISTRATA: Ah, these cursèd women! Their deeds and female
notions make me pace up and down in utter despair.

LEADER OF WOMEN: Ah, what sayest thou?

LYSISTRATA: The truth, alas! the truth.

LEADER OF WOMEN: What dreadful tale hast thou to tell thy
friends?

LYSISTRATA: 'Tis shame to speak, and not to speak is hard.

LEADER OF WOMEN: Hide not from me whatever woes we
suffer.

LYSISTRATA: Well then, to put it briefly, we want—laying!

LEADER OF WOMEN: O Zeus, Zeus!

LYSISTRATA: Why call on Zeus? That's the way things are. I can
no longer keep them away from the men, and they're all deserting.
I caught one wriggling through a hole near the grotto of Pan,
another sliding down a rope, another deserting her post; and yesterday I found one getting on a sparrow's back to fly off to Orsi-
lochus, and had to pull her back by the hair. They're digging up

all sorts of excuses to get home. Look, here comes one of them now. (*A woman comes hastily out of the Acropolis.*) Here you! Where are you off to in such a hurry?

FIRST WOMAN: I want to go home. My very best wool is being devoured by moths.

LYSISTRATA: Moths? Nonsense! Go back inside.

FIRST WOMAN: I'll come right back; I swear it. I just want to lay it out on the bed.

LYSISTRATA: Well, you won't lay it out, and you won't go home, either.

FIRST WOMAN: Shall I let my wool be ruined?

LYSISTRATA: If necessary, yes. (*Another woman comes out.*)

SECOND WOMAN: Oh dear! Oh dear! My precious flax! I left it at home all unpeeled.

LYSISTRATA: Here's another one, going home for her "flax." Come back here!

SECOND WOMAN: But I just want to work it up a little and then I'll be right back.

LYSISTRATA: No indeed! If you start this, all the other women will want to do the same. (*A third woman comes out.*)

THIRD WOMAN: O Eilithyia, goddess of travail, stop my labour till I come to a lawful spot!

LYSISTRATA: What's this nonsense?

THIRD WOMAN: I'm going to have a baby—right now!

LYSISTRATA: But you weren't even pregnant yesterday.

THIRD WOMAN: Well, I am today. O Lysistrata, do send me home to see a midwife, right away.

LYSISTRATA: What are you talking about? (*putting her hand on her stomach*) What's this hard lump here?

THIRD WOMAN: A little boy.

LYSISTRATA: My goodness, what have you got there? It seems hollow; I'll just find out. (*pulling aside her robe*) Why, you silly goose, you've got Athene's sacred helmet there. And you said you were having a baby!

THIRD WOMAN: Well, I *am* having one, I swear!

LYSISTRATA: Then what's this helmet for?

THIRD WOMAN: If the baby starts coming while I'm still in the Acropolis, I'll creep into this like a pigeon and give birth to it there.

LYSISTRATA: Stuff and nonsense! It's plain enough what you're up to. You just wait here for the christening of this—helmet.

THIRD WOMAN: But I can't sleep in the Acropolis since I saw the sacred snake.

FIRST WOMAN: And I'm dying for lack of sleep: the hooting of the owls keeps me awake.

LYSISTRATA: Enough of these shams, you wretched creatures. You want your husbands, I suppose. Well, don't you think they want us? I'm sure they're spending miserable nights. Hold out, my friends, and endure for just a little while. There's an oracle that we shall conquer, if we don't split up. (*producing a roll of paper*) Here it is.

FIRST WOMAN: Tell us what it says.

LYSISTRATA: Listen.

"When in the length of time the Swallows shall gather together,
Fleeing the Hoopoe's amorous flight and the Cockatoo shunning,
Then shall your woes be ended and Zeus who thunders in heaven
Set what's below on top—"

FIRST WOMAN: What? Are we going to be on top?

LYSISTRATA: "But if the Swallows rebel and flutter away from
        the temple,
Never a bird in the world shall seem more wanton and worth-
        less."

FIRST WOMAN: That's clear enough, upon my word!

LYSISTRATA: By all that's holy, let's not give up the struggle now. Let's go back inside. It would be a shame, my dear friends, to disobey the oracle.

(*The women all retire to the Acropolis again.*)

CHORUS OF MEN (*singing*):
        I have a tale to tell,
        Which I know full well.
            It was told me
            In the nursery.

        Once there was a likely lad,
            Melanion they name him;
        The thought of marriage made him mad,
            For which I cannot blame him.

So off he went to mountains fair;
   (No women to upbraid him!)
A mighty hunter of the hare,
   He had a dog to aid him.

He never came back home to see
   Detested women's faces.
He showed a shrewd mentality.
   With him I'd fain change places!

ONE OF THE MEN (*to one of the women*): Come here, old dame;
give me a kiss.
   WOMAN: You'll ne'er eat garlic, if you dare!
   MAN: I want to kick you—just like this!
   WOMAN: Oh, there's a leg with bushy hair!
   MAN: Myronides and Phormio
Were hairy—and they thrashed the foe.

CHORUS OF WOMEN (*singing*):
   I have another tale,
   With which to assail
      Your contention
      'Bout Melanion.

Once upon a time a man
   Named Timon left our city,
To live in some deserted land.
   (We thought him rather witty.)

He dwelt alone amidst the thorn;
   In solitude he brooded.
From some grim Fury he was born:
   Such hatred he exuded.

He cursed you men, as scoundrels through
   And through, till life he ended.
He couldn't stand the sight of you!
   But women he befriended.

WOMAN (*to one of the men*): I'll smash your face in, if you like.
   MAN: Oh no, please don't! You frighten me.

WOMAN: I'll lift my foot—and thus I'll strike.
MAN: Aha! Look there! What's that I see?
WOMAN: Whate'er you see, you cannot say
That I'm not neatly trimmed today.

(LYSISTRATA *appears on the wall of the Acropolis.*)

LYSISTRATA: Hello! Hello! Girls, come here quick!

(*Several women appear beside her.*)

WOMAN: What is it? Why are you calling?
LYSISTRATA: I see a man coming: he's in a dreadful state. He's mad with passion. O Queen of Cyprus, Cythera, and Paphos, just keep on this way!
WOMAN: Where is the fellow?
LYSISTRATA: There, beside the shrine of Demeter.
WOMAN: Oh yes, so he is. Who is he?
LYSISTRATA: Let's see. Do any of you know him?
MYRRHINE: Yes indeed. That's my husband, Cinesias.
LYSISTRATA: It's up to you, now: roast him, rack him, fool him, love him—and leave him! Do everything, except what our oath forbids.
MYRRHINE: Don't worry; I'll do it.
LYSISTRATA: I'll stay here to tease him and warm him up a bit. Off with you.

(*The other women retire from the wall. Enter* CINESIAS *followed by a slave carrying a baby.* CINESIAS *is obviously in great pain and distress.*)

CINESIAS (*groaning*): Oh-h! Oh-h-h! This is killing me! O God, what tortures I'm suffering!
LYSISTRATA (*from the wall*): Who's that within our lines?
CINESIAS: Me.
LYSISTRATA: A *man?*
CINESIAS (*pointing*): A *man,* indeed!
LYSISTRATA: Well, go away!
CINESIAS: Who are you to send me away?
LYSISTRATA: The captain of the guard.
CINESIAS: Oh, for heaven's sake, call out Myrrhine for me.
LYSISTRATA: Call Myrrhine? Nonsense! Who are you?
CINESIAS: Her husband, Cinesias of Paionidai.

LYSISTRATA (*appearing much impressed*): Oh, greetings, friend. Your name is not without honour here among us. Your wife is always talking about you, and whenever she takes an egg or an apple, she says, "Here's to my dear Cinesias!"

CINESIAS (*quivering with excitement*): Oh, ye gods in heaven!

LYSISTRATA: Indeed she does! And whenever our conversations turn to men, your wife immediately says, "All others are mere rubbish compared with Cinesias."

CINESIAS (*groaning*): Oh! Do call her for me.

LYSISTRATA: Why should I? What will you give me?

CINESIAS: Whatever you want. All I have is yours—and you see what I've got.

LYSISTRATA: Well then, I'll go down and call her. (*She descends.*)

CINESIAS: And hurry up! I've had no joy of life ever since she left home. When I go in the house, I feel awful: everything seems so empty and I can't enjoy my dinner. I'm in such a state all the time!

MYRRHINE (*from behind the wall*): I *do* love him so. But he won't let me love him. No, no! Don't ask me to see him!

CINESIAS: O my darling, O Myrrhine honey, why do you do this to me? (MYRRHINE *appears on the wall.*) Come down here!

MYRRHINE: No, I won't come down.

CINESIAS: Won't you come, Myrrhine, when *I* call you?

MYRRHINE: No; you don't want me.

CINESIAS: *Don't want you?* I'm in agony!

MYRRHINE: I'm going now.

CINESIAS: Please don't! At least, listen to your baby. (*to the baby*) Here you, call your mamma! (*pinching the baby*)

BABY: Ma-ma! Ma-ma! Ma-ma!

CINESIAS (*to* MYRRHINE): What's the matter with you? Have you no pity for your child, who hasn't been washed or fed for five whole days?

MYRRHINE: Oh, poor child; your father pays no attention to you.

CINESIAS: Come down then, you heartless wretch, for the baby's sake.

MYRRHINE: Oh, what it is to be a mother! I've got to come down, I suppose. (*She leaves the wall and shortly reappears at the gate.*)

CINESIAS (*to himself*): She seems much younger, and she has such a sweet look about her. Oh, the way she teases me! And her pretty, provoking ways make me burn with longing.

MYRRHINE (*coming out of the gate and taking the baby*): O my sweet little angel. Naughty papa! Here, let Mummy kiss you, Mamma's little sweetheart!   (*She fondles the baby lovingly.*)

CINESIAS (*in despair*): You heartless creature, why do you do this? Why follow these other women and make both of us suffer so? (*He tries to embrace her.*)

MYRRHINE: Don't touch me!

CINESIAS: You're letting all our things at home go to wrack and ruin.

MYRRHINE: I don't care.

CINESIAS: You don't care that your wool is being plucked to pieces by the chickens?

MYRRHINE: Not in the least.

CINESIAS: And you haven't celebrated the rites of Aphrodite for ever so long. Won't you come home?

MYRRHINE: Not on your life, unless you men make a truce and stop the war.

CINESIAS: Well then, if that pleases you, we'll do it.

MYRRHINE: Well then, if that pleases *you,* I'll come home— afterwards! Right now I'm on oath not to.

CINESIAS: Then just lie down here with me for a moment.

MYRRHINE: No— (*in a teasing voice*) and yet, I won't say I don't love you.

CINESIAS: You love me? Oh, do lie down here, Myrrhine dear!

MYRRHINE: What, you silly fool! in front of the baby?

CINESIAS (*hastily thrusting the baby at the slave*): Of course not. Here—home! Take him, Manes! (*The slave goes off with the baby.*) See, the baby's out of the way. Now won't you lie down?

MYRRHINE: But where, my dear?

CINESIAS: Where? The grotto of Pan's a lovely spot.

MYRRHINE: How could I purify myself before returning to the shrine?

CINESIAS: Easily: just wash here in the Clepsydra.

MYRRHINE: And then, shall I go back on my oath?

CINESIAS: On my head be it! Don't worry about the oath.

MYRRHINE: All right, then. Just let me bring out a bed.

CINESIAS: No, don't. The ground's all right.

MYRRHINE: Heavens, no! Bad as you are, I won't let you lie on the bare ground.   (*She goes into the Acropolis.*)

CINESIAS: Why, she really loves me; it's plain to see.

MYRRHINE (*returning with a bed*): There! Now hurry up and lie down. I'll just slip off this dress. But—let's see: oh yes, I must fetch a mattress.

CINESIAS: Nonsense! No mattress for me.

MYRRHINE: Yes indeed! It's not nice on the bare springs.

CINESIAS: Give me a kiss.

MYRRHINE (*giving him a hasty kiss*): There!   (*She goes.*)

CINESIAS (*in mingled distress and delight*): Oh-h! Hurry back!

MYRRHINE (*returning with a mattress*): Here's the mattress; lie down on it. I'm taking my things off now—but—let's see: you have no pillow.

CINESIAS: I don't *want* a pillow!

MYRRHINE: But I do.   (*She goes.*)

CINESIAS: Cheated again, just like Heracles and his dinner!

MYRRHINE (*returning with a pillow*): Here, lift your head. (*to herself, wondering how else to tease him*) Is that all?

CINESIAS: Surely that's all! Do come here, precious!

MYRRHINE: I'm taking off my girdle. But remember: don't go back on your promise about the truce.

CINESIAS: Hope to die, if I do.

MYRRHINE: You don't have a blanket.

CINESIAS (*shouting in exasperation*): *I don't want one! I* WANT TO—

MYRRHINE: Sh-h! There, there, I'll be back in a minute.   (*She goes.*)

CINESIAS: She'll be the death of me with these bed-clothes.

MYRRHINE (*returning with a blanket*): Here, get up.

CINESIAS: I've got *this* up!

MYRRHINE: Would you like some perfume?

CINESIAS: Good heavens, no! I won't have it!

MYRRHINE: Yes, you shall, whether you want it or not.   (*She goes.*)

CINESIAS: O lord! Confound all perfumes anyway!

MYRRHINE (*returning with a flask*): Stretch out your hand

and put some on.

CINESIAS (*suspiciously*): By God, I don't much like this perfume. It smacks of shilly-shallying, and has no scent of the marriage-bed.

MYRRHINE: Oh dear! This is Rhodian perfume I've brought.

CINESIAS: It's quite all right, dear. Never mind.

MYRRHINE: Don't be silly! (*She goes out with the flask.*)

CINESIAS: Damn the man who first concocted perfumes!

MYRRHINE (*returning with another flask*): Here, try this flask.

CINESIAS: I've got another one all ready for you. Come, you wretch, lie down and stop bringing me things.

MYRRHINE: All right; I'm taking off my shoes. But, my dear, see that you vote for peace.

CINESIAS (*absently*): I'll consider it. (MYRRHINE *runs away to the Acropolis.*) I'm ruined! The wench has skinned me and run away! (*chanting, in tragic style*) Alas! Alas! Deceived, deserted by this fairest of women, whom shall I—lay? Ah, my poor little child, how shall I nurture thee? Where's Cynalopex? I needs must hire a nurse!

LEADER OF MEN (*chanting*): Ah, wretched man, in dreadful wise beguiled, bewrayed, thy soul is sore distressed. I pity thee, alas! alas! What soul, what loins, what liver could stand this strain? How firm and unyielding he stands, with naught to aid him of a morning.

CINESIAS: O lord! O Zeus! What tortures I endure!

LEADER OF MEN: This is the way she's treated you, that vile and cursèd wanton.

LEADER OF WOMEN: Nay, not vile and cursèd, but sweet and dear.

LEADER OF MEN: Sweet, you say? Nay, hateful, hateful!

CINESIAS: Hateful indeed! O Zeus, Zeus!
Seize her and snatch her away,
Like a handful of dust, in a mighty,
Fiery tempest! Whirl her aloft, then let her drop
Down to the earth, with a crash, as she falls—
On the point of this waiting
   Thingummybob! (*He goes out.*)

(*Enter a Spartan* HERALD, *in an obvious state of excitement, which he is doing his best to conceal.*)

HERALD: Where can I find the Senate or the Prytanes? I've got an important message. (*The Athenian* MAGISTRATE *enters.*)

MAGISTRATE: Say there, are you a man or Priapus?

HERALD (*in annoyance*): I'm a herald, you lout! I've come from Sparta about the truce.

MAGISTRATE: Is that a spear you've got under your cloak?

HERALD: No, of course not!

MAGISTRATE: Why do you twist and turn so? Why hold your cloak in front of you? Did you rupture yourself on the trip?

HERALD: By gum, the fellow's an old fool.

MAGISTRATE (*pointing*): Why, you dirty rascal, you're all excited.

HERALD: Not at all. Stop this tom-foolery.

MAGISTRATE: Well, what's that I see?

HERALD: A Spartan message-staff.

MAGISTRATE: Oh, certainly! That's just the kind of message-staff I've got. But tell me the honest truth: how are things going in Sparta?

HERALD: All the land of Sparta is up in arms—and our allies are up, too. We need Pellene.

MAGISTRATE: What brought this trouble on you? A sudden Panic?

HERALD: No, Lampito started it and then all the other women in Sparta with one accord chased their husbands out of their beds.

MAGISTRATE: How do you feel?

HERALD: Terrible. We walk around the city bent over like men lighting matches in a wind. For our women won't let us touch them until we all agree and make peace throughout Greece.

MAGISTRATE: This is a general conspiracy of the women; I see it now. Well, hurry back and tell the Spartans to send ambassadors here with full powers to arrange a truce. And I'll go tell the Council to choose ambassadors from here; I've got a little something here that will soon persuade them!

HERALD: I'll fly there; for you've made an excellent suggestion.

(*The* HERALD *and the* MAGISTRATE *depart on opposite sides of the stage.*)

LEADER OF MEN: No beast or fire is harder than womankind to tame,
Nor is the spotted leopard so devoid of shame.

LEADER OF WOMEN: Knowing this, you dare provoke us to attack?
I'd be your steady friend, if you'd but take us back.
    LEADER OF MEN: I'll never cease my hatred keen of womankind.
    LEADER OF WOMEN: Just as you will. But now just let me
        help you find
That cloak you threw aside. You look so silly there
Without your clothes. Here, put it on and don't go bare.
    LEADER OF MEN: That's very kind, and shows you're not entirely
        bad.
But I threw off my things when I was good and mad.
    LEADER OF WOMEN: At last you seem a man, and won't be
        mocked, my lad.
If you'd been nice to me, I'd take this little gnat
That's in your eye and pluck it out for you, like that.
    LEADER OF MEN: So that's what's bothered me and bit my eye
        so long!
Please dig it out for me. I own that I've been wrong.
    LEADER OF WOMEN: I'll do so, though you've been a most ill-
        natured brat.
Ye gods! See here! A huge and monstrous little gnat!
    LEADER OF MEN: Oh, how that helps! For it was digging wells
        in me.
And now it's out, my tears can roll down hard and free.
    LEADER OF WOMEN: Here, let me wipe them off, although you're
        such a knave,
And kiss me.
    LEADER OF MEN: No!
    LEADER OF WOMEN: Whate'er you say, a kiss I'll have. (*She
kisses him.*)
    LEADER OF MEN: Oh, confound these women! They've a coaxing
        way about them.
He was wise and never spoke a truer word, who said,
"We can't live with women, but we cannot live without them."
Now I'll make a truce with you. We'll fight no more; instead,
    I will not injure you if you do me no wrong.
    And now let's join our ranks and then begin a song.
    COMBINED CHORUS (*singing*):
        Athenians, we're not prepared,
        To say a single ugly word

About our fellow-citizens.
Quite the contrary: we desire but to say and to do
Naught but good. Quite enough are the ills now on hand.

Men and women, be advised:
  If anyone requires
Money—minae two or three—
  We've got what he desires.

My purse is yours, on easy terms:
  When Peace shall reappear,
Whate'er you've borrowed will be due.
  So speak up without fear.

You needn't pay me back, you see,
If you can get a cent from me!

We're about to entertain
  Some foreign gentlemen;
We've soup and tender, fresh-killed pork.
  Come round to dine at ten.

Come early; wash and dress with care,
  And bring the children, too.
Then step right in, no "by your leave."
  We'll be expecting you.

Walk in as if you owned the place.
You'll find the door—shut in your face!

(*Enter a group of Spartan Ambassadors; they are in the same
desperate condition as the Herald in the previous scene.*)

LEADER OF CHORUS: Here come the envoys from Sparta, sprouting long beards and looking for all the world as if they were carrying pig-pens in front of them.
Greetings, gentlemen of Sparta. Tell me, in what state have you come?

SPARTAN: Why waste words? You can plainly see what state we've come in!

LEADER OF CHORUS: Wow! You're in a pretty high-strung condition, and it seems to be getting worse.

SPARTAN: It's indescribable. Won't someone please arrange a peace for us—in any way you like.

LEADER OF CHORUS: Here come our own, native ambassadors, crouching like wrestlers and holding their clothes in front of them; this seems an athletic kind of malady.

(*Enter several Athenian Ambassadors.*)

ATHENIAN: Can anyone tell us where Lysistrata is? You see our condition.

LEADER OF CHORUS: Here's another case of the same complaint. Tell me, are the attacks worse in the morning?

ATHENIAN: No, we're always afflicted this way. If someone doesn't soon arrange this truce, you'd better not let me get my hands on—Cleisthenes!

LEADER OF CHORUS: If you're smart, you'll arrange your cloaks so none of the fellows who smashed the Hermae can see you.

ATHENIAN: Right you are; a very good suggestion.

SPARTAN: Aye, by all means. Here, let's hitch up our clothes.

ATHENIAN: Greetings, Spartan. We've suffered dreadful things.

SPARTAN: My dear fellow, we'd have suffered still worse if one of those fellows had seen us in this condition.

ATHENIAN: Well, gentlemen, we must get down to business. What's your errand here?

SPARTAN: We're ambassadors about peace.

ATHENIAN: Excellent; so are we. Only Lysistrata can arrange things for us; shall we summon her?

SPARTAN: Aye, and Lysistratus too, if you like.

LEADER OF CHORUS: No need to summon her, it seems. She's coming out of her own accord.

(*Enter* LYSISTRATA *accompanied by a statue of a nude female figure, which represents Reconciliation.*)

Hail, noblest of women; now must thou be
A judge shrewd and subtle, mild and severe,
Be sweet yet majestic: all manners employ.
The leaders of Hellas, caught by thy love-charms,
Have come to thy judgment, their charges submitting.

LYSISTRATA: This is no difficult task, if one catch them still in amorous passion, before they've resorted to each other. But I'll soon find out. Where's Reconciliation? Go, first bring the Spartans here, and don't seize them rudely and violently, as our tactless husbands used to do, but as befits a woman, like an old, familiar friend; if they won't give you their hands, take them however you can. Then go fetch these Athenians here, taking hold of whatever they offer you. Now then, men of Sparta, stand here beside me, and you Athenians on the other side, and listen to my words.

I am a woman, it is true, but I have a mind; I'm not badly off in native wit, and by listening to my father and my elders, I've had a decent schooling.

Now I intend to give you a scolding which you both deserve. With one common font you worship at the same altars, just like brothers, at Olympia, at Thermopylae, at Delphi—how many more might I name, if time permitted;—and the Barbarians stand by waiting with their armies; yet you are destroying the men and towns of Greece.

ATHENIAN: Oh, this tension is killing me!

LYSISTRATA: And now, men of Sparta,—to turn to you—don't you remember how the Spartan Pericleidas came here once as a suppliant, and sitting at our altar, all pale with fear in his crimson cloak, begged us for an army? For all Messene had attacked you and the god sent an earthquake too? Then Cimon went forth with four thousand hoplites and saved all Lacedaemon. Such was the aid you received from Athens, and now you lay waste the country which once treated you so well.

ATHENIAN (hotly): They're in the wrong, Lysistrata, upon my word, they are!

SPARTAN (absently, looking at the statue of Reconcilation): We're in the wrong. What hips! How lovely they are!

LYSISTRATA: Don't think I'm going to let you Athenians off. Don't you remember how the Spartans came in arms when you were wearing the rough, sheepskin cloak of slaves and slew the host of Thessalians, the comrades and allies of Hippias? Fighting with you on that day, alone of all the Greeks, they set you free and instead of a sheepskin gave your folk a handsome robe to wear.

SPARTAN (looking at LYSISTRATA): I've never seen a more distinguished woman.

ATHENIAN (looking at Reconciliation): I've never seen a more voluptuous body!

LYSISTRATA: Why then, with these many noble deeds to think of, do you fight each other? Why don't you stop this villainy? Why not make peace? Tell me, what prevents it?

SPARTAN (*waving vaguely at Reconciliation*): We're willing, if you're willing to give up your position on yonder flank.

LYSISTRATA: What position, my good man?

SPARTAN: Pylus; we've been panting for it for ever so long.

ATHENIAN: No, by God! You shan't have it!

LYSISTRATA: Let them have it, my friend.

ATHENIAN: Then what shall we have to rouse things up?

LYSISTRATA: Ask for another place in exchange.

ATHENIAN: Well, let's see: first of all (*pointing to various parts of Reconciliation's anatomy*) give us Echinus here, this Maliac Inlet in back there, and these two Megarian legs.

SPARTAN: No, by heavens! You can't have *everything*, you crazy fool!

LYSISTRATA: Let it go. Don't fight over a pair of legs.

ATHENIAN (*taking off his cloak*): I think I'll strip and do a little planting now.

SPARTAN (*following suit*): And I'll just do a little fertilizing, by gosh!

LYSISTRATA: Wait until the truce is concluded. Now if you've decided on this course, hold a conference and discuss the matter with your allies.

ATHENIAN: Allies? Don't be ridiculous! They're in the same state we are. Won't all our allies want the same thing we do—to jump in bed with their women?

SPARTAN: Ours will, I know.

ATHENIAN: Especially the Carystians, by God!

LYSISTRATA: Very well. Now purify yourselves, that your wives may feast and entertain you in the Acropolis; we've provisions by the basketfull. Exchange your oaths and pledges there, and then each of you may take his wife and go home.

> ATHENIAN: Let's go at once.
> SPARTAN: Come on, where you will.
> ATHENIAN: For God's sake, let's hurry!
> (*They all go into the Acropolis.*)
> CHORUS (*singing*):
>> Whate'er I have of coverlets

And robes of varied hue
And golden trinkets,—without stint
  I offer them to you.

Take what you will and bear it home,
  Your children to delight,
Or if your girl's a Basket-maid;
  Just choose whate'er's in sight.

There's naught within so well secured
  You cannot break the seal
And bear it off; just help yourselves;
  No hesitation feel.

But you'll see nothing, though you try,
Unless you've sharper eyes than I!

If anyone needs bread to feed
  A growing family,
I've lots of wheat and full-grown loaves;
  So just apply to me.

Let every poor man who desires
  Come round and bring a sack
To fetch the grain; my slave is there
  To load it on his back.

But don't come near my door, I say:
Beware the dog, and stay away!

(*An* ATHENIAN *enters carrying a torch; he knocks at the gate.*)

ATHENIAN: Open the door! (*to the* CHORUS, *which is clustered around the gate*) Make way, won't you! What are you hanging around for? Want me to singe you with this torch? (*to himself*) No; it's a stale trick, I won't do it! (*to the audience*) Still, if I've got to do it to please *you*, I suppose I'll have to take the trouble.

(*A* SECOND ATHENIAN *comes out of the gate.*)

SECOND ATHENIAN: And I'll help you.

FIRST ATHENIAN (*waving his torch at the* CHORUS): Get out! Go bawl your heads off! Move on there, so the Spartans can leave in peace when the banquet's over.

(*They brandish their torches until the* CHORUS *leaves the Orchestra.*)

SECOND ATHENIAN: I've never seen such a pleasant banquet: the Spartans are charming fellows, indeed they are! And we Athenians are very witty in our cups.

FIRST ATHENIAN: Naturally: for when we're sober we're never at our best. If the Athenians would listen to me, we'd always get a little tipsy on our embassies. As things are now, we go to Sparta when we're sober and look around to stir up trouble. And then we don't hear what they say—and as for what they *don't* say, we have all sorts of suspicions. And then we bring back varying reports about the mission. But this time everything is pleasant; even if a man should sing the Telamon-song when he ought to sing "Cleitagoras," we'd praise him and swear it was excellent.

(*The two* CHORUSES *return, as a* CHORUS OF ATHENIANS *and a* CHORUS OF SPARTANS.)

Here they come back again. Go to the devil, you scoundrels!

SECOND ATHENIAN: Get out, I say! They're coming out from the feast.

(*Enter the Spartan and Athenian envoys, followed by* LYSISTRATA *and all the women.*)

SPARTAN (*to one of his fellow-envoys*): My good fellow, take up your pipes; I want to do a fancy two-step and sing a jolly song for the Athenians.

ATHENIAN: Yes, do take your pipes, by all means. I'd love to see you dance.

SPARTAN (*singing and dancing with the* CHORUS OF SPARTANS):
    These youths inspire
To song and dance, O Memory;
Stir up my Muse, to tell how we
And Athens' men, in our galleys clashing
At Artemisium, 'gainst foemen dashing
    In godlike ire,
Conquered the Persian and set Greece free.

          Leonidas
Led on his valiant warriors
Whetting their teeth like angry boars.
Abundant foam on their lips was flow'ring,
A stream of sweat from their limbs was show'ring.
     The Persian was
Numberless as the sand on the shores.

O Huntress who slayest the beasts in the glade,
O Virgin divine, hither come to our truce,
Unite us in bonds which all time will not loose.
Grant us to find in this treaty, we pray,
An unfailing source of true friendship today,
And all of our days, helping us to refrain
From weaseling tricks which bring war in their train.
     Then hither, come hither! O huntress maid.

LYSISTRATA: Come then, since all is fairly done, men of Sparta, lead away your wives, and you, Athenians, take yours. Let every man stand beside his wife, and every wife beside her man, and then, to celebrate our fortune, let's dance. And in the future, let's take care to avoid these misunderstandings.

CHORUS OF ATHENIANS (*singing and dancing*):
          Lead on the dances, your graces revealing.
          Call Artemis hither, call Artemis' twin,
          Leader of dances, Apollo the Healing,
          Kindly God—hither! let's summon him in!

          Nysian Bacchus call,
     Who with his Maenads, his eyes flashing fire,
          Dances, and last of all

     Zeus of the thunderbolt flaming, the Sire,
          And Hera in majesty,
          Queen of prosperity.

          Come, ye Powers who dwell above
          Unforgetting, our witnesses be
     Of Peace with bonds of harmonious love—
     The Peace which Cypris has wrought for me.

Alleluia! Io Paean!
Leap in joy—hurrah! hurrah!
'Tis victory—hurrah! hurrah!
Euoi! Euoi! Euai! Euai!

LYSISTRATA (*to the Spartans*): Come now, sing a new song to cap ours.

CHORUS OF SPARTANS (*singing and dancing*):
Leaving Taygetus fair and renown'd,
Muse of Laconia, hither come:
Amyclae's god in hymns resound,
Athene of the Brazen Home,
And Castor and Pollux, Tyndareus' sons,
Who sport where Eurotas murmuring runs.

On with the dance! Heia! Ho!
All leaping along,
Mantles a-swinging as we go!
Of Sparta our song.
There the holy chorus ever gladdens,
There the beat of stamping feet,
As our winsome fillies, lovely maidens,
Dance, beside Eurotas' banks a-skipping,—
Nimbly go to and fro
Hast'ning, leaping feet in measures tripping,
Like the Bacchae's revels, hair a-streaming.
Leda's child, divine and mild,
Leads the holy dance, her fair face beaming.
On with the dance! as your hand
Presses the hair
Streaming away unconfined.
Leap in the air
Light as the deer; footsteps resound
Aiding our dance, beating the ground.
Praise Athene, Maid divine, unrivalled in her might,
Dweller in the Brazen Home, unconquered in the fight.
(*All go out singing and dancing.*)
THE END

Rinehart Editions